BEYOND THE
RISING SUN

BEYOND THE
RISING SUN

NATIONALISM IN CONTEMPORARY JAPAN

Bruce Stronach

PRAEGER

Westport, Connecticut
London

 1995

Library of Congress Cataloging-in-Publication Data

Stronach, Bruce.
    Beyond the rising sun : nationalism in contemporary Japan / Bruce
Stronach.
      p.   cm.
    Includes bibliographical references and index.
    ISBN 0–275–95005–0 (alk. paper). — ISBN 0–275–95035–2 (pbk.)
    1. Nationalism—Japan. 2. National characteristics, Japanese.
3. Japan—Relations—Foreign countries. 4. Japan—Relations—United
States. 5. United States—Relations—Japan. I. Title.
DS889.S72   1995
305.8′00952—dc20   94–19577

British Library Cataloguing in Publication Data is available.

Library of Congress Catalog Card Number: 94–19577
ISBN: 0–275–95005–0; 0–275–95035–2 (pbk.)

First published in 1995

Praeger Publishers, 88 Post Road West, Westport, CT 06881
An imprint of Greenwood Publishing Group, Inc.

Printed in the United States of America

The paper used in this book complies with the
Permanent Paper Standard issued by the National
Information Standards Organization (Z39.48–1984).

10 9 8 7 6 5 4 3 2 1

Contents

Contents

Preface

The primary objective of this book is to give the reader an accurate picture of the extent to which nationalism exists in Japan today and the various ways it manifests itself. In the process of creating a definition of Japanese nationalism, it is also important to examine what effect nationalism will have on both the domestic polity and on Japan's role in the world. It is easy to say that nationalism exists in Japan, for it certainly does, but that statement does not tell us anything about what effect its existence has upon the institutions and policy of the Japanese state or what effect it has on the lives of its citizens. On yet another level, nationalism will also have an impact on Japan's actions in the international relations system. Because the old international order is in disarray and Japanese economic power is growing steadily, many people around the world are interested and concerned about the future role that Japan will play in Asia, in its relationship with the United States, in its relationship with Europe, in its relationship with international organizations and as a major donor of aid. Thus most of this book will be taken up with the relationship between these elements of nationalism to contemporary life and politics in Japan. But that original objective is not intended to be a simple academic exercise in defining Japanese nationalism. It is hoped that the reader will come to understand, rather than fear, Japan.

This book is not primarily concerned with the Japanese-American relationship, but it is written for an American audience by an American author who has lived and worked in Japan for many years. Consequently, although it is not a main concern, the relationship forms a constant, if not always visible, backdrop to what is written here. For this reason, and because the book is an attempt to change the way in which Americans think about Japan, the first chapter is devoted to a discussion of how Americans have come to fear a nation that is at one and the same time a defeated enemy, a devoted ally, and a cultural borrower.

One last caveat needs to be made. A significant change in Japanese politics has taken place since the main body of this book was written. In the summer of 1993, some members of the Liberal Democratic Party (LDP) bolted from their party, causing the government to lose a vote of confidence. In the elections that followed, the LDP lost control over the government for the first time since 1955, and a coalition government was formed consisting of new parties formed by ex-LDP members and long-standing opposition parties. Consequently, two other coalition governments have followed. It is too soon to tell what will be the effects of the summer of 1993 on the Japanese political system. It may be that most of the standard books on Japanese politics will have to be rewritten. Because it is too soon after the fact, I have not made a significant attempt to rewrite this book in light of those events. However, it does seem that they will ultimately reinforce the main theme of this book: that Japan is progressing away from the type of nationalism that existed in the prewar years, and has been since the occupation.

There are three major reasons for this contention. First, political changes since 1993 have effectively removed the most conservative elements of the LDP from power while simultaneously giving power to those most supportive of democratic reform. Second, the nature of the coalition that now governs Japan decreases the probability that a unified consensus of political elites can control Japanese political, economic, and social policy as manifested in a "Japan, Inc." model of elite control. Third, the events of 1993 and 1994 have demonstrated that the Japanese public is willing to participate in the political system when necessary to stimulate democratic change.

A final note: the Western style of placing the given name before the surname will be used throughout the book.

ACKNOWLEDGMENTS

As is the case with every book, there are many people who have helped me by their comments and criticisms at various stages of the writing process. The late David Wightman was one of the first people kind enough to give me his advice, and it is to his memory—as scholar, friend, and golfer—that this book is dedicated.

Among others, I would also like to thank Glen Fukushima, Kirk Patterson, Jeff Hull, James Gibney, James Marshall, Ivan Hall, the Smiths, Al Richmond, Sonni Efron, and Curtis Martin. More specifically, I would like to thank John Zeugner and Stephanie Forman Morimura for their invaluable comments on the manuscript, and Jim Impoco for the arguments, beers, and support in late-night Tokyo. Special thanks is also due the International University of Japan for supporting my research. Finally, this book would not have been possible without the support and guidance of Haru Fukui.

Introduction

The United States has every reason to rejoice in what has become of Japan since 1945. Its success is eloquent testimony to U.S. postwar policy, which during America's seven-year occupation was the most important factor in determining the contemporary development of the Japanese social, political, and economic systems. This is in great part due to the classic liberalism of those Americans who created occupation policy, General Douglas MacArthur not the least among them. American liberalism is based upon a faith in the rationality of human beings, their ability to conquer past mistakes by learning, and therefore to progress beyond the past into a better future. The idea that, given political freedom and an education, an individual can carve out of the world a productive and prosperous life that will make the world a better place for all is the essence of the American Dream. The concrete manifestation of this idealism was the attempt to graft American political values onto Japanese society.

In keeping with this liberal spirit, American policy makers believed that the people of Japan were *tabulae rasae* from which the nationalism and militarism of the past could be erased and written over with Lockean ideals of liberal democracy. They believed the Japanese to be a people as capable of reasoned, rational thought as any other, and once the repressive elite of militant nationalists was purged and the political system they created was destroyed, the Japanese people would learn liberal democratic political values and become, as a State Department policy paper phrased it in the summer of 1945, a nation "properly discharging its responsibilities in the family of nations."

Forty-two years after the occupation, all of the goals that the United States had for a post-occupation Japan have been met. Japan was one of the United States' strongest allies in East Asia during the Cold War, and it continues to be a key supporter of American policy in the region. Japan built an economy so strong that its development invigorated the rest of East Asia, making the region a preeminent center of international trade and finance. It has developed a military that is capable of supporting the United States when it is engaged in the region, capable of defending the home islands, and yet is not a threat to other states in the region. Finally, it remains tied psychologically to the United States by thousands of tiny threads, such as teacher exchange programs, sister city relations, and cultural consumption, that form an almost unbreakable bond. But why doesn't the United States rejoice in the success of its policy and the success of its ally? After such a fruitful relationship, certainly the most positive and productive relationship in the modern history of occupations, why the continuing sense of crisis?

Although the American occupiers were thorough in their restructuring of the Japanese political system and the reeducation of the Japanese people, the Japan that emerged has never been able to assuage completely other nations' fears that Japanese militarism was not dead but simply hibernating until the next spring of nationalism. The Second World War is now two generations distant, but memories remain vivid. Foreigners afflicted by past Japanese aggression are still very sensitive to any manifestation of Japanese militarism or nationalism. They fear that younger Japanese have no knowledge of the first third of the Showa era, they do not know what Japan was really like under the militarists, but they have not lost that inherent superiority toward other Asians that was a product of Japanese colonialism. Japanese people also justify their claim that they, too, were victims by nurturing memories of events such as the bombings of Hiroshima and Nagasaki and the ABCD (American, British, Chinese, Dutch) encirclement. But they have much more difficulty remembering Japan's acts of aggression in China, Singapore, and elsewhere.

It is ironic that, in the years following the occupation, the United States was the country least concerned about reemergent Japanese nationalism and militarism. The United States needed Japan as an ally and a trading partner during the Cold War, and that need forced policy makers to reverse the course of an occupation based on stern discipline, surveillance, and restrictions. In the words of one of the most important documents outlining Cold War policy in Asia, "[T]he maximum deterrent [in Asia] to the Kremlin in the post-treaty period will be a Japan with a rapidly and soundly developing economy, internal political stability and an adequate military capability for self-defense."[1] Indeed, U.S. support for the redevelopment

of Japan was so strong that other Asian nations who were the victims of Japanese aggression have accused the United States of encouraging Japanese nationalism and militarism.

In recent decades, however, American pride in the development of Japan as a staunch ally and engine of Asian economic recovery has turned bitter. The Japanese thrust into the American economy and successive trade imbalances during the 1970s rekindled American fears of Japanese nationalism, militarism, and economic mercantilism. Early warning calls were weak but have lately become more strident. By the mid-1980s, the *New York Times Magazine* was running major articles with such titles as "The Danger from Japan" and "A New Japanese Nationalism," while *Newsweek* covered the Japanese "invasion" of America via the landing sites of Rockefeller Center and Hollywood. Today the most popular books about Japan produced in America have titles such as *The Coming War with Japan*, *Agents of Influence*, *Japanophobia*, *The New Competitors*, *Japan's Pseudo-Democracy*, and *Japan's New Imperialism*.

American scholarship on Japan also has undergone a revision. Academic and popular studies of Japan in the 1960s and 1970s tended to propagate the image of Japan as unique, homogeneous, unified, and consensual. In works like William Ouchi's *Theory Z* and Ezra Vogel's *Japan as Number One*, Japan was represented as a country to be emulated in its efficient organization, work ethic, and emphasis on "human orientation." Even those works that portrayed a negative image of Japan often did so by contrasting the overly unified, homogeneous "Japan, Inc." with the diversity and freedom of the United States. In the 1980s, however, American scholarship began to place much more emphasis upon the noncohesive and negative elements of Japanese politics and society such as conflict, racism, and nationalism. James Fallows, in his book *More Like Us*, questions the wisdom of following the Japanese example by highlighting the problems of Japan, but he is but one among many who are spurning Japan as a model for the United States. Writing on Japan has changed from the days when Ezra Vogel proclaimed *Japan as Number One*. Jon Woronoff's *Japan as Anything but Number One* now seems more appropriate to many.

Today there is the smell of fear in America, a fear born of uncertainty and the unknown. The elation over the passing of communism in the eastern bloc and the victory over Iraq lasted only a few short months before uncertainty over its own internal problems and the future of its role in the world began to cloud the horizon. Just when the United States should be attaining the peak of its power, it finds itself bogged down in an economic morass. Frustrated in its inability to extricate itself, it looks for reasons for what happened and who is to blame, and its attention is often focused on Japan.

Japan seems to be everywhere in the American consciousness. The various fiftieth anniversary celebrations of the war that made America the most powerful country in the world also raise the question of why Japan seems to be winning the peace. Japanese acquisitions of land, buildings, factories, technology, and even sports franchises have put Americans, who were accustomed to being the economic aggressors, on the defensive against Japanese economic aggression. Whether the books are outrageously paranoid, such as Martin Wolf's *The Japanese Conspiracy*, or balanced and accurate, such as Clyde Prestowitz, Jr.'s *Trading Places*, the message is ultimately the same—the United States is in an important economic conflict with Japan, and it is losing. Americans look to Japanese economic success and wonder: How can they succeed when we are failing?

Fear is bred by America's uncertainty and ambivalence toward the Japanese. What do they want? For two decades they have been taught that Japanese are better workers, more productive, more sacrificing, more competitive, and more frugal. And that teaching has been accepted as gospel. But at the same time, Americans rebel against the possibility of taking second place to Japanese. Japan is still perceived by Americans to be more friendly than most of America's other allies (excluding Great Britain and Canada), but at the same time they are being told that it is the new national threat which will replace the possibility of sudden death from a Soviet nuclear attack with the slow and silent strangulation of the American economy. American presidents praise Japan as an ally in the United States' most important bilateral relationship, while the American Congress has for over a decade been sounding a call to economic war against that same ally. Who should be believed?

If the public is receiving mixed messages as to whether Japan is an enemy or an ally, the focus of its fear is even more unclear. Is Japan out to invade China and Korea again to reclaim them in the name of the New East Asian Co-Prosperity Sphere? Is it developing a nuclear capability? Will it bring about a "Second U.S.-Japanese War"? Is it subtly trying to take over the Hawaiian economy so that it will become a de facto dependency of Japan? Is it trying to ruin the American economy in order to become the number one power in the corridors of world politics? Is it bent on taking away all of the markets for American producers so that it will be the richest country in the world? Is it trying to surpass the United States as an act of dominance by one who was for so long subservient to the American master? Or is it simply a passive and peaceful state that has fashioned a successful economic policy but with no intention of threatening or dominating others? Whatever Japan's goals, and whatever the United States's fears, the re-creation of a strong Japan and the fears that others have of it are often reduced to one simple concept: a new Japanese nationalism.

NATIONALISM

Although Japanese nationalism is feared, nationalism is one of the most fundamental elements of political culture in the modern world. It has become such a basic component of modern life that it is hard to imagine individual people who do not think themselves to be part of a nation, just as it is equally hard to imagine a world that is not divided into nations. Nationalism is perceived by many to be a negative force in world events, but there are few who refute the idea of nationalism or their ties to their own nation.

Although there has been much talk since the end of the Second World War about going beyond nationalism, even today most people remain proud of their nation and their sense of nationalism. The Miller Brewing Company hopes to sell its beer by proclaiming that it is "made the American way." The French guard their language from foreign influences as if it were a sick child fatally exposed to infection. Nothing will anger a Canadian more than being told, "Ah, Canadian or American, there's really no difference, you're all the same," just as someone from Scotland or Wales would not take kindly to being called English.

For all the movement away from nationalism in the postwar world, people still have a strong and abiding desire to seek the comfort of relatively small and well-defined groups. Foreign students may find the adventure of life in their adopted countries thrilling, but most inevitably turn to their compatriots to find relaxation in speaking the same language, telling the same jokes, eating the same food, and sharing the same values. The Olympics are an occasion for all to appreciate the skills of individual athletes from around the world, and yet it is always a showcase for the skills of national teams. Victors circle the arena carrying their national flag, and when a flag and anthem are not available, as was the case for the Unified Team in 1992, the organizers of this international event are thrown into consternation. Newspapers report the results in terms of medal counts per nation. Similarly, just as it appears as if the most integrated of all regions, the European Community, is about to take another major step toward unification, the peoples of those states suddenly hesitate because they are uncertain as to what will happen to their sense of place and belonging in a Unified Europe.

Nationalism remains a core element in our daily lives, but it is also perceived as an evil force. During World War I Europe burned to the ground and millions were killed in the name of nationalism. Hitler's Germany made nationalism a force that built concentration camps and gas chambers. Today nationalism is associated with racism as in the National Front movement in Europe. It is also associated with the terrible destruction of the Soviet empire and the eastern bloc. Americans once felt joy in the death of communism and the elimination of threat from the Soviet Union, but as the disintegration of the former empire leads to greater and more senseless bloodshed, American joy turns to disgust and revulsion.

In a sense the ambivalence that Americans feel toward Japan and its increased status and power is similar to their ambivalent attitudes toward nationalism. Americans feel that nationalism in the United States is a positive force because they are responsible and can handle it, but they do not necessarily believe it is good when nationalism is demonstrated by others, especially Japan. Certainly there is a double standard when it comes to nationalism in America (or the West in general) and nationalism in Japan. Americans think nothing of their pride; they take it for granted. Americans who are not proud of being American are looked at askance as either politically dubious, immature, or simply not mentally sound. The symbols of the state and the state's connection to the nation abound. The national anthem is played at every major function, children pledge allegiance to the flag in school, celebrations commemorating past wars are ubiquitous, and "war memorials" can be found in every village and town.

Similar displays are not accepted in Japan, however. If the Education Ministry gives an administrative guidance to schools instructing them to show the flag and play the anthem at graduation and entrance ceremonies, the outside world sees it as nationalism. Japanese politicians who argue that Japan should reduce its dependence on the United States and create a more independent policy are seen as dangerous reactionaries. In fact, Americans do not trust the Japanese to handle nationalism because of Japan's past history as an aggressive, militaristic state. Just as an alcoholic cannot be trusted to take just one drink, so Japan cannot be trusted to display the slightest sense of nationalism.

Nationalism embodies all of the unarticulated and confused fears that Americans feel toward Japan. The very word has impact. Headlines such as "A New Japanese Nationalism"[2] or "Nationalistic Drift?"[3] instantly grab a reader's attention and convey a sense of threat and forboding. One of the causes of American confusion concerning Japanese nationalism has been that the books, articles, and news reports that discuss Japanese nationalism rarely define what the term means. The word is simply left hanging in the air, a metaphorical sword of Damocles, implying everything but specifying nothing.

There are, however, common elements that are often linked to Japanese nationalism. The word is frequently preceded by the modifier "new." New Japanese nationalism itself has been used both as a description of increased nationalism among Japanese youth and as a way of connoting the rebirth of nationalism in the postwar world. Most often these two elements are combined to convey the picture of a youthful Japan, free of the fetters of war guilt and ignorant of either Japan's prewar history of militarism or the hardships of the war's aftermath, yearning to stretch its adolescent muscle. Nationalism is also a code word for swagger. Japan is beginning to throw its weight around and has a new pride in itself. Japanese have a new confidence in themselves and a new sense of place in the world. Nationalism is equated with the remilitarization of Japan. As Japan grows stronger, so does its need for a military force independent of the United States and strong enough to guarantee its own security. However, it can also mean a military that is a threat to other countries in the world. Nationalism also is used as an economic term in order to brand Japanese as selfish mercantilists. In this perception they invest in the United States with the end goal of controlling the American economy. They trade with other countries only to build up huge domestic surpluses. They invest in other Asian countries and give foreign aid only as a means of building regional hegemony.

Creating a more rigorous definition of Japanese nationalism is central to the calming of American fears about Japan. Nationalism does actually mean all of the above concepts and more, but unless it is clear what type of nationalism is being discussed in each context, the word becomes meaningless. What follows is an attempt to create a clearer definition of the major types of nationalism that exist in contemporary Japan.

Since modern nationalism began in the early nineteenth century, the very heart of a political culture has been associated with "a strong sense of national identity which large numbers of individuals have been able to share."[4] In order to clarify the arguments made in this book, a distinction must be made between the associated concepts of "state" and "nation." The concept of "the state" may be understood in one sense as the coercive and legal power of government and its institutions to command compliance from the population over which it rules. A state is a purely political concept and is made up of both the machinery of the state, the laws, and the institutions of a political system, as well as the people who run it at any given point in time—the government. A state may incorporate within its territorial jurisdiction one nation or several nations. The concept of nation, in its most fundamental sense, is social and psychological. The nation is a large group of people who perceive themselves to have a common bond based upon a common ethnicity, language, history, set of behaviors, and values. The existence of this group is not dependent upon living within one country or having a government and a state. The first and foremost component of nationalism is the individual's acceptance of identity as a member of the national group.

There may be many other groups, such as family, neighborhood, town, state, trade union, church, school, and/or company, with which the individual identifies at the same time he or she identifies with the nation. One of the most important differences between these groups and the nation, however, is that the nation almost always incorporates within it the desire for self-rule, for sovereignty. The concept of nation does not refer to the relationship between ruler and ruled, between government and citizen, but rather to the bonds among the people leading them to seek to govern their own affairs.[5]

The nation is of great importance to the state because when the nation is unified under the state, it has an increased ability to rule. When there is a strong sense of national community, the power of the state is magnified because the nation will be willing to obey its commands and to work and sacrifice for it when necessary. Think, for example, of the simple act of paying taxes. In a state that does not have the support of its nation, it will be close to impossible to collect taxes without significant coercion. Because of this, states have always tried to transfer the loyalty and identity that individuals feel toward the nation to the state. All the means of socialization—the schools, media, church, parents—are a part of this connecting of the nation to the state, so that the two become inseparable in the citizen's mind through concepts like "fatherland" or "motherland." Although all states attempt to increase loyalty and support by identifying the nation with the state, this is not to say that the nation cannot exist apart from the state.

The nation and state are most closely linked in the concept of the nation-state. The nation-state denotes a people who inhabit a known and limited territory, have an economy, and control the government and state that rules it all. This is perceived as the natural condition of the world, that all peoples are divided into nations that have the right of self-rule. Although this may appear to be an ancient law of human existence, in fact it is very much a result of the French Revolution and trends that emerged in the nineteenth century. The world has been divided into nation-states only since the mid-twentieth century.

Nationalism and the actions of nation-states continue to have significant impact on the contemporary world, yet there are various competing definitions for this important concept. This is especially evident in writings on Japan, a country to which the concept is often ascribed, but rarely with much clarity or consistency. The task of this book is not so much to find the "correct" definition of nationalism as it is to find one that is appropriate to Japan and then to apply it consistently. Nationalism has some universal characteristics, but it must also, by its very nature, have different components unique to each nation. Nationalism is the ideology most fundamentally defined by the characteristics of the nation in which it is manifested.

Sociocultural Nationalism

Four specific definitions of Japanese nationalism will be used in this book, no one of which is mutually exclusive of the others. The first is a psychological phenomenon by which individuals define themselves as members of a group. Some have called it ethnic nationalism; others have called it cultural nationalism. Here the term *sociocultural nationalism* is used because in Japan nationalism is first and foremost the psychological sense of belonging to the group. Japanese nationalism conforms most closely to Max Skidmore's definition.

Nationalism involves a group's perception of itself as distinct from others, and the awareness of its members as components of the group. It also involves the group's desire to protect and preserve its identity and to enhance its power and status as a nation. It is this that leads nationalism often to become territorial, to develop an attachment to a certain land as home. It is the perception, or the belief, that is important. Many factors may serve as the explanation for "nationhood," including common culture, language, historical experiences, religion, and the like. The important factor is not whether the explanation is correct, but rather that the group believes it to be true.[6]

Sociocultural nationalism does not depend upon the existence of a state, but rather the sharing of a similar cultural history, the sharing of similar social values and behavioral norms, and especially the ability to communicate. In the words of Karl Deutsch:

It is a collection of individuals who can communicate with each other quickly and effectively over a wide range of localities and diverse topics and situations. In order to be able to do this, they must have complementary habits of communication, including usually language and always culture as a common stock of shared meanings and memories and hence as a common probability of sharing many similar perceptions and preferences in the present and near future. Members of the same people are similar to each other in regard to some of their habits and characteristics and interlocking in regard to other habits.[7]

Nations are most often conceived of in conjunction with their political control over a state—the nation-state—but nations can exist and do exist without states.[8] The Kurds and the Palestinians are both nations that have existed for some time without a state of their own, regardless of their desire for one. Other nations, such as the nations of Native Americans living within the United States, are content to exist without a state. Whether or not the stateless nation desires to create a nation-state, nations and state can exist separately. In sociocultural nationalism, it is the consciousness of the individual's relationship to the others in the nation, and not his or her relationship to the state, that is important. To paraphrase an example from Deutsch, one French person may be a Marxist and another a Democratic Socialist, but both will have more in common with each other and a much greater ability to understand and communicate with each other than would the Democratic Socialist with a citizen of Sweden or the Marxist with a citizen of the Democratic People's Republic of Korea.

Self-Determined Nationalism

The second type of nationalism is concerned with the nation's relationship to the state and can be summed up by the term *self-determination*. It is the struggle by a nation to take control of its political destiny and to create a state by which its territory and economy can be securely held and governed. This form of nationalism is best exemplified by the national liberation movement of the decolonization period, but it has been manifested in three different ways: unification, decolonialism, and Westernization. Germany in the nineteenth century is the best example of unification. The German nation suffered a long-standing political and economic disunity in conjunction with a proud cultural heritage, common history, and linguistic unity. For hundreds of years there had been attempts to pull all of the various German-speaking political entities into one unified whole, but this desire was not achieved until the French Revolution and the successes of Napoleon's national army showed the Germans the way. The power of the nation-state apparent in France's easy victory over Prussia and the lesser Germanic states, and the resultant reorganization of the Prussian military, were forces in German unification, but equally important were philosophic and cultural trends. Hegelian organicism created a rationale for the submission of the will of the nation to the good of the state, while Schlegel's *Bildung*, and Germanic romanticism in general, taught Germans that they could regain their idealized past. Thus the German people conceived of themselves as a nation, desired their existence under one state, and had the means to forge the nation-state in the face of formidable opposition.

Nationalism in the third world has been to a great extent a result of colonialism. Great powers brought the concept of nationalism to the colonies, and it was through both the teachings of the colonial masters and the desire to rid themselves of foreign rule that peoples without a strong common bond fought to create a "national" state. It is easy, for example, to imagine an Indian civil servant sent to London for his education writing a tract in English calling for the creation of an Indian nation-state based on Leninist principles. In the case of native peoples attempting to overthrow colonial domination, nationalism takes on three dimensions: the removal of the colonial government, its replacement with a unified national government, and the creation of a nation where none existed before. Whether the first was achieved by revolution or evolution, the other two dimensions often proved more difficult to attain. The colonial creation of administrative territories that encompass a mosaic of groups with no common unity has left a legacy for third world states of conflict for control of the state by various groups within the "nation" and attempts to create a nation with no historical basis.

Westernization combines elements of both unification and self-determination. Some peoples, although not directly colonized, were forced to create modern, Western nation-states from traditional political organizations by the threat of Western domination. Early Japanese nationalism is a prime example of Westernization. Although the elements of nationalism existed in the Tokugawa period, the oligarchic elite of the Meiji Era consciously forged a unified nation as a means of strengthening the state vis-à-vis the foreign powers. They knew it was a case of either emulating the West or forever remaining a "backward" people subject to the control of foreign states.

State-Oriented Nationalism

The third type of nationalism emerges when the unity of the nation and its needs and interests in opposition to other nation-states form the ideology of the state. The well-being of the nation is integrally linked to that of the state to such an extent that

"national" messages, memories, and images [are given] a preferred status in social communication and a greater weight in the making of decisions. [It] gives preference in attention, transmission, and communication to those messages which carry specific symbols of nationality, or which originate from a specific national source, or which are couched in a specific national code of language and culture. If the greater attention and the greater weight given to such messages is so large as to override all other messages, memories, or images, then we speak of nationalism as "extreme." In such cases, the messages preferred by a nationalist will outweigh and override those of humanity, prenational tradition, or world religion.[9]

This form of nationalism often makes the state upon which it is based self-centered, aggressive, and expansive.

State-Centric Nationalism

The fourth type of nationalism is based on the realist conception of the international relations system. This form of nationalism differs significantly from the previous three by its focus not on the inner unity of the nation and its relationship to the state, but rather on the relationship of the nation and the state to other nations and states in the outside world. Central to this form of nationalism is the belief that the "natural" order of international relations is the state-centric system in which independent states form the basic political and economic unit. Although a system of mutual recognition and relations exists, each state is sovereign and is in competition, peaceful or otherwise, with other states for the primary value of power. It is essentially a zero-sum game conception of international relations. The primary concern for each state when acting in the international relations system is to protect the national interest, however it is defined. It does not perceive any natural harmony of interests among the states within the system except as an overall harmony may occur, in the sense of Adam Smith's "invisible hand," through each state pursuing its own enlightened self-interest.

NOTES

1. U.S. Department of State, *Foreign Relations of the United States*, "United States Objectives, Policies and Courses of Action in Asia" (NSC 48/5), vol. 6, 1951, pp. 33–57.

2. The title of an Ian Buruma article in the *New York Times Magazine*, April 12, 1987.

3. The title of a chapter in William Holstein's *The Japanese Power Game: What It Means for America*.

4. Brian Girvin, "Conservatism and Political Change in Britain and the United States, *Parliamentary Affairs* 40 (1987), 34.

5. Curtis Martin and Bruce Stronach, *Politics East and West: A Comparison of Japanese and British Political Culture* (New York: M. E. Sharpe, 1992), 45.

6. Max J. Skidmore, *Ideologies: Politics in Action* (New York: Harcourt, Brace and Jovanovich, 1989), 260.

7. Karl W. Deutsch, *Tides among Nations* (New York: Free Press, 1979), 301.

8. Hugh Seton-Watson, *Nations and States* (London: Methuen & Co., 1977), 1.

9. Deutsch, *Tides among Nations*, 301.

Ambiguous Images

When Sony develops the Walkman, we don't say, "Nice product. Now you have to license it to GE and sell it through an American company." If they seek distribution, we don't tell them, "I'm sorry, but American stores all have preexisting arrangements with American suppliers. You'll have to distribute through an American company here." If they seek patents, we don't say, "Patents take eight years to be awarded, during which time your patent will be publicly available so that our companies can read what you've invented and copy it free of charge, so that by the time we issue a patent our companies will already have their own version of your technology."

We don't do any of those things. Japan does all of them. Their markets are closed. Our markets are wide open. It's not a level playing field. In fact, it's not a playing field at all. It's a one-way street.

—Michael Crichton,
Rising Sun

[I]n the effectiveness of its present-day institutions in coping with the current problems of the postindustrial era Japan is indisputably number one. Considering its limited space and natural resources and its crowding, Japan's achievements in economic productivity, educational standards, health, and control of crime are in a class by themselves. This success is more striking when one considers how far behind Japan was in many of these areas not only in 1945 but even in the mid-1950s, after recovery from World War II was essentially complete.

—Ezra F. Vogel
Japan as Number One

It is difficult to judge any nation's image of another nation, but the regional, economic, ethnic, racial, and political diversity of the United States makes it especially difficult to speak of one people and one perception. That notwithstanding, it can be said with assurance that America's image of Japan has changed drastically as Japan has become an economic competitor. The above quotes are typical of the dichotomous good/bad image of the Japanese being presented to Americans these days.

Crichton felt it necessary to add an afterword to his novel, *Rising Sun*, as an admonition and a warning, but his views were already quite clear in the body of the book. In it we are given a portrait of Japanese as a people who are bent on economic warfare and control of the American economy. They are portrayed as an unstable people who are superficially polite, but fundamentally ruthless and amoral. Crichton's Japanese are sexual deviants, liars, and cheats.

And they are also nationalists. What matters to them is not the gaining of wealth, but the gaining of power for Japan through economic success. They are portrayed as a people who give all for the company and the nation. They will not allow the products of other nations into the country, and if goods are forced in through trade negotiations, they will not buy them because they are not Japanese. On the other hand, Americans are portrayed as, at best, a nation of bumbling liberals who do not understand that their misguided belief in free trade is being used and manipulated by Japanese. At worst the Americans in the book are portrayed as people who are lining their pockets by selling their country down the river to the Japanese.

If *Rising Sun* represents the dark side of the American image of Japan, the bright side is represented by *Japan as Number One*. The book was first published in 1979, but is still in print and is still widely discussed. It is considered to be a paean to the virtues of Japanese society. In it Vogel lists the causes for Japan's postwar miracle, including its education system, state planning, corporate organization and management, and the group ethic of the society. In his view the Japanese are not innately bad, or aggressive, or cheats—they have simply organized their society in a highly successful and positive manner. But Vogel went beyond pointing out what was right about Japan; he also advised the United States to look to Japan as a model to emulate, where necessary and possible.

Much of the criticism aimed by revisionists at Vogel for taking an overly positive view of Japan is not deserved. He makes no bones about the purpose for writing the book and clearly states that "the focus of this book

is not on a rounded picture of Japan but on practices potentially useful for Americans wanting to improve our country."[1] But do Americans still want to hear about the virtues of Japan? Are they willing to learn from Japan if they admit that it has lessons to offer? Or would they rather hear Crichton's dictum: "The Japanese are not our saviors. They are our competitors. We should not forget it."[2]

Crichton's confused message reflects the confusion with which Americans behold Japan. They are doing all the right things, as gauged by their economic success, and yet it is instinctively felt that they have done so by cheating. They behave according to values that Americans have always held to be most fundamental and positive—hard work and frugality—and yet they are not Americans, they are different. They have been our enemies in the past, they have committed atrocities against Americans and others, and yet they have been our closest allies during the Cold War and have continued to act in concert with the United States in the political arena since its end. Are they still our economic allies now, or are they our enemies?

The American image of Japan is a classic case of cognitive dissonance, the confusion that results when presented by two seemingly contradictory, but true, facts. In this case the American people are constantly presented with very positive images of the Japanese. They are polite, they are clean, they are loyal, they are peaceful, they work hard, they save their money, they invent better mousetraps, and they produce better mousetraps. On the other hand, they also are perceived as a threat to the United States. They are taking our jobs, they do not play by the rules, they are insincere, they are buying our politicians, they are buying our land, they are xenophobic, they are nationalistic, they are our economic enemies. This cognitive dissonance is clear in polling data on Japan. Japan still ranks well up on the list of countries toward which Americans feel friendly and toward which Americans have positive images, and yet they are also seen as the greatest threat to American security in the post–Cold War era.

The instability of America's image of Japan and the vagueness of the threat that Americans feel from it put the overall relationship on an uneasy footing. Americans are ready to believe anything and everything, positive and negative, about Japan and the Japanese because they don't know what is true. If the average American reads that Japan is an unfair trader, a threat to national security and American jobs, the chances are good that he or she will believe it. If that same person reads that Japanese are actually good, kind people who want to be our allies and are investing to support the American economy, this will also be believed.

The threat projected by Japan is especially vague. Some Americans have lost their jobs, and many fear they will lose them. All can see the death of industries in their area and in other areas of the United States; they know they have been in a prolonged recession, but they often cannot see any real connection to Japan. Yet they feel that it must be there. They are suspicious of Japan and Japan's impact on the American economy, but they don't know what that effect really is or how it has come to be. There are some Americans, those in the automotive and steel industries, for example, who can point to the loss of jobs through the dominance of Japanese products in the American market, but even their situation is not altogether clear. Are their jobs lost to Japanese companies, or did their own company ship their jobs overseas? Did they lose their jobs because Japan cheated in unfair trade competition, or because Japan fairly outcompeted them in the open market? Did they lose their jobs because American labor is lazy or because American management is incompetent? What about the so-called international cars? Who can tell which components were made or assembled in what country? There is so much conflicting information and so many conflicting images available concerning Japan that one cannot help but be confused about Japan and its intentions.

Workers in other industries, and especially the vast majority who still hold their jobs, have questions about Japan that raise an even vaguer sense of dread and foreboding. What does it mean when a Japanese company buys a Montana cattle ranch? Does it mean that they are buying a piece of America, or does it mean that America is selling its heritage to the highest bidder? Does Japan really keep the products of American companies out of its markets? Does the United States need to trade with them? Why not just block them from American markets? Should I go to work for a Japanese company that has opened a factory in the area? They seem to run a good operation, but would I be working for foreign interests? Are they really quietly, secretly taking over the American economy, while playing at the smiling friend, only to rise up one day in the future on top of the world and with America in their hands? There is no proof, only concern. There is no understanding, only confusion.

It is this confusion that needs to be addressed. This chapter will examine the creation of Japan's image in the eyes of the United States and the world, but the rest of the book will be dedicated to belying some of the more negative images of Japan, especially those that relate to aggressive nationalism. The people of Japan, their behaviors, and the events that occur in Japan are as complex as they are in any other country in the world, but they are equally understandable. America's confused images of Japan are to a great extent self-inflicted. They are a result of past images that die hard, racial stereotypes, the projection of American values, and insecurities about America's place in the world after the Cold War.

IMAGES OF THE PAST

The ambivalent nature of American attitudes toward Japan is a very recent phenomenon. Since the beginning of the relationship between the two countries, the image of Japan in the minds of Americans has vacillated between positive and negative, but it was always clearly defined as one or the other.

At the beginning of the nineteenth century, it must have seemed as if neither the United States nor Japan would be a likely candidate to participate in a historic meeting of East and West. In outward appearance, Japan had not changed for two hundred years. It was still under the control of the Tokugawa Shogunate that had locked it away from the rest of the world in the early seventeenth century. Since the seclusion edicts were passed in 1637, few foreigners had ventured to Japan, few Japanese had left the country, and the only opening to the world was a highly restricted trade through the port of Nagasaki, at the most remote remove from the capital. The United States seemed almost as introverted as Japan. Isolated to both the east and west by thousands of miles of ocean, the newborn nation's main concerns were with the consolidation of its political system, the development of its continent, and staying clear of the continuous European conflicts.

The changing world of the mid-nineteenth century would no longer allow either country its splendid isolation. The Tokugawa government, weakened by Japan's long-standing domestic crises, confronted a new determination by the Western powers to open East Asia. The Russians were moving east, the Americans were moving west, and the British were moving into China. Indeed, the easy British victory over China in 1840 raised grave questions for Japan. If a Western power could so easily force open the strongest power in East Asia for millennia, then how could such a small, weak country as Japan stand up to the Europeans?

At the same time, the United States was becoming a Pacific power with economic designs in Asia. Steamships plying the China trade from the new state of California needed coaling and provisioning stations, American merchants wanted to break Holland's monopoly on trade with Japan, and the American government wanted protection for foreign sailors who shipwrecked on the archipelago.

Pragmatic pressures from merchants, Congress, and the military were not the only reasons why President Millard Fillmore ordered a naval fleet to open Japan for the United States. The United States was taking on what Rudyard Kipling, in his famous poem of the same name, would call the "White Man's Burden." The United States was the New World, a world whose development represented all that was best in the philosophy of the Enlightenment. It had turned its back on the decay of Europe, had been rewarded by God with a strong arm and abundant resources, and was now ready to bring its superior technology, culture, and religion to the dead civilizations of the East. America's blend of reform, Manifest Destiny, and white man's burden was driven by its abiding belief in Progress. Americans believed that history was progress, change was good, and civilization was a locomotive flying down a straight teleological track that started at the Creation and would end at Armageddon.

This was the irresistible force that was about to collide head on with the immovable object of Japanese Confucianism. Tokugawa Japan was heir to the Chinese tradition of perceiving time as cyclical, with each phase of life returning time and time again as it has since the beginning. Japan was a society based upon the principle of maintaining the status quo. The Law of the Military Houses promulgated by the first shogun, Ieyasu Tokugawa, locked Japan into a Confucian feudalism for the next two and a half centuries. That is not to say there were no changes, but both the institutions of the society and its isolationism remained relatively unchanged. In the eyes of those who believe in the Western philosophy of progress, then no doubt Senator Thomas H. Benton was correct when he called upon America to awaken the sleeping giant of Asia. Japan was decadent and moribund until its collision with the United States forced it into the modern world of the West. And Americans reveled in the role of reformer.

America has always cherished a weak Japan and distrusted a strong Japan. The Japanese-American relationship has run the gamut from a "special relationship" to conflict and warfare, but those times when the United States has had its warmest ties with Japan have come when Japan was at its weakest. Americans have supported Japan when it was the underdog and have succored and taught a developing Japan, but, conversely, a Japan equal in strength to the United States has always been perceived as a threat to Americans.

After the first treaties with Japan in 1854 and 1858, and even more so after the Meiji Restoration ten years later, Japan adopted its first special relationship with the United States. What was special about the relationship was the primacy of the United States vis-à-vis the other Western states in a system of unequal treaties that gave them extraterritorial and trade privileges. To be sure, the position of the United States stemmed in the beginning from the fact that it opened Japan to commerce and brought it into the Western-dominated international relations system, but the United States' position as *supra inter pares* among the Western states was due to more than its having been the first state permanently to breach the isolation of Japan.

Beyond the United States having been the primary power in Japan, its influence was also due to its status as a noncolonial, non-European state. Townsend Harris, America's first consul in Japan, was himself an anticolonialist and was against extraterritoriality, and was able to convince the Japanese of his own sincerity and of the good will and noncolonial intentions of the country he represented.[3] He levered the United States into a central position between Japan and the Western powers by convincing the Japanese that the United States had no intention of taking any colonial possessions in Japan, but that Great Britain and the other European powers did have such intentions. Therefore, he argued, it would be much better for Japan to enter willingly into a commercial agreement with the United States than to be forced into an agreement with Great Britain. The result was the Harris Treaty of 1858. It was the first commercial treaty signed with a Western state, and as such it served as the model for Japan's treaties with Russia, France, Great Britain, and the Dutch (collectively known as the Five Nations' Treaty). Although Harris was not able to keep extraterritoriality out of the treaty, it did not include any territorial concessions by the Japanese. It did include articles which stipulated that (1) upon request of the Japanese government, the president of the United States would act as a "friendly mediator" in differences between the Japanese and the European powers; (2) the Japanese government could purchase a wide selection of commercial and military vessels, military armaments, and, in general, whatever it might require from the United States; and (3) the Japanese government was given the right to hire Americans into its service, including military personnel.[4]

The good offices of the United States were often used, along with the talents of American citizens. When President Grant went on his world tour after leaving the presidency, he was often consulted in Japan. He was quizzed by the emperor about setting up a national assembly, and he was also used as an intermediary between Japan and China in order to solve their dispute over the Ryuku Islands (Okinawa). The Japanese turned to an American, Erasmus Smith, to train its diplomats, and Secretary of State William Seward was asked to mediate the boundary dispute between Russia and Japan in the Kuriles. The United States, along with Great Britain, France, and the Netherlands, had received an indemnity of $785,000 from the Tokugawa government arising from an expedition to Shimonoseki. It had been debated for a long time as to whether the indemnity should be returned, and the United States finally decided to return the indemnity in 1883. In numerous instances John A. Bingham, ambassador to Japan from 1873 to 1885, worked to secure Japanese control over tariffs and a reduction of extraterritoriality. Ultimately the trust shown in the United States by Japan (and China) resulted in the request by both countries, upon the outbreak of war between them in 1895, that the American legation in each country "take charge of the archives and protect the interests of their nationals in the enemy country."[5] It was this history of using its good offices in the service of Japan that allowed President Theodore Roosevelt to act as a mediator between Russia and Japan after their war had bogged down into a war of attrition.

American influence in Japanese education and the arts was especially great, and American teachers created an affection for the United States among their Japanese students. Those same teachers were instrumental in creating a positive image of Japan through their reports back to the United States. For example, William Elliot Griffis, who taught in Japan from 1870 to 1874, returned to write the most popular history of Japan in its day, *The Mikado's Empire*. Ernest Fenollosa, a professor at the University of Tokyo, became famous as an interpreter of cultures between the two countries and for saving traditional Japanese art from the ravages of overexuberant modernization. Along with Griffis and Fenollosa come a score of other Americans—William Clark, Edward S. Morse, J. C. Hepburn, Marion M. Scott, and David Murray, to name but a few—all well known to scholars of Japan as people who brought the two nations together. Along with the famous, thousands of unknown Americans also came to Japan to work and teach, and their letters back home, newspaper articles, and books about life in Japan also helped to forge a strong affinity for Japanese in the hearts of Americans.

To say that the relationship was one of pupil and teacher is undoubtedly true, but it also was much more complex than that. In acting as an intermediary between Japan and the European powers, and in its attempts to increase Japan's control over its own commerce vis-à-vis those powers, the United States was undoubtedly being benevolent but not altruistic. It also had its own interests in Asia and wanted to insure that it would not be locked out of Japan or China by the Europeans. The United States needed to assure itself that it could get its economic needs fulfilled in the Orient without benefit of colonial possession. Therefore it depended upon securing most-favored-nation status in Japan and China by insuring that all Western nations were allowed an equal footing and that international law and treaty commitments were secured. If conditions were to dissolve into a land grab in Asia by the European powers, the United States, undermanned and psychologically unprepared to take colonies, would be left out in the cold.[6] It was this condition that was at the root of the Open Door policy in China, one of the major factors in the falling out between the United States and Japan.

By the turn of the century the United States was a Pacific country. California's statehood came in 1850 as a result of territory gained from Mexico by war, wealth created by the gold rush of the late 1840s, and a population increase that resulted from the gold rush and the European political upheavals of the late 1840s. Commercial centers such as San Francisco looked to the west and were not content to be railheads for East Coast merchants. They wanted to be independent commercial centers. And as the United States grew in economic power, so did it grow in political power, raising a debate over the taking of colonies—the symbol of great power status. Although the taking of colonies had been held off by both Republican and Democratic administrations of the 1870s and 1880s, the McKinley administration (1897–1901) at last accepted Guam, the Philippines, Puerto Rico, and Cuba as fruits of the Spanish-American War. Hawaii was annexed shortly thereafter. Thus the American interest in Asia became more pragmatic every day, and with it came greater friction with the other power expanding in the East, Japan.

It was the Russo-Japanese War that ended the special relationship and set Japan and the United States on a course of conflict. When Japan defeated China in 1894 its victory was praised in the United States as an example of how well its lessons had been learned. In those days the sympathy had been for Japan, the underdog that had studied the lessons of modernization and Americanization well and had proven its worth. The defeat of a Western power, however, was a different story altogether. The international relations theories of the day were highly racist and were based to a great extent on social Darwinism. The defeat of a Caucasian power by a non-Caucasian race negated the concept of Western superiority upon which the legitimacy of colonialism rested. Although the United States was a newcomer to the ranks of colonial powers, the message sent out by the Japanese at Tsushima was understood equally by Filipinos as well as Indians.

The success of Japan against Russia was the beginning of the "yellow peril." The popular press began to print reports that the Japanese would not be satisfied with their victory over Russia. Now that they had tasted blood, they would soon challenge the north coast of Australia, fight the French for Indochina, beat the British and the Dutch out of Southeast Asia, and even attack Hawaii and the West Coast of North America. The war scare was especially strong in California, and it served to support an anti-Oriental immigration movement. There had long been complaints about Chinese immigration on the West Coast based on racial and cultural differences, the Asian immigrants' willingness to work for low wages and anti-unionism, and fears that unchecked immigration would leave immigrants in control of local politics. As a result, the federal government excluded Chinese from immigrating in 1882, and the San Francisco Board of Education created segregated schools for Chinese students. The combination of the yellow peril war scare and labor union control of city hall was enough to bring about the expulsion of Japanese students into the segregated schools on October 11, 1906. This segregation of Japanese came only a few months after Japan sent more money through the Red Cross for relief of the April 18 earthquake than all other nations combined.[7] It must be said, however, that the anti-Japanese racism of the West Coast was not matched by the rest of the country, as evidenced by the obvious irritation found in a *San Francisco Chronicle* editorial of November 7, 1906: "There is an astonishing disposition shown by Eastern editors to crawl on their bellies when discussing the Japanese question. Is it really a fact that the prowess displayed by the little brown men in their recent war with Russia has so frightened them that they feel compelled to ask whether American polity must be governed by fear of the consequences of the wrath of foreigners?"[8]

The impudence of the Japanese victory and the resultant Japanese swagger may have exacerbated existing racism in California, but the government of the United States was more concerned about the favorable position in Northeast Asia attained by Japan. President Roosevelt 's price for American mediation of the war was a Japanese guarantee of continued support for the Open Door policy. In addition, Roosevelt joined with the other Western powers to deny Japan's claim for $600 million in indemnities and successfully reduced its territorial gains. Even so, the territories gained in the war gave Japan a footing in Korea, Manchuria, and the Liaotung Peninsula that could be used to gain further concessions in China. Although the two governments negotiated several agreements recognizing Japan's status quo and the Open Door, and worked to calm the exclusion controversy, Japan's actions during the First World War made its intentions of economic and political control in China patently clear. It was from this time that both the United States and Japan began to plan seriously for the contingency of a Japanese-American war in the Pacific.

There were periods of amity following the First World War, most notably the Washington Conference for naval disarmament and the help both the government of the United States and the American people extended to Japan after the Tokyo earthquake of 1923, but relations continued to sour. Most destructive were the exclusion of Japanese from immigration to the United States and the steady pressure by Japan for control of China. Although Japan had been voluntarily withholding passports from Japanese laborers who wished to immigrate to the United States since the two countries entered into a Gentleman's Agreement in 1908, it still allowed a small window of opportunity for Japanese wishing to move to America, especially for women who came over as brides for Japanese men already living in the United States. Writing and passing a new immigration law that would put strict quotas on immigration was a major priority for Congress in the early 1920s because Americans were worried about a massive wave of immigration from Europe following the disruptions of the recent war. Although the quotas in the proposed bill promised to limit immigration from Japan to only about 250 people per year, anti-Japanese agitators on the West Coast lobbied strongly for total exclusion of Japanese. The Coolidge administration (1923–29) opposed it, but it was nonetheless passed as part of the 1924 Immigration Bill. The reaction from Japan was explosive. Japan had become extremely sensitive to anti-Japanese racism in the West, and this was seen as a blatant case. Massive anti-American rallies were held throughout the country, and America and its supporters were discredited. The wave of anti-Americanism in Japan created in turn its own backlash against Japan in the United States, giving greater power to those who had lobbied for Japanese exclusion.

Negative American attitudes toward Japan were strengthened as Japan moved further into China during the 1930s. Many Americans held benevolent, paternalistic attitudes toward the Chinese after decades of American missionary activities in China. The Japanese annexation of Manchuria, the bombing of Shanghai, and the invasion of China proper all confirmed the dominant American public opinion that Japan had become an evil power. The following passage in *Japan over Asia*, written on the eve of the Sino-Japanese War by William H. Chamberlin, the *Christian Science Monitor*'s

chief correspondent for Japan and the Far East, is similar in tone to most American coverage of Japan at the time.

In short, "Japan Over Asia" to-day has become a living reality, for which Japanese soldiers and sailors and airmen go to their deaths with traditional courage, with *banzais* for the Emperor on their lips, and for which the Japanese masses will have to pinch and scrape still more as the war bills fall due for payment.

The immediate response of the Japanese people to the war has been one of unanimous patriotism. Doubts and criticisms are uttered in hushed voices, if at all. Not a voice has been raised in the Diet in criticism of the war. The outward signs are all of enthusiasm: resounding cheers for the reservists who depart daily for the front; women collecting a thousand stitches on garments for soldiers, in the belief that this will serve as a talisman; long lines of people, from middle-aged business-men to little schoolgirls, filing into the War and Navy Departments to make voluntary offerings for the benefit of soldiers and sailors.[9]

The image of Japan as the scourge of Asia grew stronger as Japan cut deeper into the heart of China, but it also was becoming increasingly irrelevant. By the early 1930s Americans had turned inward to deal with their own economic problems and shut out the unpleasantness sweeping the world in both Europe and Asia. Not even the sinking of an American ship, the *Panay*, by Japan could get the United States to act. As Senator William Borah wrote, "I am not prepared to vote to send our boys into the Orient because a boat was sunk which was traveling in a dangerous zone."[10]

Although interest waned and the government would not act directly in China, newspapers and books kept the images of the bombing, the "Rape of Nanjing," and other incidents in the public's eye. The accumulated weight of American writing about Japan during the 1930s meant that it took no great effort to convince Americans that the "sneaky little Japs" were a menace to the world that needed to be stopped when the war between Japan and the United States finally came. There is no need to elaborate here about the image of Japan during the war, especially as it has been so well described by John Dower in his book, *War without Mercy*.

POSTWAR IMAGES

The American image of Japan has undergone various changes since the end of the war. When memories of the war and anti-Japanese propaganda were still fresh in their minds, Americans continued to perceive Japan as a nationalistic, militaristic country that had been foiled only by superior American military strength in its plan to stretch the Japanese empire to the "eight corners of the world." At the beginning of the occupation, the American government's policies were intended to end the nationalism and militarism that were believed to have been the root causes of the war in Asia. But initial occupation policies were much less harsh than they might have been, in part because American policy makers also held a "black top" image of Japan. They believed that the common Japanese citizen was led down the path of militarism and aggression by a nationalistic elite and that what could be learned could also be unlearned. The job of the occupation was not just to break up the *zaibatsu* (family-owned holding companies) and scrap military hardware, it was to change the very minds of the Japanese. To make them think and act in ways consistent with American democracy. In the words of *Our Job in Japan*, the government training film shown to Americans participating in the occupation, "They [the Japanese] can make trouble or they can make sense. It is our job to make sure that they make sense."

This perception of the Japanese as a people fundamentally no different from any other people but misled by a nationalistic elite aided a rapid reversal of the American image of Japan. Nearly two million Americans passed through Japan during the occupation,[11] and they brought back to Kansas and California and Maine images that were, for the most part, positive. Those GIs stationed in Japan immediately after the fighting were impressed by the willingness of the Japanese to work with the occupation forces. The extensive fraternizing that went on between the occupying forces and the civilian population, although more curtailed as the occupation continued, allowed Americans to see Japanese in their human, and often suffering, condition. Love bloomed between GIs and "Mooses" (*musume*, literally "daughter"). Mutual respect fostered cooperation, and sometimes friendship, between occupier and ex-soldier. If suffering made the Japanese seem more human, so did compassion make Americans seem more human in their eyes. Young GIs giving chocolates to children, driving them around in their Jeeps, and playing baseball with them have become such standard and hackneyed images of the occupation that it is easy to dismiss them as a Rockwellization of reality. However, the truth behind the image is revealed as one listens to so many stories told by Japanese who were those children. Sober, hardened Japanese businessmen speak with tears in their eyes about getting food and smiles and, yes, even ragged baseball gloves from the men some came to see as replacements for older brothers or fathers they had lost in the war. For all their experiences in the war, many of the GIs who took part in the initial stages of the occupation were not much older than boys themselves. For every Japanese who remembers being given a smile or a baseball glove, there is a member of the occupation who remembers bouncing about the back roads of Japan free as a bird and fed like a bear. These human bonds gave real meaning to occupation policies that were intended to fix, feed, heal, and teach.

As teachers are wont to do, Americans fell in love with their students, and the students reciprocated. In one sense the love was literal: some 20,000 GIs had married Japanese women by 1955,[12] and the unsanctioned liaisons were countless. On a more figurative level, Americans fell in love with the new Japan because it was being re-created in their own image. The popularity of American popular culture there was enormous and continued to grow throughout the postwar period. Americans brought hamburgers, bobby socks, Alan Ladd, and *Reader's Digest* with them when they came, and they stayed long after the occupation ended. Americans began to develop a "just like us" attitude toward Japan. Japanese schools had PTAs. Japanese drug stores had Coca-Cola. Japanese girls wore jeans. Japanese boys played baseball. Japanese of all sexes and ages loved watching pro wrestling. The Japanese government was "our" democracy. Even the political and social restlessness of the young "Sun Tribe" juvenile delinquents and peacenik demonstrators was an example of the changes wrought by the American occupation.

The Americanization of Japan was especially potent in the popular culture. Once the control of the media by the Japanese government had been replaced by that of SCAP (the Supreme Commander of the Allied Powers), General Douglas MacArthur, Japanese radio was reorganized by American standards. Programming schedules were divided into fifteen-minute segments. Man-in-the-street interviews, game shows, quiz shows, and variety shows became standard fare. As television replaced radio as the dominant broadcast medium, the trend continued. Two of the most popular television series in the history of Japanese television were "Laramie" (41 percent audience share) and "Rawhide" (35 percent audience share). By 1964, the peak of American programming, there were fourteen dramas, fourteen comedies, and eighteen sports shows available on Japanese television. If you had been watching television in Tokyo on a Friday night in August 1960, you would have had your choice of the "Alfred Hitchcock Show," the "Roy Rogers Show," "Wyatt Earp," "Ben Casey," or "Gunsmoke." Millions of Japanese saw the American Dream, not only in the home of Beaver Cleaver but also in movies and magazines. The economic miracle was in great part fueled by the belief that they, too, could own two cars and a lovely home surrounded by a quarter acre of lawn set with birdbaths and pink flamingos. Japanese leaders of today once pictured themselves as teen-dream dragsters rockin' out of their jeans—James Dean on the way to Dead Man's Curve. Ironically, the classic Japanese rebel without a cause was Shintaro Ishihara, ultraconservative member of the Liberal Democratic Party and author of *The Japan That Can Say No*.

The reverse of the "just like us" image was the "Tea House of the August Moon" image. Although most of the American occupiers may have been little interested in Japanese culture, they were exposed to the best of it, and some of it stuck. The occupation authorities reserved all the best houses and hotels in Japan for the occupation, and anyone in the occupation could experience the best Japan had to offer, culture or scenery, for almost literally nothing. Americans who previously had never been anywhere more exotic than Broadway were now being shown the tea ceremony, sitting legs akimbo watching *kabuki*, shouldering an *omikoshi* (portable festival shrine), or eating the quivering, translucent flesh of a still live fish. Starving families were ready to offer the most precious prints, porcelain, *netsuke* (ivory carvings), or whatever valuables they had for very little money and sometimes just for food.

Both the artifacts and the experiences were brought back with them to the United States and were quickly circulated among friends and relatives along with stories about what a good and strange time they had. The combination of being simultaneously just like us and exotic was potent, and America's interest was piqued. American tourism in Japan grew after the war, as did the importation of Japanese art and culture. *Rashomon*, *Ugetsu*, *Gates of Hell*, *The Seven Samurai*, and *Yojimbo* won over American film critics and had a strong impact on American film making then and now. Books about the exotic nature of Japan flourished, as did Japanese architecture and design. Even that most un-American religion, Zen Buddhism, became the spiritual guide of the "Dharma Bum" beat generation and the hippies who followed. The translated works of Kawabata, Mishima, Abe, and others found ready audiences in the United States. Millions of Americans took up the Japanese martial arts.

The economic image of Japan, to the extent that it existed, saw Japan as a developing economy, able to produce little more than blouses, canned tuna, and bicycles. Before the 1970s, "Made in Japan" meant shoddy and imitative. When one saw a Japanese car on the road in the United States in the 1960s, two thoughts came to mind. The first was how quaint the car was, and the other was why would anyone buy one.

While the shoddy, imitative, and quaint image of Japanese products remained ingrained in the American image of Japan during the 1960s, by the end of the decade the Japanese-American economic relationship had changed significantly. In 1965 Japan gained its first surplus in its bilateral balance of trade with the United States. Although Japan's surplus approached one billion dollars for the first time in 1969, the imbalance in bilateral trade did not become an issue in and of itself until the early 1970s. However, regenerated fear of Japanese economic strength was great enough for Richard Nixon to use relief from Japanese textile imports as part of his "southern strategy" in the 1968 presidential campaign. But by that time textiles and canned tuna were already being replaced by steel, motorcycles, automobiles, cameras, and electronic goods of every type as the real sellers in the American market.

Suddenly, the United States had discovered another image of Japan—"Japan, Inc." In the early days, Japanese economic production was still seen as being cute, imitative, and just like us, but as the deficits grew and American industries began to suffer from the competition, the images became increasingly negative and awed. Japan was pictured as some great factory of a nation where millions of indistinguishable robots rose every morning to be packed into trains and transported into Tokyo where they were plugged into their work stations for fourteen hours a day with no thoughts other than produce, produce, produce. The contemporary American image of Japan and the Japanese is now more sophisticated than that of the early Japan, Inc. days, but it is from this economic change in the relationship at the turn of the 1970s that the contemporary images, both positive and negative, are drawn.

CONTEMPORARY IMAGES

Scholars of the Japanese-American relationship frequently lament the communication gap between the two cultures. The gap comprises two basic components: there is too little information available to each country about the other, and there is more information about the United States in Japan than vice versa. This very simple set of ideas has given rise to a host of research projects sponsored by governments, research institutes, and academic institutions. The goals of these institutions and their projects—to create simultaneously realistic and positive images on both sides by closing the communication gap—are laudable, but the attempts to attain them sometimes take on the appearance of the search for the Lost Ark. I have been a member of several of these projects over the past seventeen years, and it is my conclusion that they have been invaluable in generating information about the attitudes, images, public opinion, and media of each country, but they have had mixed success in altering the process of image formation and closing the communication gap.

Certainly there is much more information about Japan available in the United States than ever before, but it still lags far behind the amount of information about the United States available in Japan. American movies continue to dominate the box office in Japan, while Japanese films, even popular films such as Juzo Itami's *A Taxing Woman*, still have limited audiences in the United States. American books are frequently translated into Japanese, but few Japanese books are available in English translation in the United States. American popular music still takes a mighty share of the Japanese music market and FM play time, but Japanese popular music is virtually unknown in the United States. Finally, news stories about the United States in the Japanese media far outnumber their opposites in the United States. This imbalance may be deplored, even though it is less than it has been in the past, but it reflects reality and is thus difficult to alter significantly. American popular culture has had universal appeal since the 1920s, and Japan is not alone in being a net importer.

The imbalance in news reporting endures because Japan continues to focus on events in the United States, while the United States continues to have many points of focus outside its borders. Specialists in the Japanese-American relationship can become very provincial. They assume the validity of Ambassador Mike Mansfield's assertion that the United States' relationship to Japan is its most important relationship, "bar none." But even as the world drifts into the new order, Cold War legacies are hard to leave behind. The United States is still the most important country for Japan, economically, politically, culturally, and militarily. But for all of Japan's economic importance to the United States, and its growing political importance, Japan is still just one of many areas of the world upon which Americans must focus their attention. Canada and Mexico, Great Britain, Western Europe, Eastern Europe, and the Middle East are all likely centers of action that affect a variety of American interests and thereby claim the attention of its media.

Most of the projects researching the communciation gap have called for broader and more balanced reporting on both sides of the Pacific. There has been an increase in the number of stories about Japan in the American media, and a broader range of stories. Economic news predominates, but cultural and political stories have become more and more common. Nevertheless, reporters on both sides say that when they want to file the broader, more objective stories, they have a hard time convincing their editors to run them. In the eyes of most editors, stories that don't have punch and are not directly related to the interests of their readers don't sell newspapers or television advertising. Stories about trade friction, the latest negative quote from a Japanese politician, or the sledgehammering of a Japanese automobile in Detroit *do* sell.

It may be that the problem in Japanese-American communication is no longer a gap but rather communication overkill. Intuitively it would seem that the more communication there is between two cultures, and the more knowledge of the other culture, the better their relations will be. That is not necessarily true. The important factors are the similarities of the two cultures involved and the negative or positive nature of the information received. If there is an increase in stories in one country's media about another country, but that information is essentially negative, then negative images will increase. However, even if the information received is objective and factual, there is no guarantee that it will create a positive feeling toward that culture. To make a simple analogy, two people of the opposite sex may develop a mutual infatuation until they really get to know each other. Once they get to know all the habits, behaviors, and idiosyncrasies of their partner, songbirds and flowers may turn to daggers and ice. Finding out that your loved one voted for Ronald Reagan, hums at the breakfast table, and is an anal-retentive housekeeper may bring a quick end to a promising start.

While this and other "marriage" analogies have been too frequently used to describe the relationship between Japan and the United States, they have within them a fundamental truth. Getting to know one another means accepting the warts along with the beauty marks. However, as long as the goal is to increase the availability of information about Japan, as opposed to creating a positive image of Japan, then there has been success. The image that Americans have of Japan has become broader and deeper, even if that increased knowledge has created problems in the short run. The ambivalence and cognitive dissonance that Americans feel toward Japan is due to the fact that they have been presented all sides of a complex people. Most people need to have, want to have, a simple view of the world, but the world is not simple; it is confusing. If we want to know about another people we must accept confusing, contradictory information. If Americans now know more about the racism of Japan as well as its work ethic, the immigrant labor problem as well as the lifetime employment system, at least they no longer think of Japanese in the hollow, one-dimensional images of *geisha* or economic animal.

Even though Americans have a broader and more knowledgeable image of Japanese than they did ten or twenty years ago, the level of knowledge is not very deep. Although 55 percent of those answering a *Time*/CNN poll taken in January 1992 said that they knew a lot (13 percent) or some things (42 percent), people may think they know more than they actually do. While we can assume that most Americans now know where Japan is (just ten years ago many Americans still thought Japan was a part of China), few seem to know many hard political or economic facts about Japan. An Opinion Dynamics survey taken in late October 1991 found that only 35 percent of those responding to their survey knew that Japan was a freely elected democracy. A fifth thought that Japan was run by the emperor, 16 percent thought that Japan was a dictatorship, 13 percent thought it was run by the military, and 17 percent were honest enough to say that they didn't know. About 50 percent of the respondents identified Japan as the United States' largest trading partner, but only 9 percent knew that it was actually Canada. These results are troublesome enough, but more problematic is the apparent lack of knowledge about Japanese policy and interaction with the United States. The same poll asked Americans to choose from a list of four figures the correct amount of money given by Japan as their contribution to the Gulf War effort. Only 10 percent correctly chose the $13 billion figure, while 56 percent thought it was less and 25 percent didn't know. This lack of knowledge about Japan's contribution to the war was made clear to me during the summer of 1991 when, months after the money had been transferred to Washington, people were asking me why Japan didn't do anything to support the war and were wondering when they were going to pay up.

There is also the problem of overintensity. The media in both countries are both oversensitive and overanalytical of what is occurring in the other country. Every misguided speech by a national legislator trying to save his or her seat in a close election by running a "save the rice" or "save our jobs" campaign is covered as if they were major statements of national policy. The media on both sides of the Pacific are ready to pounce on any pronouncement that may rock the relationship, regardless of the context, source, or significance. This overintensity of communication can cause problems where none exist. Glen Fukushima, a well-respected figure in both Japan and the United States, tells a great story about the book, *The Coming War with Japan*. In April 1991 he traveled to the United States on business and happened upon the book in the Stanford University bookstore. He questioned its worth, but thought he should purchase a copy anyway as the title alone insured that it would be a point of discussion among Japanese observers of United States-Japan relations. At Stanford, and then in his subsequent travels in Cambridge and Washington, he asked people, most of whom were knowledgeable about Japanese-American relations, what they thought of the book and found that none had heard of it. It was not until he attended a conference on Japanese-American media relations in Hawaii at the end of the month that he finally found someone who had heard of it, a Japanese journalist who informed him that articles were being written about it in Japan and that it was about to be translated into Japanese. Upon his return to Japan he found that, indeed, it was being translated into Japanese and that it was being hailed as a best seller in the United States. This was news to him. Not only was it being translated, but its authors had become celebrities in the Japanese media. Finally, he was listening to a rebroadcast of the "Paul Harvey Show" on the American Armed Forces Network in Tokyo when Paul Harvey made a comment that there was a new book written by Americans on the possibility of a coming war with Japan, and it was a best seller—in Japan.

As Fukushima puts it, here is a book virtually unknown in the United States that was depicted as an American best seller by the Japanese media, which had the effect of propelling it to be a best seller in Japan, which in turn led the American media to focus on the book because it had become a best seller in Japan. If there had been no Japanese media coverage of the book in the first place, it would have been left to die a quiet death on the remainder shelves of America, raising little or no concern or comment.

Whether the American perception of Japan is becoming more negative depends upon how the polls are read, and the polling data certainly reflect the ambivalence of American perceptions of Japan and Japanese. There are increased negatives, but whether they form a trend is open to interpretation. The American approval rating of Japan has fluctuated between roughly 60 percent and 75 percent ever since the mid-1960s and remains about 60 percent in the most recent polls. A Gallup Poll of October 1991 showed 22 percent of respondents thought that Japan was a close ally, the highest since the question was first asked in 1964. This is of special interest as it comes at the same time that Americans are more willing to see Japan as a threat. While only four percent were willing to term Japan an "enemy," many see Japan as a direct threat to the United States' national interest. ABC/Harris polls have seen those that believe the economic power of Japan is a greater threat to the United States than the military power of the

Soviet Union rise from 45 percent in February 1989 to 75 percent in March 1991. A Kyodo News Service poll conducted in November 1991 found that 89 percent of those contacted thought that Japan was either a great threat or a minor threat, but that 53 percent also called Japan a trustworthy ally. Similarly, a Gallup Poll taken from January to March 1992 showed the highest level of mistrust in Japan (44 percent) since 1960 (55 percent), but at the same time reported that their respondents' perceptions of Japan as dependable rose from 44 percent in 1991 to 49 percent in 1992.

The American image of Japan remains positive, but is increasingly ambivalent as negative perceptions are on the rise. As Walter Mead wrote in the *Los Angeles Times*, "The Red Menace is dead; long live the Yellow Peril." Ironically it may be as much a belief in the virtues of Japanese as a belief in the evils of Japan that causes fear in the United States. Americans praise the Japanese for their work ethic, industriousness, their technological achievements, their education system, management system, and the quality of their products, but these are also the things that make them such a threat to the American economy.

There are many elements fueling the recent increase in American concern with Japan. First there is a need to find a focal point in the world now that the American world view is no longer defined by its conflict with the Soviet Union. Second is a form of racism in the United States which may have more to do with the growth of an Asian people to the same status, or even higher status, than Americans than it does with the color of their skin. The third element is a perceived reverse racism and projected superiority by the Japanese. Fourth is the realization that Japanese are no longer "just like us." Fifth is the fear of economic failure in the United States and the domination of the American economy by Japanese. Sixth is the sense of defeatism based on the belief that an inept United States is rapidly losing its preeminent place in the world to an infallible Japan. Last, there is the fear of a renewed Japanese nationalism in which Japan will rise up to threaten the United States militarily as well as economically.

For the two decades between the two world wars, the United Staes was a power with little interest in the world. Its first experiences as a global power in World War I created a feeling in the United States that others should be left to fend for themselves. From the American point of view, after having come to the aid of the democracies in Europe, they ungratefully refused to pay back the loans that were made during the war. Bickering over the issue continued from soon after the end of the war until all loan recipients, with the exception of Finland, defaulted in 1935. The American reaction was to say "never again." Never again did Americans want to see young American men slaughtered in foreign fields for reasons unimportant and unintelligible. Many Americans and much of Congress was committed to isolationism until the attack on Pearl Harbor. In addition to the bitterness of America's first major military engagement outside the western hemisphere, most Americans were concerned with staying alive and well during the Depression. It was simply too much to care about what was going on elsewhere, especially as it was so far away across those two big oceans. Consequently, when Japan invaded Manchuria and then China, and even when it deliberately sank an American naval vessel, most Americans felt animosity toward Japan but not the willingness to get involved.

All that changed when the United States entered the Second World War. This was a cause worth fighting for: not only was the United Staes attacked by Japan, but Hitler and the Nazis had become identified as an evil worth fighting. This decision to fight became even more justified in the eyes of Americans by the end of the war when the atrocities that were committed before and during the war by the Nazis were publicized. Americans felt more than justified in going to war and believed the United States was the savior of the world. Thus, as the Soviet menace and Stalin replaced the Nazi menace and Hitler, Americans were willing to continue their role as keepers of the flame of democracy. The United States had taken command of the world during the war and used its power to create a postwar international system of political and economic relations which it then had a stake in protecting from its ideological nemesis. As a result, the raison d'être of the United States had become the protection of its national security, ideology, and the world from another powerful and highly visible enemy.

By 1992 there are few Americans who did not grow up instilled with a world view defined by the American victory in the Second World War and the struggle of the Cold War. Although the folly and defeat of the war in Vietnam challenged that world view, its resurgence during the Reagan years proved its strength and resiliency. Now that the Cold War is over, however, there is no one dominant threat to the United States' national interest or its ideology. Neither is there a definable world based upon such easy dichotomies as good and evil, right and wrong, democratic and communist. The United States is not, as some have made it out to be, like a soldier who finds after the fighting ends that he actually craves war and can only define himself through battle. The United States is more like the soldier who returns from the war only to find that everything has changed, his job is not there, his girl has left him, and his town has grown up. The United States is searching for a new place in the world and a new direction for its policy. In this state of global anomie, old patterns of behavior bring comfort and old fears remain. Americans are no different from the peoples of many other nations in that there is a need to identify *the* enemy, who serves as a focus for the nation's energies and a reason for national organization and unity. To the extent that Americans are convinced that the next challenge will be economic rather than military, they will increasingly be tempted to see Japan as that one great enemy to be confronted. The problem is in their perception of Japan as an economic enemy as opposed to an economic ally, and their perception of international economics as a zero-sum game conflict as opposed to a variable-sum cooperative effort.

Racism is a part of Japanese-American relations and is manifested equally on both sides of the relationship. It has always been so, and it continues to be today, although neither Japanese nor American racism is as blatant or as widespread as it has been in the past. But it exists nonetheless. Japanese racist attitudes toward America are generally expressed by denigrating the multiracial, multicultural nature of American society while praising the harmony and solidarity of a "one-blood, one-race" Japan.

There is an element of racism in American dislike of Japanese, but it has more to do with America's dislike of Japan's success than it does of their skin color. Because Japanese are not Western and of a different hue it is easier to single them out as a threat, but it is also because Americans have for so long regarded them as essentially inferior. Although there are famous individual cases of Japanese being attacked because they are the living representation of economic threat, Americans' ill feelings toward Japanese have more to do with their inability, even after two decades of Japanese economic success, to accept that the younger brother has grown up. And there is an even greater unwillingness to think of the former pupil as a teacher.

It is one thing for Americans to turn against Japanese because they think that Japanese are superior in their ability to produce products and manage their economy, but when Japanese say it themselves, it only makes Americans angrier. In their own minds many Americans can admit to the successes of Japan and even consider the possibility of learning from Japan and Japanese, but they often balk at the reality. There is a perception in the United States that Japanese people now tend to see themselves as superior, and such attitudes are not taken very kindly. A *Los Angeles Times* poll taken in January and February 1992 showed that two-thirds of respondents thought that the Japanese look down on them, as opposed to the one-fifth who thought that Japanese respect Americans; while a 1993 Opinion Dynamics poll found half their respondents looked down upon and one-third felt respected by Japanese. A February 1992 *Washington Post*/ABC News poll also found 60 percent of respondents believe that Japanese are prejudiced against Americans. The feelings are reciprocated. A 1993 CBS/*New York Times* poll found that 77 percent of Japanese felt that Americans looked down on them.

When Americans read about statements from Japanese government officials and businessmen about the incompetency of American labor and management it creates ill feelings, even though Americans may say the same things about themselves. Take, for example, the statements made by Hajime Karatsu, a respected Japanese intellectual who knows the United States well, in a *Japan Times* op ed article.[13] In arguing that the United States has no right to criticize Japan for blocking rice imports as the United States protects its own market for peanuts, he writes, "Americans should know that their faults will come out, regardless of their one-sided selfish arguments." He then goes on to say that Americans should learn to "capture the Japanese heart" by saying "thank you" for purchasing large amounts of its beef, pork, chicken, and citrus exports because if it does not, "business talks between us will not go well." The facts in these statements are true, and the sentiments are understandable, but most Americans reading his article would tend to focus on the lecturing tone of the article rather than the reasonableness of the argument.

Japanese markets are less open to American goods than is the reverse, but Japan also is one of America's best customers, and not only for agricultural goods. In 1990 the United States exported $48.6 billion of goods to Japan, second only to Canada's $83.6 billion but much higher than third-ranked Mexico's $28.3 billion. American agricultural exports to Japan comprise a significant portion of all agricultural exports in that 78 percent of pork exports, 20 percent of chicken exports, 49 percent of meat exports, 62 percent of fish exports, 20 percent of cereal exports, and 40 percent of citrus exports went to Japan. But Japan buys more than agricultural goods. In that year the United States also exported to Japan $3.7 billion of office machines and data processors, $2.4 billion of electrical appliances, $1.6 billion of road vehicles, $1.6 billion of professional and scientific instruments, and $3.5 billion of miscellaneous manufactured goods. These are substantial numbers. In most cases, they are higher than those for any other country outside Canada and Mexico. But it is still hard for Americans to be thankful that Japan imports what it does when Japanese exports to the United States are 1.8 times greater than the reverse, and are primarily manufactured goods. Under these circumstances, increasing exports to Japan is viewed as being "only fair."

The often cavalier attitude Japanese have toward the United States is exacerbated by economic problems in the United States. Americans are accustomed to throwing their weight around in other countries' markets, but feel as if they are being treated as a poor relation when they discover Japanese coming to "buy up" the United States, whether it be factories, farms, real estate, or sports franchises. This was especially disgruntling when the United States was in a recession because much of what Japanese were buying in the United States was unattainable for the average American. Whether they are businessmen in New York or golfers in California, Americans have come to perceive Japanese in America as arrogant people who act as if they are superior to those around them. This type of behavior is repulsive to Americans in general, who have a very strong sense of egalitarianism in their culture and a sensitivity to European snobbery that predates the Revolution. But when the perceived snobbish behavior comes from a people that they consider to have been inferior, then it is even harder to take.

Americans also perceive a form of racism in the "gilded ghetto" syndrome of many Japanese communities in the United States. One of the major differences for an American living in Japan and a Japanese living in

the United States is the host culture's expectation of assimilation. Americans expect foreigners to know English and expect foreigners to assimilate into the American culture. Those foreigners who do not attempt to assimilate are often looked on as not liking the United States or purposely removing themselves from Americans.

Most Japanese who come to the United States do not intend to assimilate into the culture; rather, they come on a few years' assignment from their companies and remain in the company of other Japanese and in gilded ghettos such as Fort Lee or Woodridge, New Jersey. Their nonassimilation is due to the fact that they feel more comfortable within the confines of known behavioral patterns and because they know they will be returning to Japan in a relatively short time. Grouping behavior also extends to Japanese students who come to study in the United States. This often leads Americans who have contact with them to believe that "they think they are better than us" and do not want to mix.

Americans are also put off by what are perceived as racist attitudes. Speeches by former Prime Minister Yasuhiro Nakasone and other government officials have made it clear that America's decline is in large part due to the heterogeneity of America, especially the large percentage of African Americans and Hispanics. Americans feel that they are not being treated equally by Japanese. This is certainly part of the perception that Japan is an unfair trader. It is believed that the Japanese government does not give an even break to American importers and that Japanese consumers are unwilling to buy American goods. Thus there is support for the notion that it is up to the American government to force American products on Japan.

There is increased resentment against Japanese companies who treat their American employees as second class citizens within their own country. There have been a growing number of cases of American employees who have found obvious discrimination and sexual harassment in Japanese offices. More subtly, those executives who work for Japanese companies find that there is a glass ceiling for all foreign employees and that one can rise only so far in the office. All the important positions are held by Japanese. In some ways this is exacerbated by the fact that before they entered the Japanese company they believed they would be treated better than in an American company. Those who have read the literature on Japanese management are led to believe that all people in Japanese corporations are treated equally and that the "human-oriented" nature of Japanese management means that the company melds their concern with the welfare of the employee to the production of the product. The highly touted lifetime employment system is the most obvious manifestation of this belief. Japanese companies in the United States do nothing to disabuse their American employees of these ideas and often encourage them. Thus, when the company begins to treat them differently because there are different standards for Japanese and American employees, or when the company lays them off, the feelings of anger are even greater because it was expected that Japanese corporations do not behave in such ways.

An ironic cause of American ambivalence toward Japanese is that they are less perceived as being "just like us." It is ironic because in many ways they are still just like us but, as explained above, in ways that are less than pleasant. The "Ugly Japanese" has indeed taken the place of the "Ugly American." Japanese success in the world economy has given them license to lecture to America in the way that American success gave it licence to lecture to the world. Negative similarities aside, if Americans perceive Japan as a child that has grown up, it has grown up as a wayward child. The parent observes the child's behavior and says, "We never taught you to behave like that. Don't you have any respect for us?" Americans feel responsible for having brought Japan into the postwar world and expect that the child will follow in the parent's footsteps. Thus the realization that Japanese are still Japanese, and not copies of their American parents, can come as a shock. This feeling underlies much of the belief in the United States that Japan is "unfair." The ground rules of democratic capitalism are assumed to be American ground rules, and they are disturbed when Japan plays by different rules.

The above-mentioned dislike for Japanese who are perceived to have disdain for the United States is at worst related to the fear that Japan desires, in some unspecified fashion, to control the American economy. At best, the negative perceptions that Americans have of Japan come from their fears concerning the health of the American economy and the effect it will have on them personally. A variety of polls demonstrate that the greatest increase in negative/threat perceptions are economic: Japan is to blame for the trade imbalance, Japan is an unfair trader, Japanese investment in the United States is a threat, the American economy is on the wrong track, and Americans should start buying American products.

Concern about the Japanese purchase of American assets is echoed by Michael Crichton's now famous quote from Akio Morita. "If you don't want Japan to buy it, don't sell it." The perception is that unscrupulous Americans are selling out the United States to the Japanese, allowing them eventually to dominate the United States in every way. Not only are Japanese buying economic assets, factories, cattle ranches, houses, movie studios, Rockefeller Center, technology, and financial institutions, but they are also buying American minds. The large amount of Japanese money available in the United States for academic institutions, lobbying in state and national governments, and the purchase of cultural assets raises suspicions. Why do Japanese want to buy American colleges and move their students over here? They must want to purchase movie studios so only their point of view will be shown in films. They are buying American golf courses so they can keep them for themselves. The sensitivity to the purchase of American assets by Japanese was best demonstrated by the proposed purchase of the Seattle Mariners baseball franchise by Nintendo, a Japanese-owned but locally based company. When Nintendo's name was first mentioned in connection with the purchase of the Mariners there was an immediate public outcry against it everywhere outside Seattle. The Commissioner of Baseball immediately stated that he was opposed to foreign ownership of professional franchises. Sports writers across the United States debated the pros and cons of Japanese ownership. Lost in the outcry was the fact that Nintendo did not originally seek the deal but was sought out by the city because Seattle did not want to lose its professional baseball team. Indeed, Nintendo hesitated because it knew that there would be public reaction against Japanese ownership of an American baseball team.

There is also a fear, most clearly expressed by Pat Choate in *Agents of Influence*, that Japanese money is creating a kind of fifth column in the United States. Opinion leaders from the academic, journalist, and public relations world are accepting Japanese money to spread the good word in America, while those who tell the truth about Japan (that is, those who speak about the negatives in Japan) are repressed, subtly or otherwise, by the Japanese and their minions in the United States. This kind of thinking has given rise to somewhat of a fear by journalists, scholars, officials, and other public figures that taking money from Japanese foundations, non-profit organizations, or corporations will brand them as "agents of influence." The Japanese government has put together a $375 million endowment, named for the late Foreign Minister Shintaro Abe, to fund academic and cultural programs between the United States and Japan, but there has been concern that it will result in suspicion, not cooperation. In the words of a former Japanese diplomat who was there at the creation: "Apparently the Japanese Government has become a kind of leper, with everything it approaches being seen as smeared. Why can't the government of Japan be seen as merely wanting to do good deeds?"[14]

It is Americans themselves who have created in their own minds the image of Japan as a cartoon supersociety where everything goes right and nothing goes wrong. As the old Japan-hand detective says to his partner about one of the Japanese suspects in Crichton's *Rising Sun*:

"It's hard for an American to see him clearly. Because in America, you think a certain amount of error is normal. You expect the plane to be late. You expect the mail to be undelivered. You expect the washing machine to break down. You expect things to go wrong all the time.

"But Japan is different. Everything *works* in Japan. In a Tokyo train station you can stand at a marked spot on the platform and when the train stops, the doors will open right in front of you. Trains are on time. Bags are not lost. Connections are not missed. Deadlines are met. Things happen as planned. The Japanese are educated, prepared, and motivated. They get things done. There's no screwing around."[15]

As is shown by the above quote, this attitude toward Japan has a dichotomous mirror image: if Japan can do nothing wrong, then the United

States can do nothing right. Japanese labor is as dedicated as American labor is lazy. Japanese management is concerned with the worker, but American management only cares about a fast buck. Japan is peaceful and harmonious, but the United States is a country full of violence and conflict. Japan's education system turns out highly skilled workers and managers, while the American education system is failing society. Japan is destined to be the world's next superpower, and the United States is a power in decline.

This last image in particular has taken a strong hold on Americans. Although Paul Kennedy's book, *The Rise and Fall of the Great Powers*, is not about the replacement of the United States by Japan as the world's leading power, its title kindled a new wave of theorizing about the rise and fall of the American empire which reinforced the belief that this is a natural trend of history. The United States has had its day and is now the weary giant, unable to fend off the feisty newcomer. There is a great deal of fatalism in the image. It is also summed up by the idea of the twenty-first century being the Asian century, with Japan as the leader of Asia. Japan is seen as building on its strengths, investing in markets all over the world, taking control of the world's finances, taking a growing role in world political affairs, and ever increasing the strength of its economy and society at home. The United States is tottering on the brink of collapse, having become the world's leading debtor nation (while Japan has become the world's leading creditor). Its domestic deficit has made its military strength abroad dependent on foreign investors such as Japan. The United States is no longer in command of its own destiny.

It is ironic that this dichotomous mirror image is just the same image that many Japanese have of the United States, but it is a very dangerous image for both sides. It is dangerous in that it can lead to the same underestimation of the United States in Japan that was one of the direct causes of the Second World War. The Japanese also saw the United States as a wounded giant in the 1930s and therefore believed that it would not have the economic ability or the will to get involved in a conflict against Japan in Asia. The self-pity that drives this image is doubly dangerous for Americans. On the one hand, it can lead to a national despondency, a kind of "what the hell, there is nothing we can do about it" attitude which will make it a self-fulfilling prophecy.

On the other hand, the belief that the United States is an ailing power being devoured by Japan can create a backlash in the United States in which Americans feel it necessary to fight back to regain supremacy. The "Buy American" and the "America First" movements were, in part, a result of this attitude. The fundamental belief underlying these movements was that by opening itself to the world, and sacrificing in the best interests for other countries, the United States was duped into helping them at the cost of its own success. In this view, Japan would not have become a successful economic power if the United States had not been there to guide it into the international economic system and protected its economy from outside attack. It should then withdraw from Japan, leaving it to fend for itself, while the United States' government withdraws its resources and pumps them back into the domestic economy.

This belief explicitly relates economic behavior to nationalism. If one does not buy an American product, one is not a true American. Neither of these movements gathered much steam because international involvement and leadership has become part of the American ethos, just as isolationism was sixty years ago. Certainly the major political proponent of these views, Patrick Buchanan, had little success in his challenge to the unabashed internationalist, George Bush. But the press that these movements received and the emotions they engendered in many Americans were indicative of some support.

There is also a reverse image to that of Japan as the country that can do nothing wrong and whose star is on the rise. There is a less commonly held attitude, but still widely disseminated (and hopeful) attitude, that Japan's star has passed its zenith. This attitude holds that, although Japan has had phenomenal economic growth, it is too weak to sustain it in the future. Its government is corrupt and unwilling to act. The loyalty to the company and the job of the older generation has given way to a listless and spoiled younger generation of pampered ne'er-do-wells. Its reliance on foreign sources of natural resources and foreign markets means that it will always be a pawn in international relations and never a king. Japanese industries are being hollowed out by the constant stream of investment abroad. Japanese investment in the rest of the world along with its beggar-thy-neighbor trading policies have led to a backlash of fear and distrust of Japanese investment and economic policy in the rest of the world. The older generation of Japanese leaders and managers is overconfident and unwilling to change its ways. Underneath the veneer of success lies hidden rot. This attitude has been most clearly displayed in the coverage of the decline of the Tokyo stock market in the spring of 1992. The Nikkei average lost 50 percent of its value since 1989, which was seen as a bursting of the bubble economy. This was widely reported to be the harbinger of the collapse of the whole economy.

Resurgent nationalism is the most important element in both American coverage of Japan and its image of Japan. The "new" nationalism is nothing new; American concern with a rebirth of nationalism has been around since the end of the occupation. Real concern about increased Japanese nationalism was not featured as a part of the American image of Japan until the rise of Japan as an economic power led to its "invasion" of the American market. This concern is to be found in many works on Japan since the early 1970s, but seems to take a significant increase in the late 1970s and into the 1980s. In 1972 Zbigniew Brzezinski pondered the "rising nationalism of younger [Japanese],"[16] and James Morley wrote of "a new nationalism at home."[17]

Respected scholars and journalists have expressed their fears that as Japan becomes economically dominant and more confident in its role as a political power, it will again want to become an active military power. This is related to the fiftieth anniversary not just of Pearl Harbor but of the Second World War in general. Four years of fiftieth anniversary ceremonies will constantly refresh American memories of what happened the last time that Japan was in a position of power and authority.

Articles on Japan have tended to emphasize its past history of miltarism and often describe trade relations and Japanese economic policy using military imagery. A powerful message derived from relating the events of fifty years ago to the contemporary economic power of Japan is the question of who really won the war. All of these elements are displayed in a *New York Times Magazine* article written in 1985 by Theodore H. White.

We had won out over them. We lost more than 100,000 men to prove we could not be lacerated without warning, without seeking revenge.

Except that America's revenge on Japan was of such an extraordinary character as to befuddle all scholars who claim that history has a logic of its own. What we are faced with now is the idea that events contradict history's logic. Perhaps we did not win the war, perhaps the Japanese, unknown even to themselves, were the winners. . . .

Today, 40 years after the end of World War II, the Japanese are on the move again in one of history's most brilliant commercial offenses. . . . Japanese capital is moving from penetration to control. Japanese are beginning to supply venture capital for the seedbeds of American technology, from Silicon Valley in California to Route 128 in Boston. They hover over the Draper Laboratories in Massachusetts—the national laboratories that devise the guidance systems for our missiles—and acquire what patents security lets free to the public.

They are an island nation looking out on the rest of the world as plunder from a protected bastion. . . . But it would be well for the Japanese to remember that if peace is paramount, they need us to keep the peace more than we need them. And if a ripple of depression forces Congress to act, a lockup of the open American market would wound Japan more than it would wound us. The superlative execution of their trade tactics may provoke an incalculable reaction—as the Japanese might well remember of the course that ran from Pearl Harbor to the deck of the U.S.S. Missouri in Tokyo Bay just 40 years ago.[18]

The image of a resurgent, militant nationalism in Japan combines a mixture of old and new fears. The ills of prewar Japan still exist. The military may be nominally responsible to the constitutional authority of the civilian government, but who is the government and to what extent is the constitution respected? As the journalist and scholar Karel von Wolferen argues, there is no real center of power in the Japanese government able or willing to make clear decisions in times of crisis. If elements of the officer corps were to try to assert the independent authority and power of the military, would the prime minister and the cabinet, who have ultimate responsibility for the management and supervision of the Self-Defense Forces, step forward to thwart them?[19] Similarly, the ultraconservative secret and not-so-secret societies are still around. Publicly, they race around the streets of Japan's cities waving the Japanese flag, playing the national anthem, calling for the resurrection of State Shinto and a divine emperor-ship, alternately praising the United States' battle against communism and castigating its efforts to thwart Japan's national destiny, but always calling for the remilitarization of Japan. Privately, they meet in back rooms with corrupt and sympathetic politicians of the ruling Liberal Democratic Party (LDP), slipping them huge amounts of money, raised by their connection with the underworld *yakuza*, in an attempt to influence government policy.

While the old leadership elite keep alive the flame of naitonalism that kindled their fighting spirit before the war, it also lights the spirit of a new breed of Japanese, one that was not appalled by the horrors of past milita-rism, one that has not been taught about the evils of the past, one that has seen only the success of the postwar economic development, one that, unlike its elders, has no sense of inferiority toward the Western nations but, like its elders, now sees its main rival, the United States, as an object of derision and scorn.

For all that the mass media and popular literature do to hype these images, the American public does not seem to fear a growth of militarism in Japan. However, as with other aspects of the relationship, there seems to be an ambivalence in the public's view of Japanese rearmament. The Gallup Poll taken between January and March 1992 did find that 55 percent of the public thought that Japan should not build up its defense capabilities, a finding that was up 12 percentage points from the previous year, but, on the other hand, 73 percent of the same respondents said that there was very little chance that Japan would emerge as a military power. The complaint that Japan does not carry enough weight in its own security and in defend-ing the new world order also creates a higher level of support for rearma-ment in Japan. An *Ashai Shimbun* poll taken in the fall of 1992 showed that while 77 percent of American respondents thought that Japan was a "rival," 69 percent also thought that Japan should take more military responsibility in the world. In comparison, 10 percent thought that Japan should take economic leadership, and 17 percent thought that Japan should take more political leadership. The findings that there should be a greater burden sharing, the increased spending of Japan on its own military forces in order to allow the United States to reduce its forces and not give Japan a free ride, and the feelings that Japan should do more in the world militarily, like sending troops to the Gulf, are especially interesting in light of the poll results previously mentioned that 13 percent of Americans think that Japan is under military rule.

The image that the United States holds toward Japan has changed in the past two decades in that it has become more complex. Japanese are no longer seen as only "economic animals" but a people with both good and bad traits that are simultaneously similar and dissimilar to Americans. But one component of the image that has not changed is the undercurrent of trepidation toward Japan's power—economic, political and military—and the use Japan may make of it in the future. This anxiety can also be seen in America's attitudes toward Japanese nationalism. Consequently it is imperative that we examine closely the composition of Japanese nationalism, its manifestations, and what it portends for the future of Japan and the world.

NOTES

1. Ezra F. Vogel, *Japan as Number One* (Cambridge, Mass.: Harvard University Press, 1979), 23.

2. Michael Crichton, *Rising Sun* (New York: Alfred A. Knopf, 1992), afterword.

3. Chitose Yanaga, *Japan since Perry* (repr. Hamden, Conn.: Archon Books, 1966), 26.

4. Ibid.

5. Payson J. Treat, *Japan and the United States: 1853–1921* (repr. New York: Johnson Reprint Corp., 1970), 154.

6. Thomas A. Bailey, *A Diplomatic History of the American People*, 10th ed. (Englewood Cliffs, N.J.: Prentice-Hall, 1980), 314–15.

7. Yanaga, *Japan since Perry*, 434.

8. As quoted in Bailey, *Diplomatic History*, 523.

9. William Henry Chamberlin, *Japan over Asia* (Boston: Little, Brown, 1937), 376.

10. Wayne S. Cole, "The Role of the United States Congress and Political Parties," in Dorothy Borg and Shumpei Okamoto, eds., *Pearl Harbor as History* (New York: Columbia University Press, 1973), 314.

11. John C. Perry, *Beneath the Eagle's Wings* (New York: Dodd, Mead, 1980), 168.

12. Sheila K. Johnson, *American Attitudes toward Japan, 1941–1975* (Washington, D.C.: American Enterprise Institute, 1975), 62.

13. May 4, 1992, 20.

14. *New York Times*, March 3, 1992, 11.

15. Crichton, *Rising Sun*, 68.

16. Zbigniew Brzezinski, *The Fragile Blossom: Crisis and Change in Japan* (New York: Harper and Row, 1972), 12.

17. James William Morley, ed., *Forecast for Japan: Security in the 1970s* (Princeton, N.J.: Princeton University Press, 1972), 20.

18. July 28, 1985, 21, 22, 38–39, 57–58.

19. *New York Times*, December 12, 1990, op ed page.

2

The Search for Identity

Japanese nationalism is young, but the Japanese ethnicity is old. Japanese people have a long history of similar customs, language, religions, social organization, entertainments, and other elements of common ethnicity which is the foundation for modern nationalism, but these are not in and of themselves nationalism. Nationalism is a modern phenomenon and is directly related to economic development, political development, and social modernization.[1] During the Meiji period the makers of the Japanese nationalist myths strove to make the people of Japan believe that their nation arose from the mists of antiquity unified by such key elements as Shinto, the imperial tradition, *bushido* (the samurai code of ethics), and Confucian values. But nationalism was not possible in Japan until it had contact with the West and began its modernization process. Indeed, the very myths that were intended to induce nationalism were motivated by contact with the West and were created as prescribed by Western theories of nationalism. Before the coming of the West most Japanese identified with their village, feudal domain, occupation, or family, but few would have considered themselves to be tied to a greater whole by the rites of Shinto, the values of Confucianism, and the mandate of the emperor. The vast majority of Japanese were content, or at least resigned, to toil in the fields and stay out of trouble with whatever local authority happened to be ruling their lives.

In terms of its relations with the rest of the known world, Japan had always been secure in its position as a secondary country in Asia, with little concern for what may lie beyond. It had looked to China as the dominant power and cultural influence in Asia; it had occasional interest in Korea and had trade with regions as far removed as Southeast Asia, but it remained essentially isolated. When Western encroachment in the sixteenth century became intrusive, it was dealt with by banishment and denial. The seclusionary laws (*sakoku*) that forbid foreigners to come to Japan and forbid Japanese from leaving the archipelago, in combination with Japan's relative remoteness, had been successful in keeping the world at bay for more than two hundred years. But Britain's defeat of China, and the black ships of Admiral Perry, necessitated a more positive reaction. Japan needed to open itself to the world. It had to become part of the international relations system that was dominated by Western states and their values, upon which rested the definition of statehood and international relations. It needed to reinvent itself and its nation in new, modern terms; it had to Westernize in order to survive. The quest for survival, and the shock of being torn from its secure, traditional Asian niche and thrown into a modern world, created a Japanese identity crisis.

Today Japan continues to struggle with that identity crisis, although the circumstances have changed. Japan is no longer forced to Westernize by stronger, threatening states; it stands as the unquestioned equal to the Western developed states. Racism still exists, but it is no longer a value by which states and nations are ranked in the international hierarchy. However, Japan's very prominence creates questions of identity that can be every bit as troublesome as those raised by the Western challenge of the nineteenth century. Has the very nature of its development torn it permanently from its Asian roots? Has its social development, its relationship with the United States, its position in the international councils of power, and the importance of its economic ties with the West made it, for all intents and purposes, a Western nation? Has its own perception of development been defined as a movement away from Asia to the West? Can it maintain what it perceives as its unique "Japaneseness" while being, at the same time, interdependent and open to the rest of the world? Japan could be sure of its self-identity when it was isolated from the rest of the world, but in becoming a member of the world community and the international relations system, it has had to redefine its sense of what it is, and what it is not, relative to the other nations of the world.

LEARNING FROM THE WEST

Nationalism came to Japan, as it came to all non-European countries, on the back of nineteenth-century colonialism. Japan learned from the defeat of China, and by internal defeats as well, that its reaction to the superiority of the West must not be rejection but emulation. When China was faced with modernization brought by Western expansionism, it was suffocated by the weight of its own greatness. China had been for thousands of years the central civilization of East Asia. It perceived itself as the only civilized world and was so perceived by those around it. It was not much interested in political or economic relations with the outside world and created a system of international relations based upon tributes received from those barbarian nations who wanted to trade. Neither was there much interest in ideas from outside as it was a self-satisfied culture and a self-contained economic and political system.

Both Japan and China were relatively isolated at the beginning of the nineteenth century, and both relegated those who wanted to trade with them to offshore "factories" located far from their capitals. These factories were warehouses and living quarters located on the island of Deshima in the port of Nagasaki in Japan, and in the Pearl River off the city of Canton in China. Those foreigners who wanted to trade did so at the whim of the government, and then only through government appointed and controlled intermediaries. When Japan began to seclude itself in the early seventeenth century, it was considered to be less than attractive as a trading center, and so the British left the Dutch to set up the only Western presence on Deshima.

But China was a different proposition. The demand in Europe (and later in the United States) for its tea, porcelain, silk, spices, and other rare goods had increased as centralized national economies and a middle class developed during the Renaissance. As a result, various Western nations had an interest in China, not the least among them Great Britain. As British trade in Asia grew, so did its desire to rid itself of the limitations imposed upon it by the Chinese government and the restriction of the factory system. The system limited the number of sites at which trade could take place and forced the British to deal with corrupt traders who were given a monopoly by the government, but most of all it forbade Britain to sell opium in China. The British attempted to negotiate a new trading system with China, but they were unsuccessful because China was more than satisfied with the status quo. They wanted neither opium nor foreigners freely circulating within their borders. The British alternative was smuggling, and it was the Chinese attempt to curtail opium smuggling that finally gave the British an excuse to use war as an extension of diplomacy. The British victory in the Opium War of 1840 enabled them to force China to open its trade and other relations with the outside world.

The Japanese did not need a war to realize that the technological and military superiority of the United States would be sufficient to do great damage. They learned by observing events in China. The Chinese had always assumed that outside invaders, such as the Mongols or the Manchurians, had come to rule China as it existed and wished to assimilate into the system. The Westerners did not come to assimilate, but to change. This is a lesson it took the Chinese a long time to learn. When confronted with the West, the Chinese reaction was to revert to their traditional

Confucian roles, as they had always done in the past. Japan, however, was a very different case. Japan was isolated but did not have the burden of seeing itself as superior, nor did it perceive itself as self-contained.

Japan had borrowed from other cultures since the beginning of its civilization, most especially from China. More recently, however, Western learning was widely disseminated within Tokugawa Japan after the publication of occidental books was allowed in 1720. There was a great deal of curiosity about things Western, and everything foreign was not automatically deemed inferior. Also, although Japan was more isolated than China, both geographically and in terms of its relations with other countries, Japan was more open to outside ideas and incorporated them with greater vigor. After all, Japan had borrowed much of its culture, language, and religion from China and Korea. Consequently it was able to be more flexible when confronted with the West and had fewer problems following the Western lead, as it had been following the Chinese lead for many centuries.

When it came time for Japan to follow and pattern itself after the West, it was able to do so because there was also more unity in Japan than in China. The fundamental problems of identity and direction, the questioning of the validity of traditional institutions and behaviors, brought about by the confrontation with the West, created deep fissures within China which were eventually to burst that nation into many fragments. China would not develop a unified nationalist movement as a means of confronting foreign domination until well into the twentieth century. In the case of Japan, however, the power of nationalism as means of unifying the people and the state against Western domination was more quickly understood and implemented because Japan had been to a limited extent economically and politically unified under the Tokugawa regime.

One cannot call Tokugawa Japan a nation in the modern sense of the word, but the Edo period saw the development of a greater sense of unity than had previously been experienced. Four major factors account for the greater unity. From the beginning of the fourteenth century Japan was wracked by a never-ending series of internecine wars between various feudal families. It was not until the mid-sixteenth century that one leader, Nobunaga Oda, was able to gain the upper hand against his enemies and begin to consolidate large amounts of territory under his control. Nobunaga passed his leadership on to Hideyoshi Toyotomi, who almost completed the military dominance of Japan. This task was finally carried out by Ieyasu Tokugawa, the founder of the Tokugawa Shogunate (1615–1868).

The Tokugawa government's control over all the feudal domains of Japan was by no means perfect, but there did exist a central government (*bakufu*) that had powers to keep the feudal lords and their vassals in line. One of these powers was the *sankin kotai*, a hostage system. Each feudal lord was required to keep a house and some members of his household in Edo (the Tokugawa capital, modern Tokyo), thereby enabling the *bakufu* to carry out retribution against his household if the lord took any actions against Tokugawa rule. The lords were required to spend one out of every two years in their Edo residences. This system not only helped to centralize political authority but also increased the need for a well-maintained, centralized transportation and trading system. The roads that linked the feudal domains to Edo and the consequent trade that followed those roads became the skeleton upon which a national economy would grow. The development of the roads also supported the development of centralized markets for rice in Edo and Osaka. The feudal lords and their samurai vassals could bring their rice into these two centers and have it exchanged for money. Finally, the Tokugawas encouraged the samurai to turn their attentions from war to learning in order to reduce the threat of an uprising from a rebellious domain. As we will see, the emphasis on scholarship eventually became more dangerous to the survival of the *bakufu* than a samurai rebellion.

Nativism

In the initial stages of Japan's modernization, nationalism was a result of developing Western-style systems and institutions through which the new rulers could govern the people directly. But once a truly national government and administrative system were in place, nationalism took on more importance as a means of differentiating Japan from the West and as a means of competing against other states in the international relations system. The Japanese adoption of Western political, economic, and legal systems is well documented, but the oligarchy of young leaders who led the restoration of the emperor, and who governed in his name (collectively known as the *genro*), knew that Japan was not just threatened by the physical superiority of the West; they also realized that the whole world order had changed. To insure Japan's survival and prosperity, nationalism was used both as a means of developing Japan into a modern country and as a means of exerting power in competition with other states.

These different forms of nationalism were mutually incompatible. Modernization was a necessary component of nationalism, and Western institutions had to be imported as a means of linking all Japanese to one national bureaucracy for political and economic centralization. But the very act of importing these institutions, the values upon which they were based, and the foreign experts who could instruct Japanese in their implementation were a direct threat to the social and cultural traditions that formed the essence of the Japanese nation. Thus the more modernization and Westernization progressed, the more those concerned with building nationalism on a nativist foundation feared the loss of that which made Japan different from other nations. This internal tension between the foreign elements of modernization and the native traditions of nationalism is a conundrum that is yet to be resolved, but, in the long run, Japan decided that it was necessary to go along if they wanted to get along.

Domestic politics at the time of Perry's arrival centered around a conflict between the Tokugawa *bakufu* and a group of feudal lords and their samurai retainers who thought that the emperor should be once again replaced at the top of the Japanese political system. From the very beginning of the Tokugawa era there developed various schools of scholarship which centered on the study of things Japanese and Japanese history. Those in Kyoto tended to emphasize the role of the emperor in ancient Japan, and arguments favoring a return of imperial rule began to surface by the eighteenth century. The Tokugawa regime created three categories of feudal domains. The best and most strategic lands (inner domains) were given to members of the Tokugawa family and those who had been their allies in the long wars. The next best went to related families, and the last went to families of those who had fought against the Tokugawas. These last were known as the outer domains and were mostly lands in the extreme northeast and southwest of the country, far removed from the center of power. The lords and samurai from these outer domains were most prominent in the imperial restoration, especially those from Satsuma and Choshu (today's Kyushu and Shikoku). The *sonno* (revere the emperor) movement waxed and waned during the eighteenth century but became especially strong when the decision was made by the Tokugawa government to sign a treaty with the United States and other Western powers which ended the Nagasaki confinement of foreigners.

The *sonno* movement then added a second refrain, *joii* (expel the barbarians). Samurai from the outer domains argued that if the shogun could not keep the foreigners out of Japan, he no longer could claim the mandate to rule. An especial affront in their eyes was an agreement of the shogun to an article of the Treaty of 1858 that allowed the residency of foreign legations in Tokyo. The very fact that foreigners would be treading the streets of the country's political capital was bad enough, but the residences assigned to the four major powers—the United States, Great Britain, France, and Holland—were four Buddhist monasteries. There followed, in the words of Sir Ernest Satow, a member of the British legation at the time, "a series of alarming occurrences."[2] These included the death of two British sentries at the hands of a samurai. This incident caused all foreign legations, with the exception of the United States, to retreat to Yokohama, a community created for foreigners, where they could be protected by their fleets. The Americans, as stubborn as ever, stayed in Edo to make a point, but even they were forced to remove themselves to Yokohama after a fire of suspicious origin burnt down the residence of the American legation.

The killing of a British subject by the samurai of Satsuma and the bombarding of foreign vessels by the fleet of Choshu were two of many serious attacks against foreigners. In September 1862 four British subjects, three men and a woman, were horseback riding on the major road from Yokohama to Tokyo when they encountered the procession of the father of the lord of Satsuma. It was the custom for all commoners to clear the road and let such retinues pass, but the four Britishers simply moved to the side while keeping to the road. Such disrespect was too much to endure for some samurai in the retinue and so they attacked the offenders. Two were wounded, the woman made a clean getaway, but Mr. Richardson, a merchant from Shanghai, was cut down in the saddle, his throat slashed.

The event had an immediate impact on the foreign community because this was no attack on a legation, but an open and unprovoked attack on a peaceful merchant. The British government decided that strong steps had to be taken. It demanded from the Tokugawa government an apology, an indemnity of £100,000, the arrest by the lord of Satsuma of the samurai involved, the execution of the criminals in front of a British observer, and an indemnity of £25,000 to be paid by Satsuma. These were demands that the Tokugawa government could hardly fulfill. The shogun was already under attack from the outer domains for allowing foreigners in Japan in the first place, and to capitulate to their demands would have shown even greater weakness. Getting the *daimyo* (feudal lord) of Satsuma to arrest and execute his own retainers for having upheld his honor would have been impossible. Although the Tokugawa government tried to placate both sides, neither was mollified, and, satisfaction not forthcoming, the British took things into their own hands by sending a squadron of seven ships to bombard Kagoshima.

During this same period of conflict between the Tokugawa government and the opposition domains over the exclusion of foreigners, Choshu shore batteries and naval junks began firing on Western shipping in the straits of Shimonoseki in what is now called the Inland Sea. Free passage of the straits was of great importance to Western merchants as that route was crucial to navigating the Japanese coast. Thus the threat of harassment of Western merchant vessels alone was enough to send their governments into action. British, French, Dutch, and American vessels had all been fired upon, and a coalition of their naval forces was formed to handle the task of retribution. It was first decided to entreat with the *daimyo* of Choshu to resolve the issue peacefully. In this they were fortuitously aided by two young Choshu samurai familiar with the West, Hirobumi Ito and Bunda Inoue. These two had risked their lives under the seclusion acts by secreting themselves out of the country and off to England to see the world. Having seen England and its advanced technology, Inoue and Ito were convinced that it would be folly to try to defeat them militarily. The two samurai were unsuccessful in their attempt to convince their lord that battle with the foreign powers was a lost cause, but they both went on to be two of the most famous members of the oligarchy advising Emperor Meiji after the restoration.

Finally it was decided in 1864 that a combined fleet would be sent to silence the batteries and sink the Chosu fleet in retaliation. There ensued a spirited naval engagement in which the Choshu fleet was routed. One thousand nine hundred men—British, Dutch, and French—were put ashore, captured the shore batteries, and burned part of the city of Shimonoseki. The will of Choshu and Satsuma to fight against the Western powers was drained by this defeat and by the British bombardment and burning of Kagoshima. The two rogue domains reversed their earlier position vis-à-vis the Western powers and turned to them in order to learn all they could about their advanced technology. In the final analysis, it was their skill in using modern military technology that aided them in their successful attempt to overthrow the *bakufu* and restore political supremacy to the emperor.

After the restoration, the ruling *genro* immediately began a campaign to end the feudal traditions of the past and to create a modern Japan using the West as a model. They believed that if they became like the West they would be accepted by them as an equal, and they were encouraged in this belief by the Western powers. Members of the *genro* traveled the world searching out the most modern methods of law, education, military organization, economic organization, and even fashion. Japan threw itself into the Westernization craze. The feudal past was sneered at as being a hindrance to the new, modern Japan. The government translation bureau began translating all of the most famous foreign treatises on economics, law, and politics. Western ideas became the center of debate for Japanese intellectuals and officials alike. People adopted Western haircuts, Western clothes, Western bathrooms, Christianity, the Western calendar, and the concept of holidays that accompanied it. Those who went to the West brought back stories of wealth and the obvious power of the Western nations. Japan in comparison seemed backward and inferior. It was a time when all things traditionally Japanese were disdained and looked down upon.

This headlong dash toward the West and modernization was bound to create a nativist backlash, especially as learning from the West had also demonstrated the need for developing nationalism as a means of unifying the nation behind the policies of the state. Nowhere was this more clearly manifested than in the creation of the new Japanese military. Japan took Prussia as its model for the army because Prussia had thoroughly modernized its own army in reaction to its defeat by Napoleon. The extent to which Prussia had successfully learned the lessons of modernization was demonstrated by the ease with which it used military force to unify the German states and defeat France. Prussian officers realized that the old army, where soldiers were mercenaries and commissions were purchased or passed from generation to generation in the families of the nobility, was no match for a modern, bureaucratically organized army where the soldier fought for patriotism and the survival of his nation.

The modernization of the Japanese army entailed the conscription of a national army and the dissolution of the samurai as a warrior class. The conscription of soldiers from the general population began in 1873, and its immediate effect was the creation of a new sense of unity within the military and the nation as a whole. All soldiers were now Japanese, as opposed to retainers of individual domains, and their mission was to fight for the Japanese nation and its emperor. When the soldiers were brought in for basic training, they could be indoctrinated with the propaganda of the state and made loyal to the state and emperor. Each soldier saw a new part of Japan and met with other soldiers from various regions of the country hitherto thought of as foreign domains. Once the soldiers were rotated out after discharge, they would then return home and help reinforce the idea of a unified people under one state and one emperor throughout all prefectures of the country.

By the late 1880s native nationalism began to manifest itself as a reaction against Westernization and the control of the Western powers over Japan. Even the history of the previously much maligned Tokugawa period was revised to make it more positive. Groups of intellectuals and the journals they sponsored began to spring up in opposition to Western ideas, calling instead for the rebirth of Japanese traditions. Nativists were especially concerned with implementing an ideology based upon Shinto beliefs and practices and Confucian values. The emperor was the linchpin in the system. The unbroken line of the imperial dynasty was used as the symbol of a unified heritage shared by all Japanese. That unbroken succession also linked him directly to the Shinto creation myth, enshrining him as a demigod. Finally, the Confucian values of loyalty and filial piety instilled in all Japanese an obligation to the emperor above all other people and things. The irony of the nativism of the 1880s was that it was derived from German organicist philosophy and the example of the German state.

One of the most prominent and instrumental of these nativists was Akinori Mori, minister of education from 1885 to 1889. Mori is a good example of the influence of Western thought on Japanese native nationalism. He was one of the first Japanese to be sent abroad, spent much of his time as a young man in Britain, and was a strong supporter of Westernization. But the growth of nationalism in Europe convinced him that Japan also had to develop a strong sense of loyalty to the state and nation à la Germany. Previous to his appointment as education minister, Americans had had a great deal of influence in the teaching methods and curriculum used in Japanese schools. The organization of the educational system was based on the French model, but pedagogy and curriculum were relatively liberal. In 1877 the government went so far as to turn control over elementary schools to the prefectures. Mori reversed this trend. His philosophy was, "In the administration of all schools, it must be kept in mind, what is done is not for the sake of the pupils but for the sake of the country."[3] He was especially keen on using the education of teachers to promote nationalism in the schools. He turned Japanese normal schools into quasi-military institutions in order to instill discipline and correct thinking among the teachers of Japanese youth.

The change in Japan in the 1880s is evident in two imperial rescripts on education, the first issued in 1879 and the second in 1890. The first was written by Eifu Motoda as a commentary on what Emperor Meiji had seen in the schools he had visited during a tour of the provinces. It is rather petulant in tone and reflects conservative complaints about the modernization of Japan. In it he complains that the Westernization of Japan, while necessary as a means of bringing modern technical knowledge to the country, threatens the very social fabric as Confucian values are cast aside along with the old way of doing things. The emperor observed that the sons of merchants and farmers were learning "high sounding ideas and empty theories" in a foreign language and that they had no application to their future occupations. The consequences of such an education were that the students "brag about their knowledge, slight their elders, and disturb prefectural officers." Hardly Confucian behavior. The emperor hoped that the education system would become "less highflown and more practical."

By 1890 the place of the emperor upon his celestial Confucian throne had been formalized in the Meiji constitution. The imperial rescript of that year was no longer about the problems of education, but about instructing the Japanese people in their filial piety to the emperor and, through him, loyalty to the state. It is worth quoting in its entirety because it is a succinct example of the fundamental elements of nativist nationalism: the unbroken imperial succession, the deity of the emperor, the Confucian virtue of the emperor, the need for Confucian values in society, and the mythic ties between the emperor and people that combine both filial piety to the emperor and loyalty to the state.

Our Imperial ancestors have founded our empire on a basis broad and everlasting and have deeply and firmly implanted virtue; our subjects, ever united in loyalty and filial piety, have from generation to generation illustrated the beauty thereof. This is the glory of the fundamental character of our empire, and herein also lies the source of our education. Ye, our subjects, be filial to your parents, affectionate to your brothers and sisters; as husbands and wives be harmonious, as friends true; bear yourselves in modesty and moderation; extend your benevolence to all; pursue learning and cultivate arts, and thereby develop your intellectual faculties and perfect your moral powers; furthermore, advance the public good and promote common interests; always respect the constitution and observe the laws; should any emergency arise, offer your selves to the state; and thus guard and maintain the prosperity of our Imperial throne, coeval with heaven and earth. So shall ye not only be our good and faithful subjects, but render illustrious the best traditions of your forefathers.

The way here set forth is indeed the teaching bequeathed by our Imperial ancestors, to be observed alike by their descendants and subjects, infallible for all ages and true in all places. It is our wish to lay it to heart in all reverence, in common with you, our subjects, that we may all thus attain to the same virtue.[4]

Conflict with the West

As things traditionally Japanese were reexamined in a more positive light, so were the actions of the Western powers called into question. Especially irritating were the continuation of the unequal treaties and the Western intervention after Japan's war with China. Japan maintained separate treaties with each of the Western powers, but the contents of these treaties were very similar and based upon the original Harris Treaty of 1858 signed with the United States. The treaties were considered unequal because they were not reciprocal, gave the Western powers extraterritoriality, allowed them to dictate import duties, and gave them the power to control harbor facilities and coastal shipping throughout the archipelago. The most specific goal in this drive for modernization was to end the unequal treaties, and yet all of the manifold and radical changes that had been accomplished during the first two decades of the Meiji period did not seem to be furthering treaty revision. The unwillingness of the Western powers to revise the treaties gave strength to the anti-Western, nativist movement. Extraterritoriality, or the right of foreigners to reside in Japan under the laws of their country of citizenship, was the most obvious symbol of the power of the Western states over Japan. It was believed that Japanese law was so barbaric and uncivilized that Westerners in Japan should not have to be accountable to it. Although Japan originally accepted the inevitability of extraterritoriality, its continued existence after the modernization of political and legal institutions became a fundamental insult to Japanese.

The Harris Treaty of 1858 included a clause that allowed either country to call for a revision of the treaty after July 1, 1872, which would then have to be agreed upon by both parties. As the Harris Treaty served as a model for the treaties Japan signed with other Western states, the date of July 1, 1872 loomed large in Japan's vision of the future. Some have called the effort to revise the treaties the most important element of Japan's foreign policy between 1872 and 1894.[5] As early as 1870 the Japanese Foreign Ministry informed the Western powers that it would seriously pursue treaty revision and in 1874 created the Bureau for the Study of Treaty Revision, but it was not until the 1880s that serious movement toward the revision of extraterritoriality took place.

In the spring of 1884 the British minister sent a memorandum to the Japanese government stating that "the unequal treaties would automatically be abolished when Japanese laws attained the standard which existed in various countries of the West."[6] From this point forward the Japanese government redoubled its efforts to develop Western legal codes and installed a modern cabinet system in 1885. The government had for many years been studying and debating the adoption of a Western-style constitution and it was finally promulgated in early 1889. In the wake of these actions a conference on the revision of the treaties was convened on May 1, 1886. There were a total of twenty-eight meetings lasting over a period of approximately one year. Hostility among the populace toward both the foreign powers and the Japanese government grew as the meetings dragged on and on. It finally peaked in the summer of 1887 when the government announced that it would no longer attempt a treaty revision until it had formally adopted a new legal system. The treaty revision that ended extraterritoriality finally went into effect in 1899, but by that time the general feeling in the country was that even though Japan had done what was expected of it, the Western powers were not willing to give it recognition of equality. Anti-government sentiments were particularly strong because it was believed by many that the Japanese government consistently capitulated to the demands of the foreign powers.

Another major event that created anti-Western feeling was the Triple Intervention. China and Japan had been vying for control of Korea since the 1880s and finally went to war over it in 1894. At the outbreak of hostilities most observers predicted a Chinese victory because of China's size, proximity to Korea, historical interest in it, and its history of dominance in Asia. Consequently the world was shocked when Japan was able to rout China during that summer. The stunning Japanese victory was ample proof of its ability to modernize and China's inability to do so. Its victory also labeled it, in its own eyes and in the eyes of the world, as a rapidly growing power and the strongest native power in East Asia. The fruits of its victory were a huge indemnity from China as well as the island of Taiwan, the Pescadores, treaty ports in China, and the Liaotung Peninsula in southern Manchuria. A week after the treaty terms were announced, France, Germany, and Russia stepped in to force Japan to give up the Liaotung Peninsula. Russia was especially adamant as it had its own designs on Manchuria. In the face of such overwhelming opposition, the Japanese government had no choice but to give in. The intervention was a distinct slap in the face, coming at the very time when Japanese saw themselves advancing into the world of the Great Powers. There was a violent reaction against the intervention of the three Western powers and against the Japanese government's capitulation.

Nationalism had begun in Japan as a reaction to western pressure and manifested itself in the imitation of Western institutions and modes of behavior, but by the turn of the century it had become "Japanified." The very fact that popular anti-government movements arose following the Japanese government's capitulations to the Western powers in the cases of treaty revision and the Triple Intervention is indicative of the nativism of

Japanese nationalism, based upon a belief that the Western powers had joined together to keep Japan from its rightful place in the world. This conviction was reinforced by later events. After Japan won its war against Russia, the peace negotiated by Theodore Roosevelt was again perceived by many Japanese as an attempt to give Japan less than it deserved. Incidents such as the segregation of Japanese children in the San Francisco school system convinced Japan that anti-Japanese racism was rampant in the West and especially in the United States.

This conviction was strengthened by events at the Versailles Conference at the end of World War I. During the discussions over the creation of the League of Nations, the Japanese representative offered the following racial equality clause: "The equality of nations being a basic principle of the League of Nations, the High Contracting Parties agree to accord as soon as possible, to all alien nations of States, members of the League, equal and just treatment in every respect, making no distinction, either in law or fact, on account of their race or nationality."[7] This was the only issue in the whole conference on which both Japan and China could agree. Both this original proposal and a softer compromise proposal were blocked by the Australian delegation. The American delegation did not want to oppose the clause publicly, but they felt that the Senate would never ratify the treaty if it included a racial equality clause, and so they were willing to hide behind the Australian veto. When the amendment was put to a vote, the only major power to support it was France; Great Britain and the United States abstained.

The Versailles Treaty insured Japan's place as one of the "Five Great Powers," but it did not completely convince Japanese that the Western powers considered them to be equal. In international conferences following World War I, Japan was pressured into an arms reduction treaty that gave it less naval tonnage than either the United States or Great Britain, and into relinquishing political and territorial gains made during the war in China and the Pacific. This was followed in 1924 by the passage in the United States of the General Immigration Bill which excluded Japanese from immigration. These events and others played an important role in the rise of Japanese nationalism and militarism in the 1930s.

The ultranationalism that has become a hallmark of Japan in the 1930s had various causes, not the least of which was a rejection of corrupt values imported from the West. Japanese society in the 1920s became much more liberal as the values of the postwar "new generation" took hold in the cities and democracy took root in the political system. Victory by the liberal democracies breathed new life into democracy in Japan, and party government became a reality for the first time, while the political influence of the military decreased. Western morals crept into Japan's cities, and it became fashionable for women to cut their hair, work, drink, and dance and smoke in public. Even as the Great Depression began to take hold, the *zaibatsu* continued to amass huge sums of money and used some of it to buy political power. In the countryside, however, the situation was going from bad to worse, and a great gap, both in values and income, came to divide the urban and rural areas of Japan.

To the ultranationalists, these trends signified a weakening of the nation. Democracy was an insult to the concept of imperial rule. It led to a corrupt system in which rich capitalists and politicians exploited the working people, especially agricultural labor, in order to line their pockets and gain more power. Liberal social mores were an anathema to the conservative social values of Confucianism, and libertine behavior in the cities was an insult to the peasantry, the backbone of Japan. The ultranationalists' reaction was a desire to drive the Western nations out of Asia and Western culture out of Japan. The imperial way and Confucian social values were seen as the only salvation for Japan and the rest of Asia.

As the military and their ultranationalist supporters came to have more and more political power in the 1930s, greater emphasis in government policy was placed on colonial expansion in Asia, Japanese-led Pan-Asianism as an alternative to Western colonialism, and the replacement of Western liberalism with conservative Confucianism at home. In addition, the Western reaction to increased Japanese aggression in Asia was perceived as unfair retribution and increased the belief that the West was "out to get" Japan. This, in turn, only increased Japan's distrust and dislike of the West.

A number of events leading up to the beginning of the war in the Pacific kept this negative cycle spinning. Japan increasingly isolated itself from the Western democracies through the 1930s beginning with its withdrawal from the League of Nations after that body had condemned Japan's invasion and colonization of Manchuria. After Japan invaded China in 1937, the United States terminated its commercial treaty with Japan, which dated from 1911, so that it could retaliate against Japan's economy and impose an embargo on war materials. When Japan invaded French Indochina in the summer of 1941, the United States retaliated by freezing Japanese assets and virtually ending Japanese-American trade. The Japanese perceived the American action as aggression toward it and another example of the ABCD encirclement which they had used as their original excuse for invading French Indochina. Japan used this encirclement and American economic aggression as its rationale for the attack on Pearl Harbor.

CONTEMPORARY SELF-DEFINITION

Japan's need to catch up to the West by continuing to Westernize, while at the same time maintaining distinctions between itself and the rest of the world in order to maintain its own identity, continues to be a strong element of Japanese nationalism. Defeat at the hands of the United States in the Second World War once again made it necessary for Japan to turn to the

West in order to redefine the nation and reinvigorate its political and economic systems. In part this was forced upon Japan by the American-led occupation. The emperor was stripped of all significant political and religious powers. The state was separated from Shinto, and religious freedom was guaranteed. The government was made responsible to the people, and the bureaucracy was made responsible to the government. Japanese citizens were guaranteed civil rights. The mass media and schools emphasized the development of a democratic political culture.

Although these changes were decreed by the Supreme Commander of the Allied Powers, the most powerful institution of the occupation, it was not through force alone that Japan's face was turned again to the West. The Japanese people and their government willingly collaborated with their occupiers and acquiesced in the reforms, and have remained ever since on the path set for them by the occupation. The adoption of democratic political values and collaboration in the occupation was undoubtedly a result of pragmatism. It was obvious that Japan could survive only by becoming a part of the international, political, and economic system developed by the United States and its allies during the Cold War. The pragmatism inherent in the active acquiescence to democratic reforms does not mean that they were not sincerely adopted, nor does it mean that they were temporary and superficial. Democratic political institutions and democratic political culture have become deeply and firmly rooted in Japanese society.

As occurred in the Meiji period, Japan's defeat led to a wholesale rejection of prewar institutions and a wholehearted adoption of most of the occupation reforms as a means of ridding Japan of its inferior status as a vanquished state. Once again things Western, and especially things American, were perceived as being superior to their traditional Japanese counterparts. One might say that the Japanese nation made its greatest and most consistent effort to become like the West in the postwar period. American and European popular culture began to dominate Japanese traditional culture, Japanese politics and foreign policy were tied directly to the United States, and the Japanese economy developed under the wing of American protection, as an integrated component of the Western system of international trade and finance. The Americanization of Japan continued for the entire postwar period because it gave Japan a secure base from which to develop and was successful both economically and as a means of regaining Japan's status as an equal and responsible member of the world community.

Japanese nationalism once again became defined by the relative status of Japan to the Western nations and the United States, and the Cold War played an important part in determining that status. The American connection gave instant credibility to Japan when it was anointed by the United States as its major ally in East Asia. The Japanese-American alliance reintroduced Japan once again into the councils of powers, albeit as an aide-decamp, and gave it legitimacy as an important state in the affairs of the world. As long as the cold war continued and the world economy was dominated by the United States, its position was secure and there was little reason to change.

But with the end of the Cold War, as in the Meiji period and the immediate postwar period, it has once again become necessary for Japan to adapt to changes in the world order and to redefine itself vis-à-vis the rest of the world, especially the other developed countries of the West. There are major differences, however, between the circumstances of those previous periods and contemporary circumstances. Japan is no longer at the bottom of the international hierarchy, looked down upon by others and itself as an outsider and an inferior. Japan starts this new period in its development at the top, as an equal of the most powerful and developed states of the world. Second, the history of Japan certainly demonstrates its ability to change when necessary, but the two most cited times of change, the Meiji period and the postwar period, came as a result of direct and vigorous foreign pressure. In addition, the need for change in those two periods was obvious, and the alternative to change was clearly negative. Pressures from the international community will play a role in changing contemporary Japan, but the most important forces for change must come from within. Can Japan change itself without strong and persistent outside pressure? Do Japanese even perceive the current situation as comparable to the Meiji and postwar periods in terms of the dire need for change?

Japanese society has always been extremely conservative in that maintaining the status quo has had greater salience than progress for progress' sake. Japanese society, forms of behavior, and institutions do not change rapidly, nor do they change without fundamental cause. Japan is the quintessential "If it ain't broke, don't fix it" society. Thus, when things are going fine, there is a strong tendency to continue the status quo. The vast majority of people in contemporary Japan are happy with the way things are right now, and the last thing they want is change. Especially a change that may disrupt their standard of living and their sense of well-being. Change comes only when the need for it becomes achingly obvious.

Although Japan is perceived from the outside as a highly efficient country where everything works well, in fact there are many elements of its political and social systems, and even its economy, that can be extremely dysfunctional and inefficient. The emasculation of government institutions by LDP factionalism, the inability to create equal apportionment, the pressure that "examination hell" puts on young students, and the high cost to consumers associated with an inefficient distribution system have all been identified as problems that can be solved only by fundamental reforms. And yet all attempts at reform in these areas have been unsuccessful because they have received little support from the government, the bureaucracy, or the society at large. Reforms in these areas have not been enacted or supported because, in part, it would entail changing elemental aspects of postwar Japan, all of which are perceived as having brought about prosperity. If they are changed, no one can guarantee that the new systems and institutions will be as successful as the old system in supporting the further development of Japan. One might say that the overall success of Japan in the postwar era has blinded Japanese to the myriad problems that have existed and continue to exist in Japan, despite its progress. As a friend once said, "They got the economy right, but everything else is dreadful." While this is a bit hyperbolic, there is a grain of truth. As long as the economy is functioning well, all other problems tend to be overlooked or given short shrift. Indeed, as long as the economy is functioning well, it is doubtful whether any basic changes will be supported or made. This mentality makes one question the ability of Japanese to achieve domestic change or to change their relations with the outside world.

Gaiatsu

A fundamental element of postwar Japan has been the integration of the Japanese domestic economy and the international trade and finance system. The strength of Japan's domestic economy is totally dependent upon its ability to trade, import natural resources and energy resources, utilize international financial markets, and invest in foreign markets. This integration has created two problems for Japan: economic integration frequently "spills over" into political, military, and cultural integration, and other states expect that the benefits it has gained through economic integration are reciprocal. Since the 1970s the rest of the world has had increased expectations that Japan will open its society and markets and will enter into the world community outside the economic sphere. This "internationalization" is one of the changes Japanese fear will disrupt the comfort and affluence that was so carefully developed during the postwar period.

Gaiatsu is the contemporary buzzword in Japan for pressure from outside countries for domestic change, and its use and effectiveness is a topic of hot debate. Some decry it as unwarranted and unwanted pressure from foreign countries, especially the United States, that have no right to interfere in domestic policy. Others believe it to be the only way to create change in Japan. There is a widespread perception within Japan and among foreign countries that the government actually wants pressure from the United States and other foreign powers so that it can use *gaiatsu* as an excuse for making domestic changes that would otherwise be very difficult.

The LDP was formed by a coalition of conservative parties, most of which had their roots in the rural, agricultural areas of Japan. This was at a time when Japan was still a rural, agrarian country. In 1955 about 40 percent of the laboring population was in agriculture and there were six million farm families. The LDP's four-decade tenure as the nation's government has been secured by burrowing its roots deep into these farming districts and maintaining their loyalty with policies that subsidized the price of rice and banned the importation of agricultural produce. But Japan is no longer an agrarian, rural country. The vast majority of its voters are urban consumers, and they are hurt economically by LDP policies that protect the small farmer. The number of farm families in contemporary Japan has dwindled to four million, and only 14 percent of those are farming full time.[8] In the five years between 1985 and 1990, the farming population dropped by 10 percent and is now down to about 7 percent of the nation's total labor force.[9] Along with the decline in the number of farmers, there has also been a rapid decrease in the number of people living in rural areas. A continuous migration from the Japanese countryside to large metropolitan areas and, more recently, to smaller and medium-sized cities has depopulated rural Japan. In those same five years the rural population of Japan declined by 5.5 percent.[10]

These figures have forced the LDP to consider how it will be able to maintain voter support. It is difficult to believe that the agrarian voter will continue to be the most important support base for the LDP's future. The LDP is a very pragmatic party, and farm households represent only 7 percent of all eligible voters.[11] All parties must respond to the voice of the urban consumer, and the urban consumer wants change in Japan's agricultural policy. People in Tokyo are tired of paying three times as much for meat and twice as much for milk, sugar, and vegetables as someone living in New York City. They are especially tired of paying six or seven times as much as the rest of the world for rice. A poll by the Japan Public Survey Institute showed that 65 percent of the public wants some kind of rice liberalization, while 30 percent opposes it.[12]

Yet it has been difficult for the LDP to change its agricultural policies or its orientation toward the voters of Japan. The close relationship to the farmers of Japan that has been built over the years has also incurred a great obligation on the part of the LDP toward farmers. The bonds of obligation relationships are not easily broken in Japan; they are a very important part of the social fabric. Urban consumers want changes in agricultural policy, but at the same time they would also be upset with the LDP if they thought it was ungraciously dumping its agricultural supporters by severing its obligations in haste.

Gaiatsu was one of the means the LDP used to solve this dilemma when it was in power. Recently the issue has been rice, but before rice it was beef and oranges. The Japanese government protested throughout the mid-1980s that there would be no change in its policies and that it would continue to stand fast and protect the Japanese farmer as Japanese-American negotiations on Japanese beef and orange quotas dragged on. At the same time, the United States continued to hammer Japan with threats of sanctions unless the quotas were removed. Finally, with a great show of frustration and many complaints about bullying, the Japanese government eventually relented and agreed to the removal of quotas in both areas and replaced them with a decreasing tariff schedule. In response to an outraged farming community, the LDP could point to the United States and plead "they made us do it."

The same act was played out over rice. The government steadfastly stated that it would not liberalize rice and that "not one grain" of rice would ever enter the country. Meanwhile individual but powerful politicians, among them past Prime Minister Hosokawa, could be heard admitting that rice liberalization will have to come because Japan is being pressured to do so by foreign powers. Rice liberalization eventually did come because disastrous weather caused 1993 to be the worst growing year in postwar history, forcing the government to import an estimated 2.2 million tons of rice. Although the need to cover the weather-related shortfall was the precipitating factor in importing rice, pressure from abroad—most specifically the United States and the need to finalize the Uruguay Round of negotiations of the General Agreement on Tariffs and Trade (GATT)—was the fundamental cause in ending Japan's ban on imported rice. In 1984 Japan was also forced to import rice to cover domestic shortfalls, but that was a one-shot deal. This time the market will stay open as the GATT accord calls for the liberalization of the Japanese rice market to begin in 1995.

Gaiatsu has been especially successful in agriculture, but there is a wealth of other examples. It was a major factor in the liberalization of the financial and construction industries and in the reformation of the distribution system. But if *gaiatsu* is a handy tool to be used by the government and other political institutions to force changes in the domestic political system that otherwise would be problematic, it also has a downside. For one thing, it can make the government look as if it is still under the control of the United States. In saying "the United States made us do it," the government is also saying that it does not have the will power to stand up to the United States. This substantially reduces the domestic and foreign perception of Japanese political leadership's ability to act forcefully on the world stage. Perhaps more dangerously, if *gaiatsu* is taken at face value, it can create a perception among Japanese that they are being unfairly bullied by the United States or other foreign powers, something to which Japanese are particularly sensitive.

Siege Mentality

One manifestation of Japan's belief in its national separateness or distinctiveness is a concomitant sense of isolation and detachment from the outside world. Add to this the inner-directed nationalism as described above and the result is a strong impulse toward insular attitudes. Japan has developed somewhat of a "siege mentality."[13] One element of the siege mentality is the perception that other countries are "out to get" Japan for its success. As the Japanese economy grew by leaps and bounds, so grew the pressure on Japan from the United States and other countries to open itself and conform more to their standard of doing things and the openness of their markets. Foreign criticism and pressure on Japan to change elements of what has been a successful economy is sometimes seen as a throwback to the days during the Meiji era when foreign powers did indeed act in concert to insure that the spoils of Japanese victories in China and Russia would not give Japan so much power that it would become a rival to Western pretensions in Asia and the Pacific.

It is also occasionally perceived as racism. Once again the Caucasian powers have stepped in to repress a non-Caucasian power that dares to become their equal. In *The Japan That Can Say No*, Shintaro Ishihara relates a story about talking with members of Congress and lobbyists during the spring of 1987. At that time the United States had accused Japan of not living up to a bilateral agreement on semiconductor trade and had imposed heavy duties on a wide range of Japanese imports. In addition, both the House of Representatives and the Senate almost unanimously passed separate resolutions calling for tough action against Japan if it did not open its markets. In the middle of this very charged atmosphere, Ishihara claims that there was general agreement that increasing United States-Soviet detente was based upon their both being Caucasian countries and that it might well be aimed against Japan. When a congressman said to him that the United States might abandon Japan as an ally, he wondered if the United States would ever consider doing that to France or Great Britain.[14]

Fears of an American-Russian coalition directed against Japan are a subtle undercurrent in the post–Cold War Japanese mentality. Russia and Japan have a history of conflict that dates back to the seventeenth century, and the best thing about the Cold War was a guarantee of American protection against the Soviet Union. It makes Japan nervous that Russia and the United States are now attempting to work together. The Japanese press was very conscious of the difference in treatment given to Boris Yeltsin and Prime Minister Kiichi Miyazawa in their separate meetings with President Clinton in April 1993. The "Vancouver Summit" between Clinton and Yeltsin came with all the trappings that summits are supposed to have. There were photo opportunities in scenic places, long walks in the woods, and tête-à-têtes that overran their scheduled time. About a week after the Vancouver summit, Prime Minister Miyazawa came to the United States for his first meeting since Bill Clinton took office. He was met at Andrews Air Force Base by low-level officials with little fanfare. When he did meet with the president, it was far overshadowed in the American press by the president's meeting on the same day with gay and lesbian leaders. In comparing these two meetings between the three heads of state, one

Japanese analyst wondered if it was Japan or Russia that has an alliance with the United States.[15]

Constant accusations in the Japanese media of "Japan bashing" by the United States is another manifestation of the siege mentality. Japan bashing can be defined as the criticism of Japan in the mass media and the general literature on Japan without basis and without intent to be either constructive or enlightening. Bashing is criticism for criticism's sake, with intent to harm Japan's image. There is no doubt that some of what is written in both the mass media and in the literature on Japan can be considered bashing. There are many pieces written or broadcast that are based on very little knowledge or are intended to take Japan down a peg or two. Neither is bashing an American monopoly. British press coverage of the death of Emperor Showa and Edith Cresson's attacks on Japan also gave rise to cries of "bashing" from Japan.

From the American perspective, however, much of what is perceived as bashing in Japan is actually legitimate criticism of it. Unfortunately, Japanese culture does not give criticism much leeway. In Japan criticism of someone who is your equal or superior can be made only indirectly, if at all, because it is important to maintain at least a semblance of harmony and hierarchical order. Direct and public criticism is seen as being very demeaning because it disrupts the emotions of all involved, and may lead to a real loss of "face" by the person criticized. In a manner of speaking, it disturbs the *wa*. It is also an indication that the person doing the criticizing is superior in status or rank to the one being criticized. This is not to say that direct criticism does not occur, even criticism of a person higher in the hierarchy than the critic. I have sat through many an uncomfortable silence while some young faculty member went on in a diatribe against the dean during a faculty meeting.

Japan is neither as consensual nor harmonious as it may appear from the outside, but it is most often the case that criticism of an equal or superior will be done at the proper place and time and in the proper manner. It may be while having a few drinks after work, or it may be by passing the word indirectly through others, but it has to be in the appropriate situation and time. Perhaps the best example is the way in which a Japanese husband treats his wife. Direct and public criticism of a wife by her husband used to be standard behavior by Japanese as it was recognized that the husband had a much higher social standing than did his wife. But times have changed, and as the status of wives reaches that of their husbands, the direct and public criticism of a wife by her husband is seen as demeaning and improper.

In the Japanese mind, public criticism from the United States is rude and an indication that the United States considers itself to be in a superior position in the relationship. Public criticism from the United States was tolerated for many years, and still is, because Japanese recognized the dominance of the United States in the bilateral relationship. Now that the relationship has become one of greater equality, Japan's tolerance is wearing thin. The United States is seen as the world's schoolyard bully who uses coercive tactics to intimidate Japan into making trade concessions in order to hide its own noncompetitiveness. While understandable, the bottom line is that Japan does not take criticism very well; therefore any criticism, justified or not, is perceived as bashing.

Take, for example, Clyde Prestowitz's *Trading Places*. It is an excellent book which outlines the differences between Japan and the United States in trade negotiations and gives recommendations for both sides in improving the relationship. Prestowitz is critical, but his criticism is fair and doled out evenly to both sides. But because the book does criticize Japan, it became a bashing classic in the eyes of the Japanese, even though Prestowitz is a longtime friend and student of Japan.

The Japanese media play a major role in fostering the siege mentality. Books about Japan published in the United States that are considered "bashers" are minutely dissected in the press. Pointing out criticism from abroad seems to be an obsession with the media. A study conducted for the Mansfield Center for Pacific Affairs contrasted Japanese and American coverage of three sensitive issues: the FSX negotiations, the SII negotiations, and the purchase of Columbia Pictures and Rockefeller Center. The study found that Japanese newspapers use allegations of Japan bashing "to down-play or dismiss the significance of an unwelcomed complaint." Twelve percent of Japanese stories covering FSX, 23 percent covering SII, and 41 percent covering the Columbia/Rockefeller purchases mentioned the bashing of Japan.[16]

Japan as Victim

The siege mentality is also evident in the response of many Japanese to the charges of aggression and atrocities during the 1930s and 1940s. Such accusations are perceived as unwarranted attacks because Japanese have for so long glossed over the suffering imposed on others during those years while simultaneously emphasizing their own suffering. They see themselves as misunderstood victims of the Second World War who just want to be left alone to forget, but are not allowed to by an unreasonable world that still remembers. When footage from the war is shown on Japanese television, it is most likely to show Japan and Japanese in a sympathetic light: the firebombing of Tokyo, the mushroom clouds over Hiroshima and Nagasaki, civilian casualties in Okinawa, or refugees returning from the colonies.

It is almost as if Japanese want to believe that because they lost the war they must therefore have been its victims from the beginning. Consequently there are any number of theories that reverse responsibility for the attack on Pearl Harbor. One of the most popular has already been stated above: the ABCD encirclement and American economic actions forced Japan to lash out in self-preservation. But there are many more. Shoichi Watanabe argues in a *Chuo Koron* article that Japan should not be stigmatized for the attack on Pearl Harbor because the fifty-five-minute interval between the attack and the notification to Washington was due to a bureaucratic communications error, and that the Hull Note was tantamount to a declaration of war.[17]

I used to teach a class on the history of United States-Japan relations at Keio University in Tokyo, and many of my students were fascinated by the question of when Franklin Delano Roosevelt knew about the coming attack. John Toland's book *Infamy*, was very popular with the students. In it he presents claims that President Roosevelt and his top aides knew about the impending attack but purposefully did nothing so that the United States would be drawn into the war as a unified nation. Their reasoning was that if Roosevelt knew Japan was going to attack Hawaii but did nothing to stop it, then the responsibility for the attack was Roosevelt's, not Japan's.

Japanese coverage of the anniversary of Pearl Harbor put at least as much emphasis on Japanese as victims of the war as it did on the attack itself. Nippon Hoso Kyokai (NHK) is the quasi-governmental broadcasting system for Japan, and its news broadcasts are considered to be the most authoritative. Its prime-time news program on December 8, 1991 covered the commemorative ceremonies at Pearl Harbor, including President George Bush's speech, the laying of a wreath by the president and Mrs. Bush, and the moment of silence. However, those segments were immediately followed by one showing elderly women in Okinawa carrying out a remembrance ceremony for Japanese civilians killed in the battle of Okinawa and one showing women distributing antiwar leaflets in Tokyo. The message of the concluding segments was very clear: "Japan was a victim; Japan is now a peaceful country." But NHK was not alone; the commercial networks also buffered their broadcasts of the Pearl Harbor ceremonies with images of Japan as a victim of the war.

The classic case of Japan as victim is the bombing of Hiroshima. It is the final trump card thrown down when Japan is accused of having been the the aggressor. In the Japanese mind what happened at the beginning of the war is inconsequential considering that Japan is the only nation to have been the target of nuclear weapons. The attack on Hiroshima and, to a lesser extent, that on Nagasaki are believed to be unanswerable; the atrocity committed against Japan outweighs all atrocities it may have committed. Unfortunately this attitude allows Japanese to deflect questions about Japanese responsibility for aggression and atrocities in Asia, which then becomes a reason for not teaching the history of the 1930s and 1940s, and trivializes Hiroshima and Nagasaki as antinuclear symbols.

The Japanese portrayal of themselves as "unilateral pacifists" and as the victims of the only nuclear bomb dropped in anger is laudable but diverting. There are too few books, popular or academic, like Toshio Iritani's *Group Psychology of the Japanese in Wartime*, a splendid examination of how the Japanese war mentality was derived. Examinations of the root causes of the war in Japanese textbooks are essentially forbidden, and there is still much denial of Japan's actions in Asia, especially Japanese atrocities in the 1937 capture of Nanjing. Ultimately it diverts attention from and devalues the concept that Japanese citizens were victimized more by their leaders than by either the United States or an idealized notion of "war."

INTERNATIONALIZATION

One of the most consistently fashionable concepts since the late 1970s in a notoriously fad-oriented culture has been internationalization (*kokusaika*). Its meaning is often vague, but it generally connotes a perceived need for Japan to redefine itself by opening its doors to the rest of the world. The need for internationalization springs from one basic font: Japan's economic interdependence. Trade is a two-way street that brings much more than just resources, capital, and products into Japan. Japan's economic success and high levels of trade have brought a whole new range of problems which are related to that trade, some of which are new to the Japanese experience. The number of foreign residents in Japan, both legal and illegal, has increased drastically, and they have brought with them new ideas and behaviors. Illegal aliens will be discussed later, but the legal foreign population is about 1.2 million and is increasing at about 140,000 people per year. It is estimated that the combined yearly increase in legal and illegal foreigners is roughly 216,000 per year, 60 percent of the annual growth of the domestic population.[18] Foreign governments have increased the pressure on Japan to reform its domestic and foreign policy. Conversely, Japanese feel pressured to expose themselves to peoples and cultures beyond the borders of Japan and the limits of Japanese culture.

Internationalization is at the center of the current Japanese identity crisis. For the third time in less than a century and a half, Japan is being forced to adapt to changes in the international environment. But as in both the earlier periods of adaptation, there is a growing backlash to the internationalization of Japanese culture. To the extent that Japanese believe that Japan has caught up to the West, or even surpassed the West, the backlash becomes even stronger.

One way of dealing with the need for internationalization has been to stand it on its head: internationalizing Japan by Japanizing the world. Thus, when Prime Minister Nakasone introduced his educational policies for the internationalization of Japan, the biggest component was bringing more foreign faculty members and Japanese students to Japan, not to increase the

exposure of Japanese faculties and students to other peoples and cultures but to teach Japanese language and culture to foreigners. In the words of Shuntaro Ito, a professor at Tokyo University:

The globalization of the Japanese language bears on the internationalization of Japan as a whole. Until now our understanding of the role of language in Japan's internationalization has been limited to the notion that we Japanese should learn English, French and the other foreign languages so as to be able to communicate on an equal footing with non-Japanese wherever we go. But another way of integrating Japan into the global community is for non-Japanese to learn the Japanese language and so come to a direct understanding of Japanese society. In fact, recently I've come to think that this second avenue may be the more efficient. Both routes are necessary, of course, but we haven't paid enough attention to the second.[19]

The consequence of internationalization in Japan has been to incite nationalism.[20] The increased need to learn English has made many students and salarymen resentful that they cannot do business in their own language, and the difficulties they face in learning English often increase their feelings of separation from the outside world. Businessmen ask petulantly why Japan must learn to negotiate with the rest of the world, why doesn't the world learn to negotiate with us? The need to send Japanese businessmen and their families overseas has created a whole new social problem within Japan—how to deal with returnees. Those who return from long overseas stints may become *gaijin kusai* (to smell like a foreigner) and may not be able to fit in well with either the corporate or the social culture to which they return. The new business culture that was picked up abroad has even led some to complain that foreign viruses, such as job jumping, have been brought home with the returnees. Most problematic is the fate of children who accompany their parents abroad and then are forced to return to the very in-group oriented and tracked school system as outsiders.

Both direct investment from abroad and the influx of foreign workers that accompany it attack Japanese homogeneity at its very roots. Japanese salarymen are forced to work in offices with foreigners who do not understand the rules as they know them. Increased trade relations with third world countries also often contain pressures by those countries on Japan to accept surplus workers as *gastarbeiter* to supplement the shortage of labor at the lower end of the Japanese labor hierarchy. The few enclaves of upper middle class, white foreigners in Azabu or Roppongi have never much bothered the Japanese, but the new enclaves of Iranis and Pakistanis in the Ueno and Shinjuku sections of Tokyo, and outlying prefectures, bring fears of serious challenges to the society.

An administrator at Keio University once told me: "To Japanese, internationalization is like a fashionable handbag. It is worn as a pretty accessory when outside, and it may even serve a practical purpose, but once they are home, it is thrown in the closet." I have always thought this an apt metaphor. Internationalization is welcomed in Japan as long as it is pretty, cute, superficial, and serves a pragmatic purpose. For most Japanese internationalization means such things as watching James Dean movies, being able to speak and read a little English or other European language, taking a summer holiday trip abroad, and maybe even having a foreign boyfriend or girlfriend. It does not yet imply substantial changes such as altering domestic institutions and structures to conform to world standards or accepting foreign peoples, cultures, and institutions as equals in Japan. A Japanese man with a Western girlfriend will be the envy of his peers, but envy will turn to disdain if he marries her.

Another criticism of internationalization is that it is just another form of Westernization. The basic concepts upon which internationalization is founded, and indeed, the basic values and laws of the international relations system, are all Western derived. Thus, for Japan to become internationalized, Japan must become Western. This perception of internationalization as simply another case of Japan's being coerced into molding itself to conform to the Western world raises the question of what part of the world Japan identifies with the most, Asia or the West?

ASIAN OR WESTERN?

This is a very difficult question for most Japanese. The racial and cultural origins of the Japanese nation are obvious, yet the models for social modernization and economic and political development have been Western. Certainly Japanese place the West higher than other Asian countries in their hierarchical ordering of the world. Most Asian aliens in Japan would agree that Japanese treat Western foreigners and Asian foreigners in different ways. Indeed, the most commonly used word for foreigners, *gaijin*, is used almost exclusively as a designation for Westerners. Even though Japanese have great pride in the scientific and technological achievements of their nation, they still make major efforts to learn from the West in a wide range of matters. There is no real concomitant search for knowledge from other Asian countries, not even in terms of social or ethical values. In the mid-1970s Professor Edwin Reischauer once said that to tell a Japanese person that Japan has done very well in developing far beyond the rest of Asia would be much less well received than to say that Japan has done very well in developing almost to the level of the United States. The point being that Japanese would much prefer being compared to the West than to Asia, even if the comparison was less favorable. His point still retains a grain of truth. Third world countries, including other Asian countries, rank below Japan and the West in the minds of Japanese.

Perhaps the best example of Japan's identification with the West over Asia comes in its attitudes toward foreigners in Japan. Few foreigners are allowed to penetrate too deeply into Japanese groups or into the society as a whole, but the Japanese ways of keeping foreigners at arm's length depends upon the race and nationality of the foreigner. Asians, Africans, and Middle Easterners who live in Japan often complain that they are not treated with the same respect and courtesy accorded white foreigners. While white foreigners are generally distanced from the group with polite smiles, Asians, Blacks, and Arabs are frequently treated quite rudely. When Tokushima University, in Shikoku, announced that it was going to build a dormitory for fifty foreign students, neighbors began demanding that a high fence and floodlights surround the dormitory so that the students could not get out and steal their vegetables. The majority of neighbors felt that foreigners couldn't be trusted. According to an official from the student affairs department, "some of the local people were old and had preconceived ideas about foreigners, especially Asians."[21]

Asian foreigners in Japan have an especially hard time of it as they are expected to speak Japanese and know the proper forms of Japanese behavior. Those who do not will be given short shrift. However, if a white foreigner knows only a very few words of Japanese, he or she will be invariably complimented on how well they speak the language. This double standard is also applied to Asian people who are, for all intents and purposes, Japanese in all but ethnicity. Second and third generation ethnic Koreans and Chinese who were born in Japan and have lived there all their lives are not allowed Japanese citizenship, nor are they allowed many, if any, jobs in the public service sector.

There has always been a double standard for Western and non-Western foreigners in Japan, but it has become more pronounced with the increase of foreign laborers there. Japan has more jobs than people to fill them, and this labor shortage is felt especially strongly at the bottom end of the employment ladder. The admission of foreign workers as a means of alleviating the labor shortage has been discussed over the past few years, but a comprehensive policy has yet to emerge. While the issue continues to be debated, illegal immigrants in unprecedented numbers have begun to flow into Japan. The Immigration Bureau of the Justice Ministry estimates that there were 292,791 foreigners in Japan illegally as of November 1992. This figure is just an educated guess; the actual number of illegal aliens in Japan could be anywhere from half a million to over a million. The vast majority of illegal laborers in Japan are Asian. Thais are the largest contingent (18 percent), followed by South Koreans (13 percent), Malaysians and Filipinos (each 12 percent), Chinese (10 percent), Bangladeshis, Pakistanis, and Taiwanese.[22]

Foreign enclaves are nothing new; they have been in existence ever since the coming of the Westerners in the mid-nineteenth century. Tokyo and Osaka still have well-known areas, such as Azabu and Roppongi, where Westerners have always lived, worked, and played. But the new wave of immigrants are non-Western, are coming in very large numbers, and are not confined to the major metropolitan areas. These three elements make a great deal of difference, and most Japanese have become extremely concerned about large groups of Pakistanis, Thais, Chinese, Malays, Bangladeshis, and Iranians that they increasingly encounter in train stations and on the streets. Although it is generally accepted that they are necessary to work the jobs that Japanese are not willing to do, Japanese often find their physical presence irritating and disruptive. They often gather in the thousands in places like Yoyogi Park in downtown Tokyo to meet, talk, cook their native food, and look for jobs. These gatherings have frightened local residents and unnerved city officials. Very often the police conduct sweeps of such gatherings looking for illegal workers. In April 1993 the Tokyo Municipal Government took the innovative action of planting three thousand azalea bushes in the area of Yoyogi where immigrant laborers gathered, and then cordoned off the whole area "in order to protect nature."

The immigrant labor problem was once confined to Tokyo and the other large industrial centers of Japan, but it is now spreading to all corners of the country. Farmers in the most rural prefectures are searching for Asian brides because Japanese women no longer want to marry into farm families. Factories in the more remote and rural parts of Japan are usually the ones that have the largest need for foreign labor because they have the lowest wages and the worst working conditions. Sex clubs throughout the country make use of the limitless pool of cheaper "entertainers" from Southeast Asia who come to Japan, willingly or unwillingly, to support their relatives back home.

Japanese have a cultural nostalgia for Asia in many ways, and often speak of Japan's need to "return home" to its Asian roots, but the re-Asianization of Japan is in no way evident in the barely concealed revulsion that often marks Japanese attitudes toward both legal and illegal Asian foreigners. Just as Japanese tend to be more benevolent toward other Asian peoples in the abstract than in actual contact, so do they praise Asian culture more than they practice it. The United States remains three times as popular as anywhere else as a tourist destination. American movies and television programs remain the mainstay of foreign programming on Japanese television, and American movies continue to far outdraw the movies of any other country, including Japan, in Japanese theaters. Japanese fashion is still Western fashion. If contemporary Japanese culture identifies itself with any influence outside the country, it is still the West. Japan may identify itself as a political and economic leader in Asia, or as a model for Asian development, but Japan does not accept other Asian societies as models for itself.

The most important periods in Japan's modern history have been marked by its attempts to Westernize, yet it still remains unsure of its success and the validity of the West as a model. It looks to Asia as the region of its cultural heritage and contemporary leadership, but its efforts to

Westernize have undeniably removed it from Asia. As trite as it is true, Japan is a country caught between East and West. The key to Japan's understanding its place in the world is by examining its own identity.

NOTES

1. For a fuller discussion of the relationship between traditional ethnicity and the nature of nationalism, see Anthony D. Smith, "The Myth of the 'Modern Nation' and the Myths of Nations" in *Ethnic and Racial Studies* 11 (January 1988), 1–19, and Sami Zubaida's rebuttal of Smith in *Ethnic and Racial Studies* 12 (July 1989), 329–39.

2. Sir Ernest Satow, *A Diplomat in Japan* (Tokyo: Charles E. Tuttle, 1983), 28.

3. As quoted in G. B. Sansom, *The Western World and Japan* (New York: Alfred A. Knopf, 1965), 459.

4. In Jon Livingston, Joe Moore, and Felicia Oldfather, eds., *Imperial Japan: 1800–1945* (New York: Pantheon Books, 1973), 153–54.

5. Payson J. Treat, *Japan and the United States: 1853–1921* (New York: Johnson Reprint Corporation, 1970), 114.

6. Chitoshi Yanaga, *Japan since Perry* (Hamden, Conn.: Archon Books, 1966), 193.

7. Ibid., 373.

8. *Japan Statistical Yearbook, 1991* (Tokyo: Management and Coordination Agency, 1992), 151.

9. *Japan Times*, December 1, 1990, p. 2.

10. *Japan Times*, May 22, 1991, p. 2.

11. *Japan Times*, March 7, 1992, p. 3.

12. *Japan Times*, October 13, 1990, p. 3.

13. Kenneth B. Pyle, "The Future of Japanese Nationality: An Essay in Contemporary History," *Journal of Japanese Studies* 8 (Summer 1982), 241.

14. Shintaro Ishihara, *The Japan That Can Say No* (New York: Simon and Schuster, 1991), 77–78.

15. *Japan Times*, April 21, 1993, p. 17.

16. Stanley Budner, "United States and Japanese Newspaper Coverage of Frictions between the Two Countries," paper written for the Mansfield Center for Pacific Affairs, University of Montana, Missoula, March 1992, p. 10.

17. Shoicihi Watanabe, "The Emperor and the Militarists: Reexamining the Prewar Record," *Japan Echo* 18 (Summer 1991), 72–79.

18. *Japan Times*, April 1, 1993, p. 3.

19. Interview in *Japan Echo* 16 (special issue 1989), 63.

20. Harumi Befu, "Internationalization of Japan," in Hiroshi Mannari and Harum: Befu, *The Challenge of Japan's Internationalization* (Tokyo: Kodansha, 1983), 241.

21. *Japan Times*, March 7, 1994, p. 2.

22. *Japan Times*, February 25, 1993, p. 2.

3

Nationalism and Community

Contemporary Japan exhibits all four types of nationalism described in the introduction, but the most prevalent and the most important is the first: a psychological sense of community and shared communications which is essentially nonpolitical. Japanese reverence for the nation is the result of intensely held in-group feelings, what has been called "the shared uniqueness of being Japanese."[1] Nationalism was brought to Japan by the West, and Japan's definition of self was determined through its relations with the West, but the most vital form of contemporary nationalism is distinctly nativist. For all that has been written about what it means to be Japanese, most Japanese base their identity and the identity of other members of the nation on two rather simple criteria—racial and ethnic characteristics. Neither allegiance to the state nor citizenship in the state has great importance in determining membership in the nation.

The pride that Japanese take in being Japanese, the superiority that they feel toward other nations, the psychological and cultural bonds that they feel toward other Japanese, and their sense of identity with the nation are all related to cultural traditions and societal norms of behavior. Japanese identify themselves as members of a national group, not with the state that governs the nation. Indeed, there is very little identity with the state at all. When Japanese, whether at home or abroad, proclaim themselves to be Japanese, they are not talking about their relationship to the state, either as subjects or representatives, but as members of the national group. This in-group solidarity—the sense of cultural uniqueness, racial homogeneity, collectivity, and similarity—is the nationalism that lives in the hearts of most Japanese today.

Before a discussion of Japanese sociocultural nationalism can begin, a few caveats must be issued. This chapter will argue that the Japanese are extremely homogeneous and group-oriented when compared to the peoples of most other countries of the world. However, recent revisionist studies, by both foreigners and Japanese, have begun to challenge the concepts of uniqueness, homogeneity, group orientation, collectivity, and conformity as applied to Japanese society and culture. Revisionist studies of contemporary Japan are at pains to point out that the image of Japan presented by previous scholarship—a society with no conflict and no significant differences which always operates as a harmonious whole—has been vastly overstated and is essentially incorrect. This is an especially important point as these arguments have been used to excuse a lack of knowledge by outsiders (Japanese are so different that foreigners can never understand them). It has also been used as a means of keeping the world at bay through proclamations of Japanese uniqueness (Japanese are so different that we cannot operate by any rules other than our own).

The revisionists have done a great service to the study of Japan by challenging the postwar traditions and myths that arose with the need to explain Japan's postwar economic development. They have also made Japan more accessible. There are no degrees of uniqueness, and no two nations are alike. Therefore Japan is as unique, but no more unique, than any other nation. Neither is it true that Japan, its society, its political system, or its people, can only be comprehended by Japanese. Not all Japanese conform; there is actually a rather high level of conflict in the society at any given time, and consensus does not often apply outside small groups.

Having said all that, however, one should not go too far in discounting the existence and importance of the homogeneity and/or group orientation of Japanese society. As will be demonstrated below, the homogeneity of Japan is much greater than most other nations of the world and is one of the most important factors in understanding what makes Japan different from other states and nations. Similarly, while there are other nations in the world that are as group-oriented as Japanese, they are not found among the nation-states to which Japan is most often compared, the developed democratic states of the West. Japan is not absolutely homogeneous, group-oriented, conformist, collectivist, and harmonious, but it is relatively so in comparison with other nations and states.

The other caveat has to do with change. There has been tremendous change in Japanese society over the years, while, as is normal, scholarship that records and explains these changes has lagged behind. The image we have of Japanese society is based upon what can be termed the postwar traditions. Collective scholarly and popular writings on Japan have created a certain perception of Japan and the Japanese. The totality of these postwar traditions is vast, but they include the image of Japan as consensual, homogeneous, pacific, and extremely group-oriented. The postwar traditions have given rise to a number of cultural stereotypes which are triggered as soon as the word "Japan" is mentioned. Loyalty to the family has been replaced by loyalty to the company. Blue collar, pink collar, and white collar workers all sacrifice their lives for their companies. All children sacrifice their childhood to the examination-oriented education system. All companies are human-oriented, guarantee their employees lifetime employment, and put human concerns first. But the problem with describing and explaining contemporary Japanese society is both to explain these postwar traditions, most of which have been true to a greater or lesser extent, and the changes that they have undergone in the past two decades. While these postwar traditions still serve as the foundation for understanding Japan and Japanese society, they are changing and no longer as accurately portray life in Japan.

UNIFORMITY AND CENTRALIZATION

Japan is a group-oriented society, but group solidarity may be manifested at other levels of society than the nation, and may actually compete with the nation for the loyalty of the individual. In most states the nation is comprised of different peoples who belong to various groups—ethnic, class, linguistic, religious, regional—that are in competition for their loyalties. However, in Japan not only are there few people with crosscutting loyalties, but there exists no plausible threat to Japanese national group identity. Though there are separate Japanese islands, these do not, by and large, constitute different ethnic or cultural traditions capable of challenging the majority. There is no distinct nation or territory analogous to Scotland or Wales in Great Britain. There are Korean and Chinese minorities that can be seen as analogous to African Americans and Hispanic Americans in the United States, but whereas the latter comprise, respectively, 12 percent and 8 percent of the American population, the former comprise one-half of a percent and one-tenth of a percent of the Japanese population. While these figures are not a justification for the alien status of Koreans and Chinese in Japanese society or other acts of discrimination, the small numbers do emphasize the ethnic and racial homogeneity of the Japanese nation.

The basic component of the international relations system is the nation-state, but in reality there are very few true nation-states in the world. Homogeneity has made Japan one of the purest nation-states in that non-Japanese residents, including long-term ethnic Chinese and Korean residents, account for less than 884,025 people, or about seven-tenths of a percent of the total population, the vast majority of which are ethnic Koreans. Not only are almost all Japanese citizens racially and ethnically Japanese, but very few Japanese live outside Japan. The major Japanese expatriate communities are in the United States and Brazil, but even these communities are small by any standard. In 1990 the total number of Japanese citizens living abroad rose to slightly over 600,000 for the first time, but it still only accounted for five-tenths of a percent of all Japanese citizens. Only half of those living abroad were staying for more than three months, and about a third are considered permanent expatriates.[2]

Class cleavages in Japan are negligible, as is class consciousness. Quite the opposite, rather than having class cleavages, Japanese tend to think of their society as being more egalitarian than otherwise. Most surveys demonstrate that approximately nine out of ten Japanese regularly identify with the middle class, although a third of the work force is in manufacturing. The Japanese landscape is void of class-based organizations, such as labor unions, that compete with the nation for the loyalty of the individual.

Neither do religious institutions or affiliations have the strength to compete with the nation for the loyalty of Japanese people. Only about one-quarter of Japanese report that they believe in any religion, while most have very tenuous and nonpracticing ties to both Shinto and Buddhism. The fact that most Japanese are extremely ecumenical (if one can apply that term to non-Christian religions) argues most strongly against the competition of religious loyalties with national loyalties. Japanese have a high tolerance for any and all religions.

Neither are there any linguistic cleavages within the Japanese nation. Although English is the second language of Japan, and is taught and used extensively, there is no threat whatsoever of its challenging the Japanese national language. English is not a threat to Japanese because it is neither the language of an indigenous cultural group (as is the case with French in Canada), nor is it the badge of the political and cultural elite (as is the case in India). Strictly speaking, English is not the second language of the nation, but is the first foreign language in that it is used as Japan's primary means of communication with the outside world. If the Japanese language is not challenged by any outside language, neither are there competing dialects. Regional pronunciations and diction may vary slightly, but the essential components of the language are the same throughout Japan.

Japanese identification with their local regions is strong, and it is here that possible competing loyalties may exist. Indeed, there is an interesting paradox involved in the Japanese self-perception of homogeneity. While Japanese go to great lengths to prove to themselves and the world that Japan is one unified, homogeneous whole, they also exaggerate regional distinctions. When one mentions in conversations with Japanese that the country is quite similar wherever one travels, the listener will frequently remonstrate, "Ah, but you haven't been to Shikoku," or Hokkaido, or whatever the native region of the speaker. Japanese are quite proud of regional distinctions and will argue endlessly about the qualities of rice, sake, festival dances, cuisine, and speech of the various regions of Japan.

Yet these distinctions are somewhat contrived. The more they are argued and bragged about, the more it becomes evident that there is an intent to create differences where similarities are most evident.

There are two notable exceptions to the lack of crosscutting loyalties in Japan: the Ryukyu Islands (commonly known as Okinawa) and *burakumin*. Okinawans are distinguished from mainstream Japanese in many ways. The most obvious is geographical. The Ryukyus extend between Kyushu and Taiwan, and the Okinawan capital of Naha is only 400 miles from Taipei but 1,000 miles from Tokyo. Okinawans have a separate but related history. The Ryukyu Islands became an independent kingdom in 1609, and maintained a very close contact with Japan throughout the Tokugawa reign. The islands were so tightly tied to Japan that Commodore Perry stopped there first on his way to Japan as a dress rehearsal. He also knew that the Okinawans would communicate his intentions to the *bakufu*. Okinawa was finally incorporated into Japan in 1874. Okinawans were the only part of Japan to suffer a direct invasion of allied forces, and the islands lost 150,000 people during the war, some of whom were forced to commit suicide out of respect for the emperor. The American occupation of Okinawa lasted until 1972, twenty years longer than the occupation of the other islands, and Okinawa still bears the burden of American military bases in Japan. The United States and Japan are blamed equally for the suffering during the war and for the extended occupation.

Relations between the Okinawans and mainstream Japanese have improved greatly since the end of the war. The vast majority of Okinawans think of themselves as Japanese and want more, not less, assimilation. Indeed, the major complaint of Okinawans is that they are not assimilated enough, especially when it comes to developing the islands' economic infrastructure. Since the end of the war, but especially since reversion, Okinawa has been assimilated into Japan through a centralized mass media, unitary governance, centralized education, economic unity, and improved transportation. Okinawans still represent a separate cultural and linguistic tradition, and they still think of themselves as a people somewhat apart from other Japanese, but that does not mean that they do not want to be a part of Japan. Being Okinawan is a distinction that they hold with pride, but it is complementary, and subservient, to their sense of being Japanese.

The case of *burakumin* is rather different from Okinawans. *Burakumin* have always been racially and territorially part of the mainstream, but they are segregated by their traditional caste status. Japan has always had various outcastes, especially those who engaged in trades that dealt in handling corpses, butchering animals, or working leather, as dealing with blood, corpses, and other corporeal elements was believed by Buddhists to pollute the soul. A hereditary caste system was implemented by the Tokugawa regime, and the outcastes were locked into the bottom, "untouchable," status. The Meiji restoration did away with the old caste distinctions, but societal discrimination still remained strong. Even today, many live in their own communities and still work in their traditional trades, or modern offshoots of them. Although discrimination is not as strong as it used to be, it still exists, especially in those areas of Japan, such as the Kansai area (Osaka region), where their numbers are the greatest. For example, it is not unusual for parents to check the background of their prospective in-laws in order to ascertain whether they have a *burakumin* ancestry. Although a reverse pride in being *burakumin* has grown in the postwar years, the major thrust of the *burakumin* movement has been assimilation, not disassociation.

Urbanization

There is no doubt that the different regions of Japan produce different varieties of rice, which then give rise to different varieties of sake, or that people from Kyoto use intonations different from those from the Tohoku (northeast) region. But these differences are slight when compared to the regional and linguistic differences of other countries. They cannot compare to the difference between, for example, Alberta and Quebec, or the Pyrenees and Paris. One of the reasons that Japanese are so quick to point out regional differences is that, to the extent that they do occur, they are disappearing rapidly. Wherever one goes in Japan, with the exception of the two main outer island groups, Hokkaido and the Ryukyu Islands, the countryside looks very similar. Although the development of the economic infrastructure has not been uniform, it has accelerated throughout Japan to the extent that the badges of modern Japan—high-tension wires, caravans of loaded dump trucks, and factories dotting the countryside—can be seen everywhere. The natural vistas that once made the various regions different have in many cases been reduced to a boring similarity.

This is especially noticeable in the urban areas of Japan. The rural population of Japan has been decreasing for decades and is predicted to continue decreasing by 8 percent over the next thirty-five years. In the past, most of those who left rural areas migrated to the big metropolitan areas. Now they are tending more to migrate to regional cities. In addition, village populations are decreasing because villages are tending to join together to incorporate into towns. In 1945 Japan was comprised of 8,518 villages, 1,797 towns, and 205 cities. In 1992 there were 581 villages, 1,993 towns, and 662 cities.[3]

The urbanization of the Japanese countryside has increased the sameness of Japan. As regional cities and towns expand and grow, they bring modernity to those in the rural parts of Japan who had been left behind by the economic boom and rapid development of the metropolitan areas, but at a cost of local and even regional variation. Local people are proud of their individual qualities and their local and regional heritage, but they also look to Tokyo or Osaka as a model for their own development. Thus, as regional towns and cities grew, the architecture they employed was very similar. They all built their little "Ginzas" and "Shinjukus," streets lined with shops or entertainment quarters packed closely together. Many even built miniature Tokyo Towers in order to proclaim their attainment of cityhood.

The consolidation of smaller villages and hamlets into larger towns has improved the quality of life for the community. In the early days, each small hamlet was responsible for many of its own services including daycare, elder care, post office, and fire brigade. The consolidation into larger administrative units allowed greater access to much larger sums of money for expenditures, especially as the government encouraged consolidation through legislation and put money at the disposal of those communities that unified. As a result there are now better facilities and more of them. However, the downside is that the individual hamlets have lost control over services and have a decreased sense of personal relationship to those providing them. While daycare facilities in the past were rather Spartan, at least the children were treated almost as the day care teacher's own because they were essentially all from the same neighborhood. Post offices were tiny holes in the wall that offered few services, but were run by neighbors. After consolidation, the relationship between the people and these administrative services has become as impersonal and removed as is their relationship to the government bureaucracy on either the national or prefectural level.

Mass Media

The mass media is one of the most important sources of uniformity in Japan, due in part to its highly centralized nature. Almost all major television networks, publishing houses, and newspapers are headquartered in Tokyo, from which they disseminate their offerings throughout Japan. Although there are local mass media outlets, they are not competitive as sources of national and international news and opinion.

The centralization of the broadcast media is epitomized by Nihon Hoso Kyokai (Japan Broadcasting Association, NHK), a quasi-governmental organization that broadcasts over two VHF television channels and two satellite channels. NHK is perceived as the "Voice of Japan" because it is the only network that, through the use of VHF, cable, and satellite broadcasting, can be seen throughout the entire archipelago. Even though the government emphasizes the "semi" nature of its semi-governmental status, it is also perceived as the one network representing the nation. This perception is enhanced by its programming. It alone broadcasts most important national sporting events such as sumo tournaments and national amateur competitions. Its news broadcasts are more staid than those of the commercial channels but are perceived to be more authoritative. Its Sunday evening historical dramas and its New Year's Eve broadcast bring together a large majority of Japanese viewers. However, outside of local news broadcasts, there is little local content on NHK. There are a number of programs on local lifestyles, cuisine, and culture, but these programs are produced in Tokyo and broadcast nationally. Only about 10 percent of NHK-General programming is regional, while NHK-Educational and the two satellite channels have almost no regional programming.

There are also four key commercial stations in Tokyo—Nippon Television (NTV), Fuji Television (Fuji-TV), Tokyo Broadcasting System (TBS), and the Asahi News Network (Asahi-TV)—that act as the flagships for nationwide networks. None of them covers the entire archipelago, and most of their programs are produced in and broadcast from Tokyo. There are a total of 6,718 broadcasting stations in Japan, but most of them do just that—broadcast. Very few of these stations have the capability of producing programs other than local news. Cable television has grown in Japan as a method of increasing the quality of reception for those who live in major urban areas where tall buildings block VHF transmission, but cable has not been used to a great extent as a means of expanding the range or accessibility of programming. Of the 27,527 cable broadcasting facilities in Japan, only 107 are reported to have the capability of producing their own programs. There has been much talk in Japan for many years concerning the use of its advanced technology to develop interactive media, but there remains little local content in broadcasting and little public access to the broadcast media.

Newspaper and magazine publishing is as centralized in Tokyo as is television broadcasting. Japanese are voracious readers of mass circulation magazines and newspapers. One hundred twenty-four daily newspapers publish 68.6 million copies a day. That's one copy for every two people in Japan. Compare that with the United States where 1,657 newspapers publish 62.5 million copies a day, or one for every four people. Even though Japan has 124 daily papers, there are no local or regional newspapers that are papers of record. Most Japanese get their news and information from five Tokyo-based newspapers: the *Asahi Shimbun, Yomiuri Shimbun, Mainichi Shimbun, Sankei Shimbun*, and *Nihon Keizai Shimbun*. All have morning and evening editions, and all but the *Sankei* have English-language editions. The morning editions of the big three (*Asahi, Yomiuri,* and *Mainichi*) alone account for more than a third of total daily newspaper circulation. Not only that, but each is tied to one of the Tokyo-based broadcast networks.

The mass media are located in Tokyo, and the news and information they disseminate tend to be derived from events there. Osaka is a bustling Chicago-like commercial city; Kyoto is aloof in its ancient traditions; but Tokyo is the financial, commercial, governmental, bureaucratic, communication, and popular culture center of Japan. Consequently many of the stories in the media have their origin in Tokyo. This is especially important when it comes to information that Japanese receive about lifestyles and popular culture. Japan has long been known as a society that thrives on the booms and busts of various fads, and Tokyo (or, more specifically, the Tokyo media) is the arbitrator of what's hot and what's not. The people of Japan do not have competing regional definitions of contemporary lifestyles analogous to the American Los Angeles–New York rivalry. Whether a young person wants to look punk, a middle-aged woman wants to look chic, or a college student wants to look "trad" (traditional American preppie), their behaviors and accessories are all determined by the Tokyo media.

News reporting is also unified in that it conforms to centralized and self-regulated standards. *Kisha* clubs (reporters' clubs) are the heart of newspaper reporting in Japan. All ministries, political parties, individual politicians, and the various organs of the government maintain *kisha* clubs comprised of reporters from the major newspapers. Foreign reporters are usually banned because they are too inquisitive and obtrusive. The object of the clubs is to provide the media with instant and automatic access to the news and newsmakers, but the result is often a rapport between reporters and the people they cover. *Kisha* clubs can make reporters complacent and overly sympathetic to those they are covering. There is a great deal of intimacy between the source and the reporters which is rarely questioned. There is no doubt that reporters who belong to the clubs learn a great deal of inside information, but much of it never sees the light of day. Reporters who, without permission, capitalize on the inside information they gain, will find themselves out of the club and disconnected from the source. This results in bland reportage. Few reporters who belong to the clubs go beyond what they are given, and all are given the same story at the same time.

Japanese reporters sometimes appear to combine the worst elements of pooled reporting and the excesses of the British tabloid press and Italian paparazzi. Once a story has broken, they begin schooling like sharks outside people's homes or faction headquarters, rushing in a feeding frenzy to shout questions, take pictures, and stick microphones in the faces of anyone coming in or out. But the appearance of an aggressive press belies the reality of the *kisha* club system. Few reporters go beyond accepting what is given to them by the officials they cover until the story has already broken. It is somewhat similar to the relationship reporters and politicians had in Washington before the Vietnam War and the Watergate scandal broke the bond of trust and confidentiality. There have been some instances of striking investigative reporting in Japan, but they are the exceptions to the rule. Most investigative stories are reported by the mainstream press only after they have become so far advanced as no longer to be kept under wraps, or because they have been broken first by weekly news magazines, the foreign media, or others outside the *kisha* club system.

Education

The Japanese education system also plays an important role in creating uniformity of experience and conformity to the group. The Education Ministry sets education policy for all schools in Japan and controls both curriculum and textbooks. Thus, children growing up in different regions of Japan will still experience a very similar classroom environment, study similar texts, and take similar courses. The power of the Ministry of Education to control what happens in the schools is most challenged by the teachers themselves. The teachers' union has historically been one of the most left-oriented unions, and many teachers try their best to put their own spin on what is taught by the recommended texts.

The Ministry of Education's central control over the education system and the schools that comprise it is a primary source of uniformity, but the organization of the system also creates conformity. It can be argued that, for many people in Japan, the single most important factor in their life will be the university they attend. Even if that is not objectively true, most young people and their parents believe it to be true. Students who graduate from certain universities are almost guaranteed good positions in any career they want to pursue, but entry into these Japanese *grandes écoles*, and all universities, is by competitive examination. The entire Japanese education system, especially from middle school on, is based on grouping and tracking related to the examination system. Students begin the process by studying in late primary school for entrance into middle school. All parents will be aware of the schools in the local area, or in other regions of the country, that have the best record of preparing their students for the exams of a certain high school which, in turn, is known to have a good record in preparing its students for the exams of a certain university. Location is no obstacle, as a Japanese child can go to school in any public school in Japan, regardless of whether they reside in the school district.

The examination system contributes to societal conformity in two basic ways. Because priority is placed on studying for exams, students are trained to memorize facts but not to think independently or analytically. Correct answers are important; problem solving is not. Second, the competitive atmosphere leads to rigidity and conformity. Almost every hour of the day is planned for middle school and high school students. Students fear that if they vary from the system, it will hurt their chances of success. Parents and schools present Japanese students with a one-track perception of life. They are told they must pass the examination for these schools to get into that university in order to pursue that career or join this company. Of course not all are successful. Examinations are failed; lives get sidetracked. But the overall impression that young people receive is that there are few alternative options to the one-track life plan with which they are presented. So they buckle down and lock in to the task of spending about six of the most formative years of their lives studying for exams. After four years at university, living the adolescent childhood they never had, they are ready to take up the career they worked so hard to attain.

Conformity is reinforced by the control that schools have over their students' lifestyles. School rules and regulations vary, but most schools maintain strict control over appearance and behavior. The most obvious symbol of the school's control over their students is uniforms. All students in middle school and high school have to wear school uniforms. Sometimes students use the way they wear their uniforms as symbols of rebellion. Tough guys often wear coats that are too big and baggy trousers (the effect is amazingly similar to that of a zoot suit), but these affectations are usually indulged in by those who are on the wrong track. They are students who know that the end of the line will come for them when they graduate from high school and they have nothing to look forward to after that except working in a factory or some other skilled or semi-skilled labor. The students who are on the right track, those who know they have a shot at a half-decent university, are the ones who will most rigidly conform because they recognize conformity as their road to success.

Uniforms are not the only way in which the school enforces conformity. Take, for example, the case of a female student at Shutoku Gakuin High School in Tokyo. The student was first reprimanded for getting a driver's license, which is against school rules. She then arrived at school one day with her hair in a perm and plaited. This is a style sometimes adopted by bikers or other rebellious youth. A driver's license and permed hair was too much for the school principal, and so he expelled her about two weeks before her graduation. She cut her hair, and both she and her parents apologized to the school, but the principal was adamant and refused to allow her to graduate. She sued the school and the principal to be allowed to graduate, but the Tokyo High Court ruled that expelling students from school for having permed hair was perfectly legitimate and generally accepted by society. Rather, the court put the burden of guilt on the student. Even though she had only two weeks to graduation, she knew what the school rules were and should have obeyed them.[4]

This may seem like an extreme case, but it is not. Many schools have teachers standing in the streets outside the school checking appearance and tardiness as the students file in. The teachers are constantly haranguing them to tuck in their shirts, fix their collars, or comb out their hair, while simultaneously exhorting them to "hurry, hurry" into the school grounds. School gates are closed exactly on time, and those left out may not enter for the rest of the day. A few years ago a female high school student was crushed to death by a school gate as it was closing. The girl had arrived just as the gates were being closed and tried to rush through to make it on time, but the teacher in charge wouldn't stop closing the gate. The teacher was convicted of manslaughter but was given only a suspended one-year sentence because his firing and the humiliation of the press coverage were deemed punishment enough.

Parents look to the school system as the fundamental means of socializing their children, and for the most part it works very successfully. The students buy into the need for conformity and are themselves its ultimate enforcers. *Ijime*, or the bullying of students by other students, has become over the past few years a "hot" social issue, but this form of self-enforced conformity has always been a part of the postwar education system. Students are usually singled out for bullying because they are somehow different or don't quite fit in. It can range from the wearing of glasses to having come to the class from outside the school system. Although the problem continues to exist and has had dire consequences—some of the victims commit suicide and some have been killed—there seems to be no greater emphasis on teaching Japanese students to respect differences. Indeed, the emphasis is still placed on respecting similarities.

Even the concept of who is suited to be a student is very limited. There is very little concern about adult education in Japan, even though Japan has a severe problem with the aging of its population. Although some colleges have continuing education programs, most are severely segregated from the mainstream programs. The number of mature students in regular undergraduate or graduate programs is negligible. Similarly, students who drop out of college or high school will find a hard time getting back in. The tragedy of the girl with the permed hair is not just that she wasn't allowed to graduate, but that the chances of her returning for a high school degree are very small. Students who fail their university entrance exams are forced to delay their entering a university until they pass the exams, sometimes after several attempts. But, other than those who are forced to, there are very few who willingly take a few years to mature before entering university. Similarly, it is rare for a student to drop out of one university and join another. Once you are off the track, there is little chance of getting back on it.

In the past, even those children of salarymen and bureaucrats who were sent abroad and educated there had a very difficult time getting into universities back in Japan, because they had gone to secondary school outside the Japanese education system. They didn't fit the mold. Most fathers sent abroad either sent their children back to Japan for high school or left their families in Japan. Although Japanese universities have now become more flexible in accepting students who were educated outside the Japanese examination system, it is still nearly impossible to get credit for courses taken at foreign universities. Even if one were to take courses at Harvard University or Oxford, there are few Japanese universities that would accept their credits.

Language

The final element of uniformity in Japan is its language. Japan is a monolingual nation, and there are neither indigenous languages nor foreign languages that compete with it for primacy. Homogeneity is not manifested by the language—Japanese as it is written and spoken today incorporates elements of many foreign languages—but the monolingual nature of Japanese society does reinforce uniformity. English has been the primary foreign language of the Japanese since the Meiji period, but it is a testimony to the strength of Japanese that even though English has existed in Japan for all those years, few people are fluent and it has never even approached parity with Japanese. In the past, local dialects created differences in spoken Japanese, but the centralized education system beginning in the Meiji era and the advent of Tokyo-centered broadcast media have, for all intents and purposes, eliminated major differences in the way Japanese is spoken and understood in the major regions of Japan.

Japanese national identity is strongly connected to the Japanese language. There is a prevalent belief spread by social critics, academics, and the government that Japanese is a unique language and is used only by the Japanese. This is simply not true. There are hundreds of thousands of Koreans, Chinese, and other immigrants who have grown up in the Japanese school system and have true native fluency. There are also many others around the world who have studied the language and understand it better than the average Japanese. For a sterling example, read Roy Andrew Miller's book, *Japan's Modern Myth*. Nevertheless, the use of Japanese remains one of the major identifying factors for Japanese themselves and is the means they use to separate themselves from others. Its difficulty becomes both a point of perverse pride and a badge of nationality. Only the Japanese use Japanese, so if you speak Japanese, you must be Japanese.

Once Korean, Chinese, and other ethnic immigrant groups are overlooked, it was easy for Japanese to use their language as a means of keeping foreigners at bay. This, however, is becoming more difficult. One of the greatest differences in the Japan of the mid-1970s and contemporary Japan is the Japanese language ability of most foreigners. Back then, if you were a foreigner and could get along in the language, most of your foreign friends would say, "Boy, that's great, how can you do it?" The expectation was that Japanese was almost impossible to master. These days the expectations are just the opposite. If you are a foreigner and residing in Japan but don't know the language, the reaction of other foreigners tends to be, "What's the matter with you?" It has created a real conundrum for the Japanese. If speaking the language is one of the major identifiers of nationality, what happens when Kenyans, Canadians, and Thais can speak the language? Although the internationalization program encourages the learning of Japanese by foreigners, it also creates a great deal of discomfort. It is very common to be praised by the Japanese for one's language abilities when they are minimal. However, when they approach fluency there is a distinct negative reaction. Foreigners are not encouraged to become Japanese.

Uniformity in class, religion, lifestyles, information, education, and language, when taken together, create in Japan a relatively high level of shared values and cultural understanding. They are important factors in making Japanese feel that they are one people, one group. Not all Japanese loosely adhere to Buddhism and/or Shinto. Not all Japanese believe they are members of the middle class. Not all Japanese get their information from the Tokyo media. Not all Japanese are educated in the same way. Not all Japanese speak exactly the same language. But so many Japanese do have such similar lifestyles and backgrounds that the vast majority perceive themselves to be very similar to all other Japanese and are very proud of it. Japanese believe that it is a good thing to be a typical Japanese, whereas an American would not want to be perceived as typical or "just like everyone else." This is the heart of the matter. The extent to which similarity among Japanese exists is less important than the extent to which they perceive its existence, because socio-cultural nationalism is a state of mind. It exists when the individual believes himself or herself to be a member of the national group.

But that belief does not exist alone; it is based on the reality of the uniformity described above. It is that uniformity which forms the basis of Japan as Deutsch's communication community. Japanese are able to communicate relatively easily, they understand each other's implicit signals, they expect certain behaviors from others, because they expect to see in others around them the same values, communication patterns, and patterns of behavior that they themselves exhibit. This holds true in the most general sense, no matter what the attributes of the other person. Although the person may not expect to know what the personality of others he or she encounters will be, they can expect that it will be encased by familiar behaviors.

CONFORMITY AND THE GROUP

Japanese sociocultural nationalism is manifested by the way in which Japanese identify with each other as a distinct cultural group, the primacy of that group identity, and their adherence to the norms of the group—the behavioral and social norms of Japan. Takie Sugiyama Lebra has coined the phrase "social relativism" to describe the Japanese preoccupation with social interaction. Japan is the quintessential "how am I doing?" society. Just as Japan as a state is constantly concerned about how others think of it, Japanese people have been taught to take their cues of appropriate behavior from others around them. They rely upon others, especially members of their group, to tell them what is right and wrong, good and bad. They become very sensitive to these cues in their communication with others.

In this sense, Japanese behavior is quite different from that in an individualist society such as in the United States. Americans are also concerned with the essential question, "how am I doing?" but Japanese and Americans are asking the question to two different audiences. Japanese ask it of others; Americans ask it of themselves. The United States is an individualist's society that believes in both Sigmund Freud and Samuel Smiles. The teachings of these two seemingly disparate people reflect the American belief that the answers to most problems are to be found within one's self. On the one hand, there's no problem that can't be solved if one just goes out and takes the bull by the horns. Or, as grandfather said, "Never borrow and never loan, save your money and buy your own." The stereotypes are endless: Horatio Algier, *Mr. Smith Goes to Washington*, the pioneers. On the other hand, Freud taught the children of the pioneers that not all problems are external, sometimes they exist within our minds. Thus the other means of solving problems is to turn inward to examine the inner soul and/or the subconscious. Life can be won by pursuing the "inner game."

These traits of American society are mentioned in order to highlight the group-oriented nature of Japanese society. Japanese turn outward toward the other members of the group, not inward, in their search for solutions to life's internal and external problems. As is the case with consensus, this concept is most accurate when applied to individual-small group relations. The operative parable for life in Japan is the one in which a father shows his sons that a single twig can be easily broken but a bundle of twigs is rock-hard.

It is not that Japanese do not value individualism; sometimes they idealize it. American loner heroes, such as James Dean, have a great popularity in Japan. Rocky and Rambo are both big heros in Japan because they present their viewers with wish-fulfillment. It is very common for Japanese to tell their American friends or co-workers that they wish they could be like Americans, speak out against conformity, and go their own way. Many Japanese admire America most for its individuality.

And yet all those salarymen singing "My Way" in karaoke bars all over Japan know that, in reality, existence is only possible within the group. The housewife depends upon the neighborhood association for information concerning garbage collection, evacuation in case of earthquakes, and the donation of money for a neighbor's funeral. The salaryman cannot get anything done at work unless he does it within his working group, discussing ideas with others, and getting their help and consensus. The university student's life rotates around one of the many university clubs he or she attends. Even those who are rebellious tend to do so in groups of their fellow rebels. Those groups most removed from the mainstream of Japanese society—teenage delinquents, gangsters, leftist student organizations—rely on a strong group ethic as a means of supporting themselves against the rest of the system.

Messages in the popular culture constantly reinforce the group ethic. Most police and samurai dramas follow the pattern of one of the most popular television shows in recent Japanese history, "Seibu Keisatsu" (Western District Police). The story line of each show invariably followed the same sequence. People involved in the crimes committed often had some connection to a member of the police group. That individual member would then try to go it alone in the solution of the crime, only to be thwarted by the criminals, pinned down by gunfire, or confronted with a bomb set to go off in minutes. At the climax of the show the rest of the group would swoop in and, guns blazing, save the day. The message was symbolized by the stock ending in which the group walked off the screen arm in arm and laughing: the group works, individual effort doesn't. Game shows and variety shows are very popular in Japan because they bring large casts of performers together as a single group. Comedy shows are built around troupes of performers, not individual comedians.

Groups give Japanese individual purpose and identity. Life in Japan can be very simple and free of stress because there are implicit norms of behavior that pertain to every possible situation. Once the norms are learned, one will rarely be caught in a situation that is ambiguous. Whatever the situation, one knows how to act and expects that the people with whom one is interacting also know "the rules of the game." The predictability of both actions and reactions between strangers greatly enhances social interaction. When you meet someone, cards are immediately exchanged in order that the other will know just who you are and what is your relative position in the situation. If you are equals, you act as equals; if one is lower or higher in the hierarchy, then you act appropriately. People who enter meeting rooms with others they have never met before know exactly what to do and where to sit because the seating arrangement for the relative hierarchy in a business group, for the host and the guest, for juniors and seniors, and so on, is prearranged.

Group allegiances are held together by the glue of these behavioral norms. Dependence and obligation are the two most important in maintaining the collectivity of the group. If the individual looks to the group to define his or her identity, then the individual is obviously very dependent on the group. But, on the other hand, the group cannot exist without the involvement of the individual. There is a quid pro quo: the group will forgive the individual for various transgressions, as long as the individual confesses his or her sins, and promises to continue to submit their will to the group. The apology is the concrete manifestation of the quid pro quo. The apology is an act of contrition, a baring of the neck to the group. Its acceptance is the group reaffirming its collectivity and superiority.

Apologies are so common and expected that there are apology forms ready and waiting to be produced at the proper moment. One evening years ago when I was a student in Tokyo, I walked across the street from my apartment to buy a package of cigarettes from a vending machine. Just as I was retrieving them a policeman on a bicycle pulled up and asked me to produce my alien registration card. Foreign residents are supposed to carry them at all times. It seems that there had been an incident in the area involving a blond-haired foreigner. As I fit the description and hadn't bothered to pocket my card when going out, I was taken down to the ward police station for questioning. The incident involving the other foreigner was cleared up and my innocence on that count proven, but there was still the transgression of not having had my alien registration card. I was parked in the lobby of the police station and wiled away a couple of hours with various policemen who stopped by to practice their English with me. ("Have you lived here long?" "Do you like Japanese girls?") Eventually I was sent upstairs to the detective bureau where I met a stern-faced officer who instructed me in the seriousness of my offense. He ended by saying that they would let me go this time but that I would have to apologize to the Japanese people. For a moment I was nonplussed. Just as I was wondering how I could apologize to the nation for my actions, he reached in his desk and pulled out a mimeographed apology form. It was written in English especially for foreigners who had forgotten to carry their alien registration cards. I signed the form and everyone was happy. After a cup of tea with the boys, they sent me on my way with an escort who checked to make sure that I really did have the card in my apartment.

Obligation is the other major factor that glues the group together. Obligation relationships are one of the most important factors in Japanese interpersonal relations. Once you become a member of the group— whether it be the family by birth, the neighborhood by chance, or the company by design—you are obligated to the other members of the group, and they are obligated to you. The problem is that it is not as specific as simply returning a favor for a favor of equal value. It is a sense of indebtedness to the group for being a member of the group which has no specific value and exists as long as you are related to the group. There are many active obligation relationships among people from the same university class decades after graduation.

Again, it is not that people necessarily like being under obligation to other members of the group. One often hears Japanese grumbling about *giri*, as this obligatory responsibility is called. If a company employee goes out with the rest of his or her office mates to a Sunday function when they would much rather be at home relaxing, it is an obligation to his or her work group. When an executive gives a speech at yet another junior's wedding ceremony, it is an obligation to his employees. When a patient sends a year-end gift package to his or her doctor, it is an obligation for the services of the doctor. In all of these cases, if they were asked why they are doing these things they really don't want to do, the response, "Oh, it's *giri*," would come with a wry grimace. Yet the deed would still be done because it is reciprocal (the person expects others to do the same for them), and because it is a necessary duty.

The preoccupation of the Japanese with their social environment and the group is overwhelming. This is not to say that Japanese have no internalized values of right and wrong, good and bad. However, the external social environment does play a very important role in determining behavior. The company employee often decides when to leave work not by the time on the clock or the completion of his or her tasks for the day, but by whether his or her fellow workers are leaving. The company determines when it is time to switch from long-sleeved to short-sleeved shirts. Popular magazines are full of articles telling their readers how to eat spaghetti, how to ask a woman out on a date, how to find your boyfriend's erogenous zones, and what socks to wear with what ties. In short, Japanese are more conformists than free spirits.

Although Japanese may not like to conform, or to be dependent on the group, or to be obligated to the group, all these are much preferable to being left out of the group. The person who does not belong to a group will have few friends and no identity to the others around them. The group ethic makes Japan a comfortable place to live if you are in the group, but for those outside the group, life can be hell. Thus one of the great Japanese fears is to be ostracized from the group.

I remember the state police films of accident scenes that we were forced to watch when I was a high school student taking driver's education classes in the United States. Almost thirty years later those graphic images of mutilated and burned bodies still remain in my mind. The message was simple and clear: if you speed, if you drink and drive, if you don't pay attention to the rules of the road, you will end up looking like this. I also remember the film we were forced to watch when I got my driver's license in Japan. In that film a happy young husband, after taking leave of his beautiful wife and two lovely children, ran over and killed a bicyclist on his way to work because he was speeding and not paying attention to the road. There were no graphic pictures of death. The film quick-cut from scenes of the rising speedometer, a look of horror on the face of the bicyclist, a look of too-late recognition on the face of the driver, to a scene of the bicyclist covered by a clean white cloth, while the driver, held by policemen, looked down at the victim. As I recall, the driver was not even sent to prison, but he and his family became social outcasts. They tried to pay their respects at the victim's funeral but were shunned. His wife's friends would not visit her anymore, and his children's classmates pointed at them at school. Everyone at work looked at him as he walked by. The message of this movie was as clear as that of any American state police shock movie: the punishment for breaking the law is ostracism and shame.

Changes

Thus far this chapter has reinforced the standard postwar traditions of homogeneity, conformity, uniformity, dependency, obligation, and collectivity, but it is now time to discuss the second caveat to the postwar traditions—change. While none of the postwar traditions have ever been absolutely true, their relative truth is decreasing as Japan attains the economic and social rewards of development. In the words of Professor Sumiko Iwao, a member of Keio University's Institute for Communication Research and a leading social psychologist: "The norms and attitudes that shape Japanese life styles and Japanese society as a whole have undergone crucial changes over the past decade. Indeed, a number of tendencies once cited as distinguishing characteristics of the Japanese people actually appear to have reversed themselves . . . we can isolate three changes in the Japanese character over the last decade: a tendency toward diversity and individuality, a need for swift results and instant gratification, and a desire for stability."[5]

Just as the postwar traditions of Japan were a result of the need for economic development, the reaction against those postwar traditions, individualism in particular, is a result of the abundant affluence created by successful economic development. The consumer is inundated with commercial images promising liberation from the dronelike existence of the mass to the new, exciting, liberated world of the individual. Travel ads emphasize getting away by yourself (as opposed to the old group tours). In a Coke commercial the music rises, a spandex-encased dancer collapses in exhaustion on the floor of her spacious urban apartment, and pops open a Coke as the Chinese character for "me" covers the screen. Japan is the land of my home, my life, my car, my stereo, my credit card, and my loan.

Postmaterialism is a concept used to describe the drift toward more collectivist values in postindustrial Western societies. But the postmaterialist social drift in postindustrial Japan has been just the opposite, from collectivism to individualism. The process of industrialization in the West was socially atomizing and gave popularity to concepts such as anomie. The process of postwar development in Japan was unifying and gave rise to concepts such as the company as ersatz family. Just as Western society attempts to rediscover the group ethic (as indicated by its desire to learn from Japan), Japan is more actively seeking individualism.[6]

Japan's younger generation has been in the forefront of these postmaterialist changes in Japan. The *shinjinrui* ("new breed") differ from their elders, and from all past generations of Japan, in two significant ways. They assume that their world will be stable and affluent. Few previous generations of Japanese have been affluent, and those that have been never were able to assume that they would remain so in the future. This relative sense of complacency negates the traditional belief that you have to work hard just to stay even, to say nothing of getting ahead. There is a feeling in the air that personal economic goals have been attained and that Japanese should now have the time to relax a bit and enjoy them. There are many economic goals that have yet to be attained, such as roomy, affordable housing and a reduction in prices of agricultural consumer goods to equivalents in the developed world, but still there are money and goods enough for all. Now that Japan has reached the upper rank of economic powers, Japanese want more space, more housing, more parks, but they especially want more leisure time. The Japanese government has for years been pressuring companies to reduce the number of working days from six to five, has increased the number of national holidays, and has even taken the drastic step of beginning the gradual reduction of school days from six to five.

Young people are not the only ones affected by Japan's increased affluence and the security of its domestic society in the postwar years. Japanese of all ages have made Japan the epitome of a nouveau-riche society in which nothing succeeds like excess. Before the economic "bubble" of the 1980s burst, Japan resembled the filming stage for *Bonfire of the Vanities*. Rent-a-car companies offering an afternoon in a Mercedes or a Ferrari proliferated. Elderly couples or people who lived alone could rent a "family" of actors to come and spend the day with them, as if they were their real family. Everyone had to get the first bottles of Beaujolais Nouveau as soon as they left France. People paid up to a thousand dollars for the privilege of eating in garish and ostentatious restaurants, and for the pleasure of telling their friends where they ate and what it cost.

Personal spending has decreased since the beginning of the recession, expense accounts are way down, and the entertainment districts that thrived on them are hurting. People are more cost-conscious than they were in the 1980s, but the changes are more relative than absolute; Japan is still a nouveau-riche society. Designer clothes are still de rigueur, but they are more likely to be purchased at reduced prices in wholesale outlets than from designer boutiques at full prices. Japanese of both sexes and all age groups have come to expect only the best. Companies pander to the growing consumer mentality of the Japanese and sell them on the consumer dream, which has led to a rapid increase in misuse of credit cards and personal bankruptcy. And it starts right from the beginning. A couple getting married in Japan can expect to pay about $60,000 for engagement, wedding, and honeymoon expenses.[7]

Affluence compliments other factors that have increased the atomization of Japan society. Women are accustomed to spending less time in the house and want to be taken more seriously in the work place. In 1980 40.5 percent of female college graduates in their late twenties were still single, but in 1990 it rose to 56.2 percent.[8] This indicates that women are staying in the work force later and that they also want to remain in the work force. A 1992 Health and Welfare Ministry survey reports that 52 percent of married women plan to join the work force after having children (up 10 percentage points from 1982), and 67 percent of married working women said that they planned to continue working (up 13.4 percentage points since 1982).[9] Older people have also come to realize that they are one of the largest and most rapidly growing segments of the population, and they want their demands met.

The vast majority of literature concerning the postwar traditions of Japan is related to the cultural underpinnings of the Japanese economic "miracle." Whether it be the human-oriented nature of Japanese management or the employee's transference of loyalty from the family to the company, the group ethic and conformity are perceived to have been fundamental to the success of Japanese capitalism. The conformity of the employee to the demands of the work place were evident in the following truisms. The worker's loyalty to the company and the working group takes precedence over all other groups. The individual worker sacrifices and suffers for the good of the group. If it is necessary to go out drinking every night with clients or co-workers to the detriment of his or her family relations, it will be done. The shop-floor worker arrives early in order to participate in quality control group meetings. All members of the company wear the same uniform. Everyone engages in calisthenics and sings the company song in the morning. Each department and working group within the organization has their own year-ending parties and new year's parties. If the company orders an employee to move abroad or relocate to another city, it will be done without question.

If the Japanese management and corporate-employee relations have been the most obvious manifestation of conformity and group orientation in Japanese society, then it is also in these areas that the changes in Japanese society are most obvious. Younger employees are no longer as willing to put up with the long hours, short vacations, involuntary transfers, separations from their families, crowded commutes, and other inconveniences that have always been the sacrifices once thought must be made for the company group. Older employees are finding that they can no longer expect the loyalty from their companies that was expected to be the reward for a lifetime of sacrifices. On the other hand, companies are having to adjust their organization and traditional management practices. Some firms have begun laying off salaryman employees, while others have reneged on offers to prospective recruits. Two-thirds of Japanese companies with over ten thousand employees now have some form of flex-time, and almost as many have reworked and expanded their vacation schedules to suit the needs of their employees better. Traditional studies of Japanese management have always stated that head-hunting of mid-level employees was impossible because a new manager would not be able to fit into the already solidified company group, but now mid-level job jumping is the norm among Japanese corporate employees. Seniority-based salaries and lifetime employment have been two of the most fundamental elements of postwar Japanese management, but the former is under attack and the latter is almost dead. Many companies are beginning to switch to contracts with annual salaries geared to ability rather than seniority. In addition, most Japanese executives believe that lifetime employment is becoming a thing of the past.[10]

COLLECTIVISM AND THE STATE

Although the group ethic in Japan may be changing, it is still the dominant social value, and conformity to the group is still the dominant behavioral norm. If the strength of sociocultural nationalism stems from the homogeneity and collectivity of Japanese society, what are the political implications? The widely held perceptions of homogeneity, one race, collectivity, consensus, harmony, and uniformity are assumed to have an important impact on the political system. Conformity and collectivity in particular are often perceived as attributes enforced by an authoritarian political system. Especially important is the assumption that high levels of conformity and collectivity are not to be found "naturally" but have to be created in order to exist. The refusal to accept the idea that a harmony of interests may exist among the members of Japanese society is reminiscent of Thomas Hobbes' belief that conflict is the natural condition of man. This point of view as applied to Japan is best demonstrated by Karel van Wolferen when he writes that the high collectivity and conformity of Japanese political and social life are "the result of political arrangements consciously inserted into society by a ruling elite over three centuries ago, and the Japanese today are given little or no choice in accepting arrangements that are still essentially political."[11]

Van Wolferen is correct in arguing that the application of Confucianism to the feudal political system of the Tokugawa period was the political enforcement of a social hierarchy intended to lock Japan into a harmonious status quo. Indeed, the political enforcement of collectivism predates the Tokugawa period by at least a thousand years. But political coercion and propaganda are not the immediate causes of contemporary Japanese collectivism and conformity. The role of the Japanese government in encouraging conformity is not so much greater or lesser than in other developed democracies.

The political enforcement of collectivism in the modern era began with the Meiji government's need to unify the nation in support of the new Japan they were creating out of the chaos of Tokugawa decay and foreign intervention. The *genro* consciously created what Carol Gluck has termed Japan's modern myths,[12] including *kokutai* (national polity as embodied by the Meiji Constitution) and *tennosei* (the emperor system), as a means of encouraging political loyalty through the use of cultural and religious myths and traditions. The divine status of the emperor in the Meiji Constitution combined Shinto tradition with traditional Confucian ruler-subject relationships and Buddhist morality. Japan under the Meiji Constitution approximated a democratic system for a few years after World War I, but for most of its existence it was an authoritarian government. Japanese society was rid of the social and economic castes of the Tokugawa period, but the relationship between the political elite and the mass remained hierarchical and authoritarian. The presentation of the emperor as a revered father figure to his family of Japanese subjects reflected a melding of Confucian relationships, Buddhist teachings, and Shinto myths. The people's acceptance of the *tennosei*, and the supporting mythic *kokutai*, guaranteed the continued existence of the hierarchically ordered, authoritarian political system. Finally, the immense coercive power of the state was applied to those who did not heed or accept the modern myths.

Although the collectivity and conformity in modern Japanese society is a creation of central political authoritarianism, they are no longer imposed by an authoritarian state backed by repressive laws and the secret police. Rather, contemporary authoritarianism in Japan stems from the social group and social relations. In part it has become self-sustaining. Gluck's "modern myths" created for political control have been continued in modified form to serve as the foundation for the postwar traditions based upon the superiority and uniqueness of Japanese culture. What was created as a means of identity with the state is continued as a reinforcement of national identity.

The Japanese government has a role in reinforcing collectivity and conformity, but it is rather indirect and minimal. Coercion is no longer used as a means of creating support for the government, state ideology, or state institutions. The state does have an active role in the socialization process, but to no greater extent than does the state in any developed democratic political system. The state proposes and presents political and social values to the public, but it does not require or enforce their acceptance. Van Wolferen's political arrangements were a primary cause of collectivity and conformity, but they are no longer essentially political. Rather, they are essentially social.

The values of collectivity and conformity are imposed upon the Japanese public by the society itself, not the political system. In the words of John Owen Haley: "Societal order has been maintained in Japan more by a complex network of interpersonal and informal obligations and sanctions than those imposed by law. As a result, the predominant controlling norms of Japanese society have depended directly upon consensus and the structure of authority within particular groups as well as raw exercises of private power—both physical and economic."[13]

Japan is what Alexis de Tocqueville once described American society to be: "the tyranny of the social majority." This concept was adopted by John Stuart Mill, who wrote in *On Liberty*:

But reflecting persons perceived that when society is itself the tyrant—society collectively, over the separate individuals who compose it—its means of tyranniz-ing are not restricted to the acts which it may do by the hands of all its political functionaries. Society can and does execute its own mandates: and if it issues wrong mandates instead of right, or any mandates at all in things in which it ought not to meddle, it practices a social tyranny more formidable than many kinds of political oppression, since, though not usually upheld by such extreme penalties, it leaves fewer means of escape, penetrating much more deeply into the details of life, and enslaving the soul itself.[14]

Japan is a tyranny of the social majority, but while Mill expresses his conviction that the social majority "enslaves the soul," the average Japanese would be more inclined to think of it as conferring a sense of place and belonging. Social values and behavioral norms related to collectivity and conformity do limit the individual freedom of Japanese, but they are not enforced by the state. Rather, they are enforced by other Japanese, espe-cially the other members of the group.

Daily life in Japan brings constant reminders of what behavior is per-missible and what is not. It is sometimes as removed and distant as the magazine articles that instruct their readers on social etiquette, but it is usually much more immediate and personal. The senior members of a bank's office staff will let a junior member know in no uncertain terms that a checked tweed sport coat is not acceptable attire for a loan officer. Lovers who display their affections on the subway will receive hard stares and reproachful looks from their fellow passengers. Japanese have the feeling that they are being constantly watched, not by the secret police, but by others around them. I lived years ago in a suburban neighborhood of single family houses. There was a rare snowfall in the evening, and when I left for work the next morning I could see that there was only one patch of snow left on the road, and it conformed perfectly to the dimensions of my house and extended exactly to the middle of the road. Everyone else in the neighborhood had arisen early in the morning and swept up the snow immediately in front of their houses. Having grown up in a place where it snowed frequently and heavily, and where snow removal was the job of the government authorities, I ignored the situation and began my walk to the train station. I had taken no more than a few steps when a neighboring housewife ran up to me calling "Good morning, Professor Stronach."

"Good morning, Mrs. X."
"Well, it certainly snowed last night, didn't it," she said while looking signifi-cantly at the lone patch in front of my house.

"Yes, it did," said I, stubbornly refusing to see the message in her eyes. "I love the snow, but I must be off to work now."

"Ah." Her obvious but implicit opening gambit had fallen on deaf and foreign ears. She cut the cackle and got to the point. "It seems as if everyone has already cleared the snow off the road."

"Yes. You know, in the States the town does that for you."

"Oh, really? Here we do it ourselves before we go to work."

Egalitarian Hierarchies

The importance of rank, role, and hierarchy in the group reinforce the belief that Japanese collectivism is authoritarian. Japanese groups are hierarchically ranked, and it sometimes seems as if Japanese are obsessed with rank ordering everything from universities to blood types. Each rank within the group has its own distinctions, even though they may only be formal distinctions (*tatemae*) that do not conform to the real power relations within the group (*honne*). It is important to know the other's rank within the group because forms of behavior, speech, bowing, and other mannerisms in Japanese society differ according to the situation and relative levels of the individuals interacting. For example, one would use different levels of formality in speech and bow in different ways when greeting someone above you, someone below you, and your equal in the group.

Rank is related to role. The group fulfills its function only as long as each individual member performs his or her assigned role. Identification with rank and role are so strong that people are often addressed by their rank or role in the group rather than by their names.[15] Office workers call their manager "manager" (*bucho*). A senior member of the group is called "senior" (*sempai*). Teachers and doctors are addressed by honorifics only (*sensei*). It is the sense of role, and the ability to accept one's role and rank in the hierarchy, that makes the Japanese group tight and cohesive. It is also the outward manifestations of *tatemae* rank that make the group appear so authoritarian. Everyone defers in gesture and speech to their seniors. Seniors act with hauteur and disdain toward their juniors. However, outward appearances are not always what they seem. Even though juniors and seniors conform to the behavior expected of them, it may be the case that the junior actually has more power and authority within the group than the senior.

Collectivism in Japanese society is simultaneously hierarchical and egalitarian. In the broadest sense, the melding of the individual into the group means that all are subservient to the group. While their various roles within the group may have different rankings, no one individual is superior to any other individual in the group. This is reinforced by many behavioral patterns in Japan, often expressed by the phrase "the nail that sticks up gets hammered down." Thus, while everyone in an office is extremely sensitive to the slightest nuance of ranking—who went to which university, whose children are going to which kindergarten, who married into what family—the office is open, everyone has the same desk, carpet, and telephone, the department manager is there in the office with everyone else and has a company work-jacket to put on when he goes down to the shop floor.[16]

The acceptance of rank and role in a hierarchy also pertains most appropriately to the interaction of individuals within a small group. Individuals will willingly defer to seniors and mold their individualism to fit the form of their role in the group. But they are not willing to do so in relationships outside the group. Although Japanese perceive themselves to be ranked vertically within the group, they certainly do not see themselves or their group as existing in a vertical/authoritarian relationship with the government. The government is a separate, but not superior, world to the one in which most people live. Indeed, rather than being perceived as superior to the world that the average citizen lives in, they are more likely to perceive it as being inferior. Thus, while there are hierarchical rankings within the group, those rankings do not exist outside the group, most especially in the individual's relationship to the state.

Neither are the acceptance of role and the behavior that accompanies that role reflective of an authoritarian relationship between the citizen and the state. The individual in the role will defer to seniors and/or the group as a whole because it is in his or her best interest to do so. It is understood that the group, whether it be a quality control group on an assembly line or a university tennis club, will only function for every member's benefit if all members submit to the rules of the group. But once outside the group relationship, there is no inherent behavioral or pragmatic reason for Japanese to defer to others they perceive as being senior or superior to them. Quite the opposite, Japanese take a great deal of pride in the egalitarian nature of their society and often adopt an "I'm all right, Jack" attitude toward others.

Nation/State Dichotomy

In the modern use of the terms, nation and state have become almost interchangeable, but a state can exist without a nation and a nation can exist without a state. In the case of Japan, the two do coexist as a true nation-state, but nationalism is not determined by the nation's relationship to the state. Indeed, there is a strong dichotomy between the two, with the emphasis on the relationship between the individual and the nation, not the relationship between the individual and the state.

In most countries membership in the nation[17] is determined by political loyalty. This is especially true in countries that have a variety of ethnic and other minority groups because loyalty to the state becomes the one primary factor in unifying those various ethnic and racial groups that live within the borders of the country. Thus, to use the United States as an example, an

American is one who is a subject of the United States government. Within that classification there are various subgroups depending on racial and ethnic background such as Japanese American, African American, or Mexican American. In Japan, however, the fact that one is a subject of the state does not automatically confer membership in the nation. Membership in the Japanese nation has little to do with being a citizen of the Japanese state but is primarily ethnic and racial.

Once a foreigner has become a naturalized citizen of the United States, most other members of the nation will then accept him or her as a fellow "American," or member of the nation. It is citizenship that confers nationality. In Japan, however, becoming a citizen of the state does not make one "Japanese." The importance to other Japanese is not if you are a citizen of the political system, but whether you are a member of the national group. In order to be accepted as a member of the nation, one must fit all the sociocultural requirements. One must be a member of the Japanese race, be ethnically Japanese, speak the Japanese language, and behave according to the mainstream cultural values and social norms. This is a manifestation of the priority given in Japan to the social system over the political system. Even if a person has Japanese citizenship, if that person is obviously racially or ethnically different from Japanese, then they will not be accepted as a member of the nation.

To use a practical example, imagine a native Japanese customer walking into a store in the United States and an African-American customer walking into a store in Japan. Because there are so many different races and ethnic groups of people who are citizens of the United States, the American shop owner's first assumption would be that this is a "normal" person. That is, an American who speaks English and who understands how things are done in an American shop. The shopkeeper would not know that he or she was dealing with a foreigner until the customer spoke with an obvious Japanese accent or paid with Bank of Tokyo traveler's checks, or did any number of other things that would signal "foreigner." On the other hand, if an African American were to walk into a Japanese shop, the shopkeeper would automatically assume that the person was not Japanese and had none of the attributes of a Japanese. That is, the shopkeeper would assume that the person could not speak Japanese, didn't really know what he or she was doing in the store, and would need help immediately.

The definition of nationality by race and ethnicity rather than citizenship is one aspect of the separation of nation and state in Japan, but there are others. As has been discussed elsewhere, Japanese believe themselves to live in various groups and "worlds," and the social world is perceived as being quite different from the political world. This leads to what is described in Chapter 4 as the spectator political culture—a gap between Japanese and their political system. This gap extends itself to a differentiation between citizenship and membership in the nation. In the prewar years, nationalism was induced in Japanese from the top down as a way of creating political support for the newly created, modern Japan. Postwar Japan has maintained the sense of community created in the prewar years, but it has lost its ties to the political system. The modern political systems have not had their roots in traditional Japanese culture and therefore have not yet become integrated into the culture (especially now that there is no enforcement from the top), as have the political institutions of countries like the United States and Great Britain where political systems did evolve organically. Postwar nationalism has been a grassroots phenomenon developed from the bottom up and as such is less concerned with creating bonds of loyalty between the nation and the state.

The separation between state and nation can also be clearly seen in the way national pride is manifested. Many studies have demonstrated that Japanese have relatively less pride in the "nation" than other nations, but it all depends upon what is meant by the "nation." A 1985 study showed that Japan and Germany were the least proud of fifteen countries surveyed.[18] The preliminary results of a cross-national study on pride and patriotism supervised by Ronald Inglehart and carried out by the Dentsu Institute for Human Studies and MITI's (Ministry of International Trade and Industry) Leisure Development Center show that while 62 percent of Japanese respondents demonstrated pride in the country, that was the lowest in the ten-nation survey. Among the other countries surveyed were the United States, Korea, Spain, Poland, Mexico, Nigeria, Chile, and Czechosolvakia. All other nations were above 80 percent.[19]

To explain what has appeared to be relatively lower Japanese expression of national pride, it may be necessary to distinguish between pride in the state and pride in the nation. Japanese are not especially proud of the former, but they are quite proud of the latter. Japanese, far more than the peoples of other industrial states, are likely to express a belief in their cultural superiority. In several polls, nearly 90 percent of respondents agreed that the Japanese were "by nature better than most other peoples. By contrast, 47 percent of Americans considered themselves "better."[20] It is most clearly manifested when the sources of pride are separated from the expressed level of pride. While less than 10 percent of Japanese express pride in their political institutions, over 90 percent express pride in Japanese arts, culture, economics, science, and technology.[21] Similarly, in a 1991 poll on the Japanese people's attitudes toward the society and state taken regularly by the Prime Minister's Office, those respondents who answered that they felt some degree of patriotism were asked what they meant by "patriotism." Slightly over 60 percent responded love of the physical country of Japan and its nature, as compared to 20 percent who responded protecting its independence and security.[22]

These figures indicate that Japanese do make a distinction between state and nation, and their allegiance to the latter is stronger than their allegiance to the former. However, Japan also has a democratic political culture that necessitates some role for citizens in their political system. The conservative political elite would like to bridge the gap between the separate worlds of Japanese society and Japanese politics by mobilizing sociocultural nationalism to support government policies, state institutions, and the symbols of the state. In other words, people should use their national identity as a means of promoting loyalty to the state. However, these attempts have been successfully resisted, and, as we shall see in the next chapter, state-oriented nationalism is not strongly supported among the Japanese masses.

NOTES

1. Robert E. Ward, *Japan's Political System* (New York: Prentice-Hall, 1978), 66.

2. *Japan Times*, September 14, 1991, p. 2.

3. *Asahi Shimbun*, April 22, 1992, p. 6.

4. *Japan Times*, October 31, 1992, p. 2.

5. Sumiko Iwao, "The Japanese: Portrait of Change," *Japan Echo* (special issue, 1988), 2.

6. Curtis Martin and Bruce Stronach, *Politics East and West* (New York: M. E. Sharpe, 1992), 40–41.

7. Stephanie F. Morimura, "Japan's Marriage Industry Is Booming," *Japan Scope* 2 (Spring 1993), 39.

8. *Japan Times*, July 26, 1992, p. 2.

9. *Japan Times*, July 25, 1992, p. 2.

10. Ibid.

11. Karel van Wolferen, *The Enigma of Japanese Politics* (New York: Vintage Books, 1990), 3.

12. See her book, *Japan's Modern Myths* (Princeton, N.J.: Princeton University Press, 1985).

13. John Owen Haley, *Authority without Power* (New York: Oxford University Press, 1991), 199.

14. J. M. Robson, ed., *The Collected Works of John Stuart Mill*, vol. 18. (Toronto: University of Toronto Press, 1977), 219–20.

15. Takie Sugiyama Lebra, *Japanese Patterns of Behavior* (Honolulu: University of Hawaii Press, 1976), 84.

16. Martin and Stronach, *Politics East and West*, 16.

17. For the purposes of this discussion, the author wishes to differentiate between "membership in the nation" and "nationality" in order to emphasize the separation of nation and state. The former connotes a sense of belonging to the nation as a sociocultural group (*minzoku*), while the latter connotes citizenship in the state (*kokuseki*). Japanese nationality can be conferred by the state, but membership in the nation cannot.

18. Richard Rose, "National Pride in Cross-National Perspective," *International Social Science Journal* 36 (1985), 88.

19. *Japan Times*, June 13, 1991, p. 2.

20. Nippon Hoso Kyokai, *Nihonjin to Amerikajin* [Japanese and Americans] (Tokyo: Nippon Hoso Shuppan, 1982), 69.

21. Martin and Stronach, *Politics East and West*, 61.

22. Prime Minister's Office, *Public Opinion Survey on Society and the State* (June 1991), 9.

4

Nationalism and the State

The previous chapters have established that high levels of nationalism, especially sociocultural nationalism, exist in contemporary Japan, but what effect does nationalism have on the political system and policy outputs? On the one hand, the state cannot implement policy without general unified support from its citizens. The sense of unity that nationalism creates is necessary to maintain domestic peace, creates a sense of sacrifice for the good of others, and allows the government to carry out national policy without interference or disruption. All these conditions are necessary for any state to govern its people without coercion. On the other hand, too much citizen support for the state can be a terrible thing. When the bonds that tie the people of a nation together are equated with the bonds that link the citizen to the state, it can create a situation in which the nation is identified by one particular ideology, one set of political institutions. In extreme cases, national identity is linked to one government or one leader. The citizen's ethnic identity becomes so entwined with his or her political identity that the two become inseparable. In such a case, criticism of the state is considered to be an act of disloyalty to the nation. In addition, a strong sense of national unity linked directly to the state can create an us/them perception of the nation-state's relations with the rest of the world.

Japan has been a good example of this Dr. Jekyll/Mr. Hyde aspect of nationalism. Its strong sense of national unity was instrumental in its rapid modernization and in the phenomenal economic development of the postwar period. But it was also instrumental in the development of authoritarian governments, the colonization of Asia, and in a lingering sense of isolation and separateness. Japan went through the Dr. Jekyll/Mr. Hyde transformation in the prewar years, and now some observers wonder if it is not about to go through the transformation once again. They wonder if Japanese nationalism will remain the constructive force that built the postwar economic miracle. Japan's new assertiveness and pride are, to some, signals that Japan is on the verge of regressing to the authoritarian and aggressive policies of the prewar era. If the Japanese people's strong group solidarity, ability to sacrifice, willingness to follow political leadership, and belief in the superiority of their race and culture could be linked to identity with the political and economic goals of the state and government, Japan's quest for power would become a threat to the world.

A superficial look at Japan would indicate that such fears are not groundless. Japanese society often appears to be so regimented as to have authoritarian political overtones. The state's bureaucracy maintains strong control over the society through a centralized police force, centralized economic planning, administrative guidance, and a centralized education system. People are obsequious to police and government officials. Children line up in formation to march into classrooms. Public address systems broadcast messages into every neighborhood. Schools gloss over the problems of prewar history. Executives perceive themselves to be the descendants of samurai warriors. Boot-camp type training centers teach corporate employees to lose their sense of individualism and submit their will to the group, the better to follow the orders of their superiors mindlessly. Young people, from their perch of affluence, view the rest of the world with disdain. The government demands more and more political power in international forums, and the military, for the first time in the postwar era, has been deployed overseas.

These images make it easy to believe that Japan is again sipping from the cup of power and is about to forget its vows of abstemious pacifism, but they are the images of superficial perception and have little basis in reality. State-oriented nationalism is the weakest type of nationalism in contemporary Japan, and it will remain so for some time to come. Japan is a highly regimented society in many ways, and sociocultural nationalism is strong. But social regimentation is not easily linked to political authoritarianism, and neither is sociocultural nationalism easily harnessed to support state-oriented nationalism. Some members of the political and cultural elite have been trying to link these elements ever since the end of the occupation, but have been completely unsuccessful in doing so for a number of reasons.

JAPAN, INC. AND CONSENSUS

Japan is often perceived as a unified, seamless whole bound together by consensus and conformity. One element of this perceived unity is a return to the "black-top" image of prewar days. It holds that there is a high degree of communication and consensus among a broad elite that forms a cabalistic relationship known as "Japan, Incorporated." This perceived cabalistic elite is comprised of the leadership of the LDP, the government (often seen as one and the same), ultranationalist groups, the administrative civil service, big business, and out-groups such as the *yakuza* (organized crime). In this model, the elite works together to reduce democratic elements of the constitution by increasing the power of the emperor, remilitarizing Japan, reintroducing conservative Confucian moral values, and, in general, increasing the authoritarian control of the government over the polity. There is no doubt that the cabal exists; there are members of the above-mentioned elites who would like to see political and religious authority reinstated in the emperor, greater authoritarianism in the political system, and the codification of traditional Confucian, hierarchical values. But the breadth of the cabal, the extent to which members of those elites work together to achieve these various goals, and the extent of their influence on policy making is seriously in doubt.

It is also true that conservatives have been working throughout the postwar era to achieve these regressive reforms, but the policies of the far right have never been implemented. Article 9 is still part of the constitution, the status of the emperor remains unchanged, the Self-Defense Forces (SDF) retains a low profile, and the younger generation of Japanese seems to be even more "Western-oriented" and less adherent to traditional Confucian values than any previous generation. One might even argue that this cabalistic nexus was more important years ago when Yoshio Kodama was funneling money into the LDP, Bamboku Ohno was leading a major faction of the LDP, and Prime Minister Nobuske Kishi was planning to use *yakuza*-ultranationalist groups to protect President Dwight Eisenhower on his trip to Japan following the passage of the 1960 United States-Japan Security Treaty.

A close examination of postwar history demonstrates that attempts to introduce more nationalistic policies have failed, ties between state-oriented nationalism and sociocultural nationalism are hard to forge, and the existence of a highly unified, effective cabalistic elite is a myth. The image of Japan, Inc. was created in the 1970s as a way of comprehending why Japan was able to develop its economy so rapidly. It was, in part, an excuse used by some in the United States to explain why Japan had been able to outcompete the United States in its own markets. After years of perceiving the Japanese as somehow lesser than Americans, the only way to understand their success in competition with the United States was to portray them as cheats. Japan was successful because the LDP, the bureaucracy, and major corporate interest groups such as Keidanren and Nikkeiren worked together to create and direct economic policy. Individual American corporations were not able to compete successfully because they were not competing one-on-one with their Japanese counterparts. Rather, they faced a whole unified team comprised of the government, bureaucracy, and groups of companies. The perception of Japan, Inc. was also supported by Japanese themselves who proudly pointed to their work-together attitude, cultural homogeneity, and government-business solidarity. The original perception of an economic Japan, Inc., spurred by Japan's unexpected and pheonix-like rise into international preeminence, was soon expanded beyond economic policy to include political and social policy as well. It was believed that Japan's economy was able to grow so rapidly because Japan was still an authoritarian society ruled by a closed elite of decision makers controlling a pliant population that simply did as it was told. It would only be a matter of time before Japan used its economic power to enter the international political arena, by military means if necessary. Once the ball got rolling, Japan would shed its pacifist veneer and democratic institutions would fall by the wayside.

The above-described model of Japan, Inc. is predicated upon a highly consensual elite, but consensus among a controlling elite is more myth than reality. Recent studies of Japanese policy making have demonstrated that the power of "big business" interest groups has never been that great, and the ability of the bureaucracy to lead government policy making has significantly declined over the past two decades.[1] In the early years of LDP rule, the ruling party was heavily dependent on the bureaucracy for policy-making advice. This was in part a leftover from earlier years. Under the prewar constitution the civil administrative service was directly responsible to the emperor, and its members were seen as his representatives in the real world. The authority and aura of the emperor thus also clung to the bureaucracy. In a more pragmatic way, this also meant that their power was much greater than that of elected politicians. Although the occupation reforms intended to make the bureaucracy the servants of the people and not the emperor, the bureaucracy's power remained strong because the occupation was carried out through the Japanese bureaucracy. The Americans preached grassroots democracy, but they ruled Japan through top-down decision making and a highly centralized bureaucracy. In addition, the Japanese bureaucracy was the home of Japan's "best and brightest," experts who had the best interest of the whole country in mind and who knew what they were doing. Nowhere was this more evident than in their control over economic policy and their guidance of the growth of what Chalmers Johnson has called the "developmental state."[2] The politicians of the LDP were happy to follow their dictates and ride the crest of the resulting economic boom.

By the 1970s, however, the situation had changed. The LDP was faced with a tighter government budget, grassroots political movements concerned with the environment, small business grievances, consumer movements, and challenges from opposition parties. These changes forced the LDP to reject "plan rational" decision making for more political decisions that may have been economically irrational but that satisfied the demands of important blocs of voters. It also had to bring opposition parties into consensus on policy in order to get its legislation passed through the Diet with the minimum amount of turmoil. In addition, after a decade of rule and the incorporation of many ex-bureaucrats into the party, a growing number of LDP politicians began to feel competent to make policy themselves. The result has been what Michio Muramatsu and Ellis Krauss term patterned pluralism;[3] the government and bureaucracy remain strong, but social interest groups and the opposition parties maintain a number of contact points through which information and influence is channeled.

The heart of the Japan, Inc. model of Japanese policy making is consensus, but the extent to which Japan is actually a consensual society has also recently been called into question. Many differentiate the Japanese political process from the political process in other developed democracies by emphasizing the cultural differences between Japan and the Western democracies. The need for maintaining consensus as a political and social value is high on the list of these cultural differences. Maintaining harmony is an important part of societal behavior for Japanese, and there are various ways in which the need for maintaining harmony can be manifested. There are intense pressures on the individual to conform to the group, and they can be transferred from individual norms of behavior to institutional norms of behavior. This is especially true when group decisions have to be made. Each member of the group is exposed to strong pressure (sometimes directly, sometimes obliquely) to reach a unanimous, consensual decision with the other members of the group. Attempts are usually made to avoid the direct expression of contentious opinions that can create friction among members of the group. Rather than the direct, head-to-head debates and arguments that take place in a formal meeting (the hallmark of American group decision making), opinions are expressed in more informal settings, such as over an after-hours drink with co-workers, so that the person expressing the opinions does not have to be held to them and bad feelings can be more easily diffused. At the same time, those participating in the decision-making process can get a feel for who is supporting what position and line up behind a budding majority. Although the process forces "unnatural" unanimity where it may not exist in reality, it is also very inclusive and egalitarian in that all members of the group are included in the process. The final verdict may be a foregone conclusion, but all voices, from the most junior to the most senior, will have been heard by the time the formal meeting to make the decision is finally held.

Individual Japanese are socialized to conform, and conforming is one means of creating a consensus within groups, but consensus-building behavior is also attributed to institutions and groups and their interactions with other institutions and groups, especially in the Japan, Inc. model of Japanese policy making. Group or institutional behavior cannot be extrapolated from individual behavior in the case of consensus building. Groups and institutions interacting with each other cannot develop the kind of unanimity that exists among individuals working within a small group. The broadest and most general models of consensus formation in Japanese policy making are those with the least validity. While it is easy to conjure up an image of cabalistic behavior, the reality is somewhat different. There can be close ties between members of the various elites, but there is no special cohesiveness or consensus when it comes to policy. There are many conflicts between the LDP and the bureaucracy, between the LDP and private enterprise, between private enterprise and the bureaucracy, and among the factions that exist within all three of these broader institutions.

The value of consensus can even be harmful because creating consensus among various groups is so difficult and time-consuming. Harmony and collectivity may be the hallmarks of Japanese society, but when one member of the group cannot be cajoled or coerced into submitting his or her will to the will of others, communication rapidly breaks down. Japan is a society that attempts to avoid conflict through consensus, but it has few built-in means of resolving conflict. There is so much reliance on consensus in decision making that when parties in conflict are unable to build a consensus, there is no tradition of adversarial debate that allows them to maintain both dialogue and conflict.

Fragmentation and consensus exist simultaneously, and this dichotomy can create very dysfunctional systems in which there are so many competing centers of power, any one of which possesses a relatively limited ability to negotiate with the others, that no one institution has the ability to lead others to the necessary consensus. This is the condition so well described in Karel vanWolferen's *The Enigma of Japanese Power*. A plethora of tightly knit groups all hold some power, compete among themselves for more, and have a relatively hard time coalescing to support policy initiatives. This lack of leadership and resultant logjam in policy making leads in turn to public apathy toward the entire political system.

The lack of unity and consensus that often exists in Japan is demonstrated by the ubiquitousness of factionalism. Factions, or *habatsu*, are formed within larger institutions or groups by individuals who have specific common interests, backgrounds, or needs. The most well known and powerful factions in Japan are those within the LDP and are based on personal leadership, issue interests, or background (e.g., those that have worked their way up through the ranks as opposed to those that have descended into the party from the bureaucracy). In the administrative civil service or in private enterprises, they are most commonly based on one's alma mater. Tokyo University graduates wield tremendous power in the civil administrative service, and Keio University graduates wield a great deal of power in certain corporations and banks. The common ties that form the initial selection criteria for joining a faction are then reinforced by patron-client relationships and bonds of personal obligation that enhance solidarity and consensus.

Factional consensus and solidarity, however, by their very nature reduce the same qualities in the larger group or institution in which the factions exist. When factions within the group compete for commonly sought scarce resources such as finances, policy, or positions for its members, they become potent forces of fragmentation. The LDP is the epitome of factionalism in Japan, and the party has been the perfect demonstration that unity is rarely found in reality. There have been many instances when factions within the LDP have been the most important opposition to government policy in the Diet and in the public consciousness.

In the elections of 1979 the LDP was able to secure a working majority only by bringing successful independent candidates into the party. But even as the party teetered on the edge of losing its majority in the lower house for the first time since 1955, it was racked by a power struggle between the two most important factions, one led by former prime minister Takeo Fukuda and the other by Masayoshi Ohira. Both ran for prime minister before the Diet, and Ohira was finally elected in a run-off ballot. Members of the Fukuda faction were able to gain their revenge when the Social Democratic Party of Japan (SDPJ) called for a vote of no confidence in the government in the spring of 1980. The Fukuda faction abstained from voting, which led to the first (and only) successful vote of no confidence against a LDP government and the fall of the Ohira cabinet.

Similarly, but not as drastically, the original debate over the bill authorizing the deployment of Self-Defense Forces on United Nation-sponsored peacekeeping missions (from this point on referred to as the Peacekeeping Organization, or PKO, bill) was strongly influenced by factional struggles within the LDP. The PKO bill was immediately attacked by the opposition parties upon its submission by the government to the Diet in October 1990. The LDP held a comfortable majority of twenty-four seats in the lower house, but instead of rallying round the bill with the strength of its majority, the LDP was unable to offer unified support. The bill was the brainchild of a leader of the Takeshita faction, Ichiro Ozawa. His initiation of and support for the PKO bill ruffled the feathers of many in the party (even within his faction) who thought he was out to garner too much power too soon, by attempting to become the power behind the throne of the Kaifu cabinet and take sole control of the Takeshita faction. In addition, there were those within the LDP who opposed the PKO bill because they opposed Prime Minister Toshiki Kaifu. Many in the mainstream factions of the LDP believed (and rightly so) that he had been lifted into the party presidency and the prime ministership only because he was from a minor faction and had a clean record, and not because he actually deserved the position. Most of the leading LDP politicians of the time who believed themselves to be in line for the position, and deserving of it, were removed from consideration because they were tainted by involvement in the Recruit scandal.

Eventually, factionalism within the LDP led to the loss of its parliamentary majority in 1993. But even before it fell from power, factionalism in the LDP created breakaway political parties, which had the effect of further fragmenting an already highly fragmented party system. In the early 1970s, the scion of an important LDP family, Yohei Kono, led a drive to reform corruption within the party but was blocked by the party leadership. He then went on to form a new party, the New Liberal Club, after the LDP did little to reform itself even after the Lockheed scandal. The New Liberal Club eventually disbanded, and Kono was reincorporated into the LDP, eventually becoming the leader of the party.

But it was conflict between the party factions over political reform that finally led to the creation of three new parties and the loss of the LDP governing majority. It began in 1992 when a prominent, young LDP politician, Morihiro Hosokawa, broke away from the LDP to form the Japan New Party. Hosokawa was more concerned with reforming the highhanded nature of the LDP and the apathy with which most Japanese people approach politics, both of which he sees as the root causes of financial corruption and political indecisiveness. Then, in June 1993, the government of Prime Minister Kiichi Miyazawa lost a vote of no confidence when a large group of LDP members, including the Hata faction, refused to support their own party. Those renegade members went on to form two new parties; the Hata faction formed the Shinseito (referred to in English as either the Renaissance Party or the Japan Renewal Party), and the other defectors formed the Shinto Sakigake, or Harbinger Party.

In the election following the successful vote of no confidence, seven different parties, including those formed by the breakaway members of the LDP, were able to forge a coalition led by Hosokawa which had enough seats to remove the LDP from power for the first time since its inception. It is too soon to tell what effect this will have on Japanese politics in the long run. There are those who believe that, with the large number of ex-LDP members in the coalition, politics will continue more or less as before, and there are those who believe that the Japanese political system has been irrevocably changed. Whichever is the case, the events of 1993 support the theory that consensus is an important political and social value, but conflict is more often the reality in Japanese politics.

Events in the fall/winter of 1993–94, and especially in late January–early February 1994, indicate that conflict and fragmentation will only increase as the seven different parties that form the coalition start fighting among themselves over policy, and as the LDP begins to exert its power as a mighty opposition party. The coalition has a seven seat majority (262 seats) in the House of Representatives, but it has been able to bring those votes to bear only after long and agonizing negotiations among party leaders, and sometimes not even then. The LDP has 224 seats and has been able to use them in a more unified manner. The loss of the rebels may have increased the unity of the remaining party members, and from the very beginning the LDP has demonstrated a willingness to struggle with the coalition on major policy. Hosokawa's inability to unify the members of coalition parties behind government policy significantly weakened his hand when negotiating passage of reform legislation, tax legislation, and the budget.

Reforming the Japanese political system is the very raison d'être for the coalition, but the reform bill agreed upon by the coalition leadership was defeated in the upper house by the defection of twenty backbenchers from the SDPJ. The setback allowed the LDP to force significant concessions in electoral system reform and campaign financing reform from Hosokawa as the price of passing the overall reform bill. That embarrassment was equaled, if not surpassed, just a few weeks later when Hosokawa announced that he was replacing an unpopular 3 percent consumption tax with a 7 percent national welfare tax. The immediate reaction of other members of the coalition, especially the SDPJ, was so negative that he was forced to backpedal quickly on the national welfare tax.

Now that a coalition government is ruling Japan, relations among the coalition members and between the government and the opposition LDP make conflict, not consensus, the reality of domestic policy making. But even during the reign of the LDP, its relationship with the opposition parties was another major fissure in the purported unity of the Japanese political system. It was often assumed in studies of Japanese politics that the LDP had the ability to run roughshod over the opposition parties because it had been in power for the past four decades, and because it was assumed the legislature has no power in policy making. Although recently more attention has been given to the role of opposition parties in the political system and the policy-making process, the traditional view equated the LDP with the government. Nearly forty years of governing gave the LDP a great deal of control over the policy-making process and a great deal more power than any one opposition party, or even all of them combined. It is also true that the legislature had relatively little power in the policy-making process. But that is not to say that both the procedures of the legislature and the actions of the opposition parties within the legislature could not cause severe problems for the LDP and the bureaucracy. They could then, and they can certainly do so now in the hands of the LDP as opposition party.

Twenty years ago the opposition parties began to increase the number of their seats in the Diet as LDP majorities got thinner and thinner. More seats in the legislature translated into more seats in legislative committees and more chairmanships of those committees, which has forced the LDP to rely more and more on the support of opposition parties for passage of government legislation. Although the strength of LDP majorities has fluctuated wildly since the mid-1970s, there is no doubt that, whatever its majority, it has a hard time forcing legislation through the Diet if it is adamantly opposed by a unified opposition. That has been especially true since the 1989 election when the LDP lost its majority in the upper house. An increasing number of bills are being introduced from the floor of the legislature by private members, and the number of government bills amended in committee has also been increasing. In addition, by the early 1980s only approximately 5 percent of legislation was being passed by LDP strength alone, while the rest need some form of opposition support.[4] The important point is that the LDP, as the conservative party, in combination with the bureaucracy or alone, never had the power to force ultraconservative bills through the legislature. Now that it is in opposition not only is it as a party less able to pass ultraconservative policy, but the diversity of the parties that contribute to the process of governing insure that a conservative, cabal-like consensus cannot gain control of Japanese policy.

The LDP's procedural ability to railroad legislation through the Diet varied with the strength of its majorities. The mathematics were simple: if it held more than 50 percent of the seats in the upper and lower houses and all members voted as a bloc, it could have passed any piece of legislation it wanted. But the simple quantitative power to pass legislation is not enough; there must be at least the appearance of consensus. Given the importance of harmony and consensus as societal values, the public expects consensus from its political leadership. The need for consensus in policy-making led the LDP and the opposition a merry dance for many years. The LDP always had the numbers, even if they were only minimal, to pass legislation, thereby leaving the opposition with only one major weapon to stop the passage of government legislation it adamantly opposed—painting the LDP as a nonconsensual bully. The opposition would signal the country that it is being railroaded by bogging down the legislative process through highly colorful means that were made for media attention. The two most common means were boycotting debate and slowing down voting procedures.

Once these tactics were put into use, and the boycott of committee hearings on the disputed bill was usually the opening move, the dance began. The LDP would always allow the boycott to continue for some time and made a show of trying to bring the opposition into agreement while attempting to demonstrate to the public that it was simply a responsible government party attempting to do what government parties are supposed to do—pass legislation which will help them run the country well. The longer the opposition stalled, the more the LDP could paint them as obstreperous nay-sayers that are good at attacking policy but who could not do anything constructive. The tactics of boycott and delay could backfire because the voting public did indeed hold this passive-destructive image of opposition parties, and especially the major opposition party, the SDPJ. The poor showing of the SDPJ in the 1992 upper house elections is in some part due to the public's disfavor with the manner in which it opposed the PKO bill in the months preceding the election.[5]

On the other hand, the opposition parties tried to portray themselves as a collective little Dutch boy, holding back both the bill in question and, more figuratively, a sea of authoritarianism as represented by the LDP's power politics. The voting public was also apt to perceive the LDP as a bully driving a steamroller, and so both parties were playing on the other's weaknesses. If no compromise could be worked out, the dance would always end with the LDP simply passing the legislation over the veto of the opposition party.

There was one final opposition tactic, used most often by the Japan Communist Party (JCP) and the SDPJ, and it was the most obvious example of the disunity of the Japanese political system. Opposition party members would rush headlong down the aisles in an attempt to wrest the microphone by force from the chairman of the committee or the speaker of the house in order keep him from either calling the vote or certifying the results. The ensuing melee can be astounding for those who believe in the harmony of Japanese society. The picture of legislators wrestling among themselves, standing on chairs shouting, fighting with security guards, and pushing elderly men down on the floor is equally disconcerting to the Japanese public.

The Black Nexus

The most nightmarish scenario conceived by those who fear the rebirth of Japanese nationalism centers on the shadowy world of the various ultranationalist groups. The tendrils of this giant octopus are everywhere. Here they work with legitimate businesses and the underworld to gain vast amounts of money; there they distribute that money to buy both political and physical muscle. There is a relationship between ultranationalist groups and the LDP, and it does represent the darker side of Japanese politics. These groups are in the forefront of the fight to tie the nation to the symbols, institutions, ideology, and policies of the Japanese state, and they are not hesitant to use whatever means are necessary. Like their prewar predecessors, they tend to be based on traditional, Confucian morality and hierarchies, love of fatherland, *kokutai, tennosei*, Shinto, anti-communism and, for some, a Japanese-led Pan-Asianism.

The revival of ultranationalism has been a concern from the beginning of the occupation. By the mid-1950s hundreds of ultranationalist societies had arisen, and, according to police statistics, there were 840 ultranationalist groups representing 125,000 members by the end of the 1980s.[6] They are a highly visible presence in Japan, mostly through their use of sound trucks and demonstrations. Their sound trucks, covered in slogans, blasting out martial music, and flying the national flag, can be seen cruising streets throughout the country. They stop occasionally at busy intersections to allow members to mount the roof of the truck and deliver impassioned speeches calling for the return of the northern territories, the revision of the constitution, remilitarization, the political empowerment of the emperor, or to comment on the issues of the day. They also cruise regularly outside the old Soviet (now Russian) Embassy and the American Embassy, and one can always find at these locations a phalanx of police whose job it is to keep them at a safe distance.

Ultranationalist groups also conduct mass demonstrations. Their three favorite occasions for demonstrating have been the annual meetings of the Japan Teacher's Union (Nikkyoso), Anti-Soviet Day, and Northern Territories Day. Ultranationalist groups believe that the Japan Teacher's Union, which is strongly supportive of the SDPJ, is poisoning the minds of Japanese children with socialist propaganda and so converge on their annual convention in order to blast its slogans and generally disrupt the proceedings. Anti-Soviet Day is on August 9, the day the Soviet Union declared war on Japan and invaded Japanese-held territories in Korea and Manchuria. Northern Territories Day is officially recognized by the Japanese government and is a day commemorating the loss of Japanese territories through agreements at Yalta between Stalin and Roosevelt. The fight to return the islands to Japan has become of special importance since the dissolution of the Soviet Union.

The ultranationalists are not content to carry their banner through the streets, play their music, hold demonstrations, and give speeches. Like their counterparts in the prewar period, they also attempt to have a direct impact on the nation through the politics of intimidation. The use of sound trucks itself is inherently intimidating, but their behavior has also been expressly violent. Communist Party offices have been broken into. The leader of the SDPJ, Inejiro Asanuma, was stabbed to death in 1960 while making a televised speech. The mayor of Nagasaki was shot by an ultranationalist after he intimated that the war responsibility of the emperor should be more openly discussed. The employees and property of the *Asahi Shimbun* often come under attack because it is the leading left-oriented newspaper in the country. To give just a few recent examples, an ultranationalist burst into a branch office of the *Asahi* in 1987 and shot a reporter to death, and a lighted smoke bomb was thrown through the window of a branch office when the paper reported in 1988 that the emperor was stricken with cancer.

But the left is not the only target of ultranationalist intimidation tactics. Until his disgrace and eventual arrest, Shin Kanemaru was one of the major forces in the LDP. He held many important party positions, was a leader of the Takeshita faction, had many connections to members of the far right, and was considered to be in the right wing of the party. Yet he was also a favorite target of ultranationalists because his positions on a number of issues upset the right wing. He supported a foreign policy led by the United States, wanted Japan to take more responsibility for Japan's prewar actions in Asia, and while on a trip to North Korea he even stated that North Korea should be compensated not only for the prewar colonization of Korea by Japan but for the postwar effects of neo-colonialism. In November 1991 there were two aborted attacks on his home, and he barely escaped being assassinated in March 1992 when an ultranationalist fired three shots at him from close quarters but missed.

As was the case in the prewar years, ultranationalists often despise political parties for their ties to unclean commercialism. The linkage between big business and the political parties, especially the LDP, is believed to be a corrupting influence on the country. Thus, even though Yoshio Kodama was one of the most important linchpins in the LDP-*yakuza*-ultranationalist nexus, six weeks after the Lockheed scandal broke in 1976 a young ultranationalist flew his Cessna into Kodama's home in a kamikaze attack to protest Kodama's role in the scandal. In the past, rightists have regularly attacked the homes and persons of senior members of the LDP and corporate executives, and have attacked the LDP headquarters building to protest financial scandals and what might be seen as a collaborative exploitation of the Japanese people by political and corporate interests. In the most recent incident, in 1992 an ultranationalist torched a truck filled with propane gas and then set it rolling toward the prime minister's official residence in protest of the government's decision to allow the emperor to visit China that October. Ultranationalists were opposed to the trip because they feared that the emperor would have been demeaned and made to apologize for Japan's actions in the prewar years.

Harassment by ultranationalists and their sound trucks is a nuisance and adds greatly to Japan's noise pollution problem, and the use of violence for political ends endangers the public, but neither have much effect on the political system, nor are they often taken too seriously by the public. It is their connections to mainstream elements of the Japanese political elite that constitutes a more important concern and is perceived as a real danger. Some influential, conservative political leaders have been very active in developing ties to new and prewar ultranationalist organizations as well as *yakuza* organizations. They, in turn, are very closely connected with the ultranationalists. From the time of the occupation, when General Charles Willoughby recruited *yakuza* to intimidate and control trade unions and other activist groups of the left, organized crime groups and punk hotrod (*bosozoku*) groups have been used by conservative politicians as fund raisers and enforcers. The nexus between the ultranationalists, the underworld, and the LDP has been documented,[7] and most LDP prime ministers have relied upon those who lead in the world of shadows, such as Yoshio

Kodama, Kenji Osano, and Susumu Ishii, as fixers and financiers. These connections have often been exposed during the investigation of the many financial scandals to which the LDP is prone.

The Tokyo Sagawa Kyubin scandal (or simply Sagawa scandal), the most recent and the largest since the Lockheed scandal, offers an excellent example of both cooperation and conflict among members of the black nexus. The scandal broke as a large but relatively common case of graft and illegal political donations. Hiroyasu Watanabe, the president of Tokyo Sagawa Kyubin, a trucking and package delivery company, and another top executive were arrested for causing a loss of about 95 billion yen to their company through making illegal loans to other companies. As investigators burrowed into the case, it was discovered that Watanabe received kickbacks from the loans from which he distributed over two billion yen to various politicians. Among the top recipients was Shin Kanemaru who received 500 million yen. One of the companies in particular was controlled by *yakuza*, and Watanabe was found to have close ties to the late Susumu Iishi, the past leader of the Inagawa-kai, one of the largest *yakuza* groups.

The plot became thicker when it came out that Watanabe used his connections with the underworld to act as a go-between for the LDP, *yakuza*, and an ultranationalist group. In the fall of 1987 former prime minister Noboru Takeshita was campaigning to be elected as the president of the LDP, which would allow him to take over the prime ministership from outgoing Yasuhiro Nakasone. An ultranationalist organization called Nihon Kominto was conducting a harassment campaign against Takeshita. The group was upset because Takeshita was ex-prime minister Kakuei Tanaka's closest aide, and they claimed that he stole the leadership of the LDP's largest faction away from Tanaka after he suffered a stroke. Kanemaru was one of Takeshita's main backers and so asked Watanabe to get Iishi to put pressure on Nihon Kominto's leader, Torao Iwamoto, to stop the anti-Takeshita campaign. Iwamoto agreed, but only if Takeshita would apologize to Tanaka. Takeshita tried to visit the Tanaka residence but was turned away. He was alleged, however, to have written a note that read, "I promise you to protect Kakuei Tanaka."

The scandal is still running its course as of this writing. Takeshita gave up the leadership of his faction and has effectively been removed from Japanese politics. Kanemaru also has no power as he quit the Diet and the LDP, but his case continues. He originally told prosecutors that he donated the 500 million yen to sixty politicians, but it was later discovered that he and an aide used the money for personal investments. He was arrested in March 1993 for tax evasion. The ultimate result of the scandal was the call for political reform that led to the rebellion of LDP members and the success of the anti-LDP coalition in the elections of July 1993.

The Sagawa scandal demonstrates that corruption is endemic in Japanese politics, and that connections between the LDP, the *yakuza*, and ultranationalist organizations do exist. The causes for political corruption in Japan, and why it has been tolerated by the public in the past, are outside the scope of this book. The point I want to examine is the extent of influence that the connection brings to the *yakuza* and ultranationalist groups. Members of the LDP use their connections in the black nexus to raise funds and get favors done, and the *yakuza* use theirs to get protection and contracts for their companies, but the ultranationalist groups seem to get little other than a tacit acceptance of their existence. The LDP, ultranationalist groups and organized crime do not form a unified whole, and neither have the latter groups had an important effect on national policy making. Ultranationalist groups use violence for political ends, but their violent acts are directed against the establishment and the leadership of the LDP, as well as against the left. Ultranationalists attack the LDP because it is perceived as corrupt, venal, and more interested in political power for power's sake than for the ideological causes of the far right. But in the final analysis, what separates the ultranationalists and the LDP is the past. The ultranationalists want to recreate what they perceive to be the glory of Japan's prewar past, but the LDP is tied to the present and the future. The LDP is a party defined by its postwar successes, and the past is more an embarrassment than a model for the future.

Death of an Emperor

The continuing conflict between ultranationalist groups and the government and LDP politicians demonstrates that the ultranationalists have not been able to affect government policy in any major way, regardless of the informal ties that do exist. There are many areas of policy that demonstrate the ineffectualness of the ultranationalists, but perhaps the best example is their desire to "restore" the emperor's power, à la the Meiji restoration. If the ultranationalists ever had a chance to change the postwar system back into a more conservative reflection of its prewar self, it came during the years from 1988 to 1990. At that time the eyes of the nation were focused on the institution of the emperor as Hirohito died and Akihito ascended to the throne.

There was a strong upswing in sympathy for the emperor when the seriousness of the emperor's illness was first announced in the fall of 1988. The conventional wisdom of the day judged it to be increased support for the institution as well as the individual. Numerous articles were written speculating whether, with the passing of Emperor Showa (formerly Hirohito), the emperor would become a more politically powerful institution as a result of increased support for the institution, and because the new emperor was not tainted with the failures and actions of the prewar period.

Again it was a case in which superficial appearances were quite different from the fundamental reality. Some occurrences during the period beginning with the announcement of the emperor's illness and lasting into the official period of mourning certainly gave rise to fears that Japan was regressing back to prewar behavior. The government displayed nascent authoritarian tendencies by flooding Tokyo with police prior to the funeral services for Emperor Showa and the enthronement ceremonies for Emperor Akihito. For months on end the police were out in force carrying out car searches and sweeping the areas in which these events would occur. The government was also able to effectively censor news reports concerning the state of Hirohito's health during his illness. Pressure from the government and, to some extent, implicit threats from the ultranationalist groups were able to change public behavior. During his illness weddings, concerts, parades, and celebrations of all types were canceled. One major department store even went so far as to remove stocks of red fish paste from its shelves because it is considered to be a celebratory food. Normally ebullient television variety shows were toned down or canceled, as were many public events, and the festive New Year's holiday season took on a more somber tone.

Taking all this into consideration, it would appear as if the passing of Emperor Showa occasioned a new turn to the right for Japan, but what actually happened was quite the opposite. Those who wanted to use the occasion of his passing to create conservative changes in the political system totally misread the feelings of the people. The groundswell of attention and respect given to the emperor had much more to do with nostalgia for the passing of an era than support for the institution of the emperor, to say nothing of increased political power for the institution. Emperor Showa reigned sixty-three years, longer than any other emperor. Most Japanese were born under his reign, and he became symbolic of the tremendous changes that Japan has undergone over the past sixty years. His passing was a visible indication that both the prewar and postwar eras had ended. It symbolized a postwar acceptance of his benign, constitutional status; it did not symbolize a turning back to the prewar adulation for the emperor. While the people of Japan mourned the death of a long-known symbol of the nation, in some ways the end of the Showa monarchy also allowed Japan to move out from under the shadow cast by Hirohito's prewar leadership. Sighs of relief could also be heard among the sighs of nostalgia and mourning.

Most media coverage emphasized the national focus on the transition, but sometime between the protracted illness and the long period of mourning, most Japanese lost interest in it all. The Japanese people began to resemble children at a great-uncle's funeral. They were quiet and kept their heads down while respect was paid, but at the same time they kept looking up from their attitude of prayer and wondering when they could go home and play, watch TV, and get on with their lives. Even before the official mourning period was over, people rushed to return to life as normal. The crowds lining the streets of Akihito's motorcade were respectful but not too enthusiastic and, in some places, fairly thin.

Even the complications of maintaining the old Shinto rites under the new "separation of state and religion" constitution did not create that much concern or interest outside the media. While political commentators and scholars at home and abroad wrung their hands over whether the new emperor should be allowed to conduct this or that ceremony because of the religious implications, the public was not really very much interested. The participation or nonparticipation of the new emperor in Shinto rites had very little meaning for the public. In the first place they had very little understanding of what the rites were or what they symbolized. It was all very quaint but relatively uninteresting. In the second place anything the emperor did, short of walking on water, would not have deified him in their eyes. The attainment of high levels of affluence and education mean that the average Japanese is no longer willing to accept the notion that his or her emperor is a divine being.

In the end, when the national period of mourning had ended and Akihito had gone through the last ceremonies marking his ascension to the throne, it was a period that marked the passing of the last emperor to be considered a deity and the last emperor to hold real political power. The passing of the emperor was indeed a period in which the role of the emperor in Japan was reevaluated, but the result was a strong reconfirmation of the emperor's limited role under the postwar constitution. All the attempts by right wing politicians and ultranationalists to use the passing as a means of changing the status quo came to nought.

State and Bureaucracy

Since the end of the occupation, the LDP and the bureaucracy have consistently tried to enhance some of the old conservative values and engender more respect for the Japanese state. As early as the fall of 1951, Minister of Education Teiyu Amano announced his intention to introduce a moral code as a guide for national education as soon as the occupation ended. Many older leaders of Japan felt that it was necessary to reestablish a national ethic through moral instruction to stop the postwar moral decline, to counter the mistaking of democracy for license, and to restore a sense of pride and patriotism in the nation.[8] There was a strong element of Confucianism in the code, reflecting the relationship between moral and political order. The Confucian elements of the code were so obvious, that many compared it to the Imperial Rescript on Education of 1890. Most important was the code's section on the state.

The State is the parent body of the individual; without the State there would be no individuals. It is wrong for the State to think of individuals solely as a means to an end, and it is wrong for individuals to think of the State solely as a means to an end. The two are in a close and indivisible relationship.

On tradition and creation: This state has its own traditions, and if we are to create a new age, we must be firmly rooted in these traditions.

On patriotism: The fortunes of a country depend on the patriotism of its people. We are responsible for taking over the State from our forefathers and passing it on to our descendants.

On politics: Politics must not be conducted in the interests of party or faction or class. When a class of interests arises . . . a solution must be sought . . . with full regard for the interests of the nation as a whole.

On the emperor: We possess an Emperor who is a symbol of the State, wherein lies the peculiar nature of our national polity. It is a special characteristic of our country that there has always been an Emperor throughout its long history. The position of the Emperor partakes of the nature of a moral focus as the symbol of the state.

On the ethics of the state: Morality is the lifeblood of the State. The state, in essence, is founded more deeply on its moral than on its political or economic character.

The public outcry was immediate and forced the minister to withdraw his code, but the Ministry of Education remains today a driving force for the "moral education" of the Japanese people. It has often been accused of "cleaning" the image of prewar Japan, presenting the blandest, most positive image of contemporary Japan, and socializing students into the use of state symbols. The ministry has now mandated that all eight social studies texts used in the sixth grade state that the Hinomaru is the national flag and the "Kimigayo" is the national anthem, and that the flag be flown and the anthem be sung at all school entrance and graduation ceremonies. In addition, there are accusations that the ministry's "control over what subject matter social studies textbooks should contain has become stricter and forced them to become more nationalistic in tone."[9]

The textbook issue is particularly sensitive because the Ministry of Education has the ability to control what school children think and know through its regulation of texts. All textbooks used by Japanese schools are purchased only after being read and approved by ministry officials. If the officials do not like what they read, they issue "requests" to the publishers for changes in the text. A publisher who does not accept the requested changes will not have its textbooks purchased by the national school system. Ministry inspectors expressed an average of fifty comments per text on social studies textbooks in 1992, a rather low figure in comparison with other years.

The ministry's censorship of passages dealing with Japan's prewar history and its colonization and invasion of other Asian countries has drawn the most attention over the years, but its coverage is much broader. It has also requested changes in the ways textbooks have portrayed the U.S. military effort in Vietnam, the status and role of the SDF, the government's nuclear power policy, and its foreign aid policy. Most recently, an author writing a text on contemporary society inserted part of an editorial by Yukichi Fukuzawa, the founder of Keio University and one of the most admired men of the Meiji restoration, that encouraged following the Western model by taking colonies. The ministry advised the author to drop the editorial and quote only from Fukuzawa's autobiography. The author is taking the ministry to court over the question of censorship, but he is not likely to get very far. In 1965 Saburo Ienaga took the ministry to court over nineteen deletions it had made from his history text. Twenty-eight years later the Supreme Court ruled that the deletions did not constitute a violation of Ienaga's freedom of speech. According to the court, the ministry has the right to screen texts in order to promote standardization and to safeguard the mental development of the nation's students.

The trouble with textbook screening is not that it inculcates nationalism into the nation's students, but that it encourages standardization and promotes a collective forgetting of inconvenient past occurrences. Both are deplorable, but they should not be confused with the former. When that which is "nationalistic in tone" is examined, it pales in comparison with the more blatant nationalism that is taught in other school systems around the world. Take, for example, a change in social studies textbooks for junior high schools that went into effect in April 1993. Previously the texts stated that "the government holds the view" that Japan has the right of national self-defense. The new texts simply state that all nations have the right of self-defense and all have defense forces to protect that right. In the opinion of this author, it is a true statement of fact and not excessively militaristic. Those who are against the change accuse the government of teaching children that the Self-Defense Forces (SDF) are legitimate under the constitution.[10] In general, the treatment of militarism in Japanese texts compares very favorably with the idolization of the military and military heros found in American school texts.

Another major policy area that has been a controversial focal point in the linkage of sociocultural nationalism to state-oriented nationalism is the visitation of government officials to Yasukuni Shrine. The shrine is the resting place of the spirits of all those who have died in battle for Japan and as such is a potent symbol of militarism and the state. Although it would be normal for members of any country's government to visit a state memorial for those who had died in the service of their country, the situation at Yasukuni is made more complex by the fact that it is a Shinto shrine. Members of the government visiting Yasukuni in an official capacity to offer prayers to the dead goes beyond paying respect to deceased veterans. In a symbolic way it evokes many images of the past, including the prewar era of *kokutai*, and in a constitutional sense it embodies the joining of state and religion.

The controversy over members of the government making official visits to Yasukuni was rekindled in 1985 when Yasuhiro Nakasone became the first prime minister of the postwar era to visit the shrine in an official capacity on the fortieth anniversary of the end of the war. The outcry against the visit at home and abroad was so great that no other prime minster has dared to repeat his visit, but other members of government have done so, including eleven cabinet ministers who attended ceremonies marking the end of the war in 1991 and fifteen who visited in 1992. The informal ban on prime ministerial visits to the shrine continues to be upheld by the coalition government.

Another controversial policy in which personal behavior of Japanese citizens was linked to the good of the state had to do with the Japanese government's desire to increase the population. The decrease in the number of children being born in Japan is considered to be one of the country's top problems. Japan's birthrate in 1990 was 1.53, and it is projected to sink to 1.35 by 1996.[11] The decline in the birthrate is a fundamental element in many of Japan's contemporary social issues: the severe labor shortage and the consequent need to import labor from abroad, the aging of Japan's population, and the change in role of Japanese women. The government has been doing everything it can to encourage women to have more children and suppress birth control. It has long banned birth control pills while rewarding families that have more than one child with tax breaks and cash incentives. Rural communities that have the worst depopulation problems often offer hundreds of dollars per child born. Takao Nishioka, at one time the chairman of the LDP's Executive Council, stated that it is in the best interest of the nation for Japanese women to "bear and multiply" and that they should have at least three to five children. This statement came as a shock in that it was reminiscent of language used by the Japanese government during the war when Japanese women were expected to produce more babies in support of the war effort.[12]

Japanese women and their husbands are not paying much heed to the exhortations of the government. Although the pill is banned, other methods of birth control, especially abortion, continue to be very popular. Women are just now beginning to move into positions of importance in the work force and are less willing to take on the traditional roles of wives and mothers. Even those families that are having children usually limit the number to one or two. Their desire to limit their families is directly related to the standard of living and quality of life in Japan. Raising a child is very costly, especially in a country where everything from housing to weddings is tremendously expensive. In addition, people simply think that Japan is crowded enough as it is. Land and services are scarce now, and a larger population would significantly decrease the standard of living.

Militarism

No issue associated with the "new nationalism" carries more emotion-ally laden trauma than the remilitarization of Japan. The fear of Japan regressing to its militarist past underlies all the surface concerns over economic power. Of all the ambiguous fears that others have concerning a strong Japan, the fear that Japan will again become an aggressive military power is the lowest common denominator. Japan's economic success will always carry with it the fear that its fiscal resources and technological capacities will enable it to become a military power rapidly, if it so decides. It seems that no matter what Japan does or says, no matter how long it continues to conduct itself reasonably and peacefully, memories of prewar military aggression will always determine others' predictions of Japan's future. In the late 1960s when Japan's economic success first became apparent, "experts" such as Herman Kahn were predicting remilitarization and even the acquisition of nuclear armaments.[13] A quarter of a century later the same things are being predicted of Japan's future.

Any discussion of the role of a Japanese military force must begin with Article 9 of the constitution: "Aspiring sincerely to an international peace based on justice and order, the Japanese people forever renounce war as a sovereign right of the nation and the threat or use of force as means of settling international disputes. In order to accomplish the aim of the pre-ceding paragraph, land, sea, and air forces, as well as other war potential, will never be maintained. The right of belligerency of the state will not be recognized."

For all the concern abroad, the debate over Japanese remilitarization and the possibility of militarism has been carried on largely within Japan. The domestic debate has focused on the legality and legitimacy of the Self-De-fense Forces, the name given the Japanese military. Many articles have been written about the debate since the SDF's inception in 1954, but it remains quite clear that the SDF is unconstitutional. It is a land, sea, and air force maintained by the Japanese government. Even those who support it argue that the constitution should be changed to make it constitutional. But, for reasons too lengthy to detail here, questions of strict constitutionality are often unimportant in Japanese politics. What is important is the question of legitimacy. That is, even given its unconstitutionality, should it be sup-ported by the Japanese public as a necessary component of a sovereign state as a means of protecting that sovereignty, while simultaneously keeping Article 9 as a statement of Japan's pacifism and commitment to using the SDF as a solely defensive force?

The debate over legitimacy, over whether the SDF should continue to exist, endures but it no longer has much meaning. After forty years of coexistence with the SDF, most Japanese have come to accept its legitimacy, a fact clearly indicated by polls. According to a survey of 2,374 Japanese done by the Prime Minister's Office in January 1988, about 75 percent had a positive image of the SDF, a result that has not changed significantly since the mid-1970s.[14] But perhaps the best indication of the acceptance of the SDF's legitimacy by the Japanese people is the change in opposition parties' policy. For many years opposition parties denied the legitimacy of the SDF by claiming that its existence was unconstitutional. In the late 1980s, however, the SDPJ and other smaller opposition parties changed their policies to accept the existence (if still questioning the constitutionality) of the SDF. This policy change was a belated recognition of the general public's support for the existence of the SDF.

The existence and legitimacy of the SDF are no longer the issues; the new issues of debate are its size, role, and public perception. There is a vague belief among many Japanese that it is necessary to maintain a military force because that is what other powers do. As with many other aspects of their political system, Japanese are satisfied with the military status quo. When asked in the above survey whether the size of the SDF should be increased, decreased, or left the same, 64 percent wanted it to remain the same, while 10 percent wanted an increase and 13 percent wanted a decrease. Similarly, 58 percent were satisfied with defense spending as it is, 11 percent wanted an increase, and 19 percent wanted a decrease.[15]

Japanese are not too fearful that Japan will ever have to go to war—only a fifth of the population believes that there is a danger of Japan getting into a war—and they don't even perceive the SDF's sole, or even most important, function to be maintaining national security. Seventy-seven percent of the respondents to the survey thought that disaster relief was the most important function of the SDF, followed by national security (8 percent) and maintaining law and order (6 percent). Japanese do not even expect the SDF to be able to defend the homeland by itself. Seventy-eight percent of the respondents believe that the Japan-United States Security Treaty is useful, and 67 percent think that Japan should be defended by both the United States and Japan. Only 6 percent thought that Japan should defend itself by itself.[16]

Nothing is impossible, but it is very difficult to conceive of Japan developing a militaristic state or a popular militaristic nationalism. It is true that Japan has the sixth largest military in the world and the third largest budget, but size and funding do not immediately translate into military power. It is easy to assume that because the Japanese economy has been run successfully, then all other elements of life in Japan will operate in the same efficient and effective way. Foreigners with little knowledge of Japan tend to believe that any endeavor undertaken by Japan will be approached with total commitment and will end in success. This image of Japanese as an infallible super race is often projected by Japanese themselves, but it can be counterproductive. Because others think Japanese will throw themselves wholeheartedly into any endeavor, they believe that if Japan begins to remilitarize, they will approach it with the same enthusiasm and unrelenting commitment as they applied to their economic development. In this perception there is no room for moderation; it is all or nothing. Thus, when foreigners, especially those who felt the negative consequences of Japanese militarization in the prewar period, learn that Japan is increasing its military strength, they can only project a combination of the fanaticism of the 1930s with the technology and efficiency of the 1990s.

The efficiency of the economy itself is questionable, but that aside, there is no automatic transference of Japanese know-how from the economy to other areas of life. Japanese economic development was a result of a combination of factors that included a great deal of aid and support from the United States as well as a rapidly expanding international economy that was tailor-made for the export-driven Japanese economy. Japanese culture, behavioral traits, and cooperation among various private and public institutions certainly played a role in fostering rapid economic growth, but had they not been supported by the international environment and other structural factors, it is doubtful whether Japan would have the economic power and affluence it has today. It is therefore a fallacy automatically to assume that Japan will redevelop its military in the same way and with the same result as it redeveloped its economy.

Indeed, although Japan has had a military force for about forty years, it is actually rather inefficient and ineffective. Japan's military budget is in the world's top ten, but that figure is somewhat deceiving. The military budget increased about 5 percent per year during the 1980s, but much of that increase was due to the growing strength of the yen against the dollar. Because spending is reported in dollars, the amount goes up as the value of the dollar goes down. Measuring military spending as a percentage of gross domestic product (GDP), Japan is far behind most other countries. It spends only 1.5 percent of GDP as opposed the Germany's 3.1 percent. And about half of Japan's defense expenditures are spent long before any equipment is actually purchased. About 40 percent of total defense spending goes to wages, and about 10 percent goes to help pay for the maintenance of U.S. forces in Japan. Japan pays the United States for about 50 percent of the cost of maintaining U.S. forces in Japan, or about $3.5 billion per year. Finally, much of defense spending is inefficient. Like everything else in Japan, military equipment costs two or three times what it would cost in the West. As journalist James Fallows said in an interview with the *New York Times*, "This may be the only military force in the world that makes the Pentagon look like it gets bargains."[17]

Another important consideration in the numbers game is the amount of investment it would take for Japan to remilitarize successfully. There is no doubt that, if public opinion and government policies support rearmament, Japan has the technological capabilities to do so, but at what cost? Japan's postwar economic development was in part due to the relatively small amount of its GDP that it had to invest in defense. As a result, both the public sector and the private sector have become accustomed to spending relatively little on defense. A government budget that included the astronomical sums necessary to become a power strong enough to challenge the South Korean and Chinese armies or the Soviet and American navies would simply be unacceptable. Japan appears to be a country with unlimited financial resources, but the government budget is actually rather tight. As it is, the government is having a hard enough time trying to balance the budget.

The creation of a conventional military force powerful enough to match the great military powers of the world, or even Asia, would be difficult enough, but more than conventional weaponry would be needed. There would be no real military security for Japan, especially if Russia, China, or the United States is a possible enemy, without a nuclear deterrent. Building a credible nuclear *force de frappe* in Japan is almost inconceivable. Japan has built its postwar identity around its opposition to nuclear weapons and its role as the only victim of nuclear attack. It has staked its international reputation on that identity. It would have to renounce that fundamental and crucial identity, and the Nuclear Non-Proliferation Treaty, in order to build a nuclear capability. Technological and cost considerations aside, neither Japanese citizens nor the other nations of the world would accept such a renunciation.

The bottom line is that Japanese citizens support the existence of the SDF, but they are not active supporters of the military or militarism. For all the young Japanese who love to watch American guns 'n' ammo movies, and for all the older generation who sing old war songs in karaoke bars, the military is still a pariah. Japanese people accept the legitimacy of the SDF, but they really don't want to have much to do with it. The SDF exists in a world far removed from the average Japanese, and that is the way they want it to remain. One gets the feeling that Japanese people are supportive of the Japan-United States Security Treaty because they would rather see an American in a military uniform walking down the street than a Japanese in a military uniform. Even a former president of the Defense Academy, Masamichi Inoki, has said that it is better for Japan to rely on the security treaty with the United States for its defense because the United States can defend Japan and act as a guarantee that the Japanese military will not once again try to become too powerful.[18]

An incident in the fall of 1992 demonstrated how much attitudes among the military and the public have changed since the prewar era. Major Shinsaku Yanai of the Ground Self-Defense Forces wrote an article for the October 22 edition of the *Shukan Bunshun*, a respectable weekly magazine, castigating bureaucrats for betraying the public and railing against political corruption. His solution to these problems was to call for a revolution or a coup d'état. The call for a coup d'état by a member of the armed forces was a national news sensation and an extreme source of embarrassment to the

SDF. When I asked my friends in the SDF about it, they simply mumbled that Yanai had always been known as a crackpot. The public's reaction was humorous disbelief, as opposed to outrage. The idea of a coup d' état in this day and age was simply laughable.

The shame at the loss of the war and the anger at the military for having brought about such a disaster are still at the back of the mind of many Japanese, even though it is a few generations past the war. Pride in the military services does not exist. The average Japanese looks down on the military. It is extremely rare to see a member of the SDF wearing his or her uniform on the street, and most of the officers I have known from the SDF Agency and the Defense Academy usually wear mufti. Certainly it is not a career that would be chosen by most Japanese. Japanese recruiters have a difficult time finding people to enlist in the SDF, and it is becoming harder as SDF personnel may now actually be involved in some danger abroad through participation in the United Nations peacekeeping organization. It is hard enough recruiting young people into "three-K" jobs—*kitanai* (dirty), *kiken* (dangerous), and *kitsui* (difficult)—in the private sector. It would be almost impossible to convince them to join the military because not only is it a three-K job but recruits also lose their freedom, face the possibility of being in combat, and become members of a distinct out-group. Of the 494 graduates of the Self-Defense Forces Academy in 1991, 19 percent declined to go into the SDF. Many of those who opted out did so because the SDF was not a desirable employer.

Although the government says that morale in the SDF is high, many in the enlisted ranks think otherwise. As a private in the SDF said, "only 40 percent of the soldiers have a positive attitude, while 60 percent have a negative attitude. I would put myself in the latter group." Although service personnel are given many more amenities and treated much better than they were in the past, they still have to put up with living conditions that make even life in the crowded apartments of Tokyo look like heaven. Making such sacrifices as living in a room with twelve other people and taking fifteen-mile hikes with a full pack are not the kind of sacrifices that Japanese young people are willing to make, nor do they have to. The labor shortage in Japan waxes and wanes, but no one is forced to join the military because they can't find a job in the private sector. But perhaps the worst thing about being a soldier is being perceived as an "outsider," a member of an out-group by the members of mainstream society. According to that same soldier, "the thing I like least about being in the SDF is what happens when people find out I'm a soldier. When my friends and I go out at night, we always have to hide it from anyone we meet."[19]

Finally, there is the ability of Japan to use its military as a coercive means of gaining political and economic advantage over other states in the world. Even if Japan were able to develop a truly powerful offensive military force, what would be its strategic goals? Fears of Japanese remilitarization are inexorably linked with prewar events, but there is little similarity between the prewar international system and that which exists now. The expansion of the Japanese empire through military means depended on the military's ability to control domestic politics, the strength of the Japanese military vis-à-vis the other states of Asia, and the weakness of an international deterrent force. This chapter is concerned with the first element, but the other elements must also be considered. Even if conservative elements in the Japanese government or the military elite were able to control policy to such an extent that the use of force for political and economic gain were feasible, how would other Asian countries and the rest of the world react? Other states would not stand still and let Japan gain predominant military power. Korea and China, both victims of prewar Japanese militarism and the two countries most sensitive to Japanese rearmament, are quite different from what they were in the prewar period. They both have strong militaries more than able to counter any Japanese aggression in Asia. Indeed, they are already on the alert for such a possibility even now when the Japanese threat is so minimal. A recent South Korean annual white paper on defense stated that Japan was making a concentrated effort to develop its military and would shift from a defensive military to an offensive military capability within the next few years. It warned that such behavior would be a direct threat to South Korea. In addition, a South Korean public opinion poll conducted in February 1992 showed that 66 percent of Koreans believed that their country should be on guard against Japan, as opposed to 18 percent who stated that they want South Korea to establish friendly relations with Japan.[20]

Neither would non-Asian countries quietly accept a strengthened Japanese military. If Japan were to remilitarize aggressively today, the United States would be one of the first countries to react. It is true that the United States has been the biggest supporter of Japanese rearmament, but it has always played a "double game" in its policy toward Japan's rearmament. It wants Japan to be strong enough to support the United States in Asia, but it does not want Japan to become too strong or to use the power of its military in any way that is contrary to American policy. Similarly, while American forces are stationed in Japan to protect Japan and the international peace of Northeast Asia, the unstated secondary reason is to act as "the cap in the bottle" of Japanese militarism.

Mass-Elite Linkages

The above are just some of the manifestations of state-oriented nationalism among the Japanese elite, but the real question is whether they have support among the public. Even if there are members of the political elite who want Japan to adopt more conservative, nationalistic policies, they are not able simply to implement such policies by decree. Japan is not just a

democracy in name. Democracy in Japan is not pseudo-, tenuous, temporary, or shallow. Democratic values and institutions have taken deep root
in the political culture,[21] and consequently any attempt to implement
conservative, nationalistic policies must be supported by the public. Either
that or the political institutions themselves must be changed to give the
political elite the ability to act without public support.

Assume, for the sake of this argument, that the "Peace Constitution" and
its democratic political institutions will remain in place and that conservative politicians do have a nationalistic agenda for which they want to
develop popular support. Under those conditions the ability of conservative
politicians to create public support for state-oriented nationalism is highly
questionable because the Japanese public wants to maintain the status quo,
is output-oriented, does not have a state-oriented sense of patriotism, does
not have trust in politicians, and is not given to ideological, normative
support for the state. Japanese people have a strong commitment to the
status quo because they perceive it as having brought affluence and peace
to their lives. Making major changes of any kind or adopting policies that
will disturb the rest of the world can only threaten the peace and security
that most are enjoying. Eighty percent of Japanese believe that their country
is pursuing a peace policy, and 73 percent rate the best thing about life in
Japan to be its peacefulness.[22] Sixty-three percent feel satisfied with their
present life (a figure much unchanged since 1958), and 60 percent feel that
it will remain so in the future.[23] Sixty-two percent of Japanese believe that
Japan should safeguard its security by "maintaining the status quo."[24]

To stand the famous line from John Kennedy's inaugural address on its
head, the Japanese public asks what their country can do for them, and not
what they can do for their country. The Japanese public is accustomed to
positive outputs from their government. They believe that government
policy has been at least partially responsible for the rapid economic development of Japan and continues to do well in consolidating its gains. There
are increasing demands for better government policy in some areas such
as housing and the environment, and there is some concern with government policy during the recession of the early 1990s, but on the whole the
public is satisfied with the government's domestic and foreign policy
record. The public voted the LDP out of office because it was unable to
reform corruption within the party, but the public does not want to change
either the political system or the fundamental LDP policies of the past.
Indeed, the coalition government was elected in part by promising to hold
to LDP domestic economic policy and foreign policy.

In sum, the average Japanese person is mostly concerned with his or her
individual life and the well-being of their families, and want to maintain
the status quo. When asked by a government survey whether people
"should pay more attention to state and social affairs" or "should attach
more importance to enriching their personal life," 34 percent chose the

former, 41 percent the latter, and 20 percent made no decision. When asked if there was any group (political and/or social) to which they felt a strong affiliation, or to which they wanted to be of service, 69 responded "no." When asked if they wished to receive benefits from the state or render help to the state, 42 percent responded the former, 15 percent the latter, and 34 percent said that they wanted it to be both ways.[25]

It does not seem at all likely that the Japanese public will develop a sense of state-oriented patriotism. Asked whether people "should attach more importance to national interests even at the sacrifice of personal benefit" or "emphasize their own benefit over that of the entire nation," 31 percent favored the former, 30 percent the latter, and 34 percent found it hard to decide. A majority (52 percent) did feel that they had a strong sense of patriotism, but when asked to describe specifically what they meant by patriotism, 60 percent answered that it meant a love of nature and the physical country itself, while only 20 percent replied that it meant the protection of independence and security.[26]

Japanese love their country, the beauty of their land, and the art of their culture, but they are not patriotic in their devotion to the state. When asked by a national defense survey what they would do if Japan were invaded, only 7 percent said they would either put up guerrilla resistance (2 percent) or join the SDF (5 percent). Ten percent said they would put up no resistance whatsoever, 19 percent said they would resist by other than military means, and 40 percent said they would support the SDF "somehow."[27] In the previously mentioned ten-nation survey conducted by the Dentsu Institute for Human Development and MITI's Leisure Development Center, Japan recorded by far the lowest levels of patriotism. Only 10 percent of Japanese said they would die for their country. The second lowest was Spain at 47 percent, and the highest was South Korea at 85 percent.[28]

Separate Worlds

The conservative elite's task of linking the public and their sociocultural nationalism to the state and political institutions is made especially difficult by a wide gap that separates the political elite and mass in Japan. In most political cultures where there is a gap between the elite and the mass, it is in nondemocratic (and often developing) political systems where the elite does not need the full support of the citizens, and the citizens do not expect to have any input into the formation of governments or their policy making. These are termed subject political cultures because the mass acts as subjects of the elite. This is not the case in Japan. The results of the above survey on the relationship between the citizens and their state indicates that Japanese citizens are more concerned about outputs from the state than inputs to the state only as long as those outputs are positive. Japanese citizens recognize their right to have a say in government policy making and will act on that right if they see a change in the positive nature of the outputs they receive from the state.

A gap exists between the public and the political elite, but it is not strictly hierarchical. It is as true for Japan as any other country that the political elite have more political power than the mass, but the political elite still remains dependent upon the mass for support and legitimacy. In addition, there are many members of the mass, such as artists, social critics, and university professors, who have a higher ranking in the various Japanese social hierarchies than do members of the political elite. Indeed, the social ranking of Japanese politicians is generally quite low.[29]

It is more fruitful to think of the gap separating the political elite from the mass as horizontal rather than vertical. Japan has sometimes been called a spectator political culture. That is, Japanese recognize the existence of different "worlds" within their society that are separate from normal life. There is the world of kabuki, the world of sumo, and the world of the *yakuza*. Politics is also seen as being a different world. Japanese people are interested in politics, but they do not believe that it is really part of their everyday life. They watch it from afar, as they would watch a baseball game. They get involved, they cheer, they boo, they buy tickets or they don't buy tickets, but the one thing they do not contemplate is jumping down from their seats and running on to the field. Here the analogy breaks down, however, because Japanese citizens are not completely passive. They do get involved in the political system when they think it necessary and important to do so. Baseball fans do not have the ability to vote for their managers and players. Neither do they hold massive demonstrations or petition drives in reaction to their team's policies.

Because Japanese believe that the world in which they live and the political world are two separate entities, it is difficult to get the public to identify with the state and political institutions.[30] As was pointed out earlier, the social system has a higher importance in Japan than the political system, and political institutions have very little cultural meaning to Japanese. When Americans see the Stars and Stripes, when a Briton sees the Parliament Building, or when a French person hears "The Marseillaise," they become more than just the symbols of the state and political institutions; they also symbolize the nation, its history, and its culture. Japanese have no such cultural and political synthesis in their political institutions or state symbols.

The separation of the public from their political system is also due to perceived differences in role, lack of trust in politicians, and a belief that the common citizen lacks empowerment. Japanese people think that their political system tends to be corrupt; they do not trust their politicians and believe them to be dishonest. Neither do they believe that they have much say in what goes on in the political system or much ability to change the government. But, on the other hand, they believe that the running of the political system should be left to the politicians. There is a great deal of political cynicism in the Japanese public. The role of government is to govern, and so they are left to do so. Politicians are corrupt and think mainly of themselves, but that is the way of all politicians. From the viewpoint of Japanese, that is the way of the world. Things may change now that the LDP is no longer in power, but it is too soon to tell. The fact that those who brought about the downfall of the LDP and created the new government used to be members of the LDP has done nothing thus far to decrease the cynicism of the Japanese public. The public is perhaps willing to be persuaded that things have changed, but it is maintaining a wait-and-see attitude.

This picture of Japanese citizens as apathetic and cynical[31] might mean that political elites will have an easy time enacting any policies they like without interference from the public. It is a dangerous picture wherein conservatives could be able to push the system toward more nationalistic policies. But this has not happened because there are limits to both the apathy and cynicism of the public. Even though there is a lack of trust in politicians and political institutions, Japanese support their state and its democratic ideology and acquiesce in government decisions. Even given the above conditions, the government is not simply allowed to pass any legislation it pleases. Opposition parties in the Diet and public opinion in general are potent controls on government policy. Only by understanding this can one explain why governments have gone to such lengths to avoid opposing public opinion and to garner public support for its policies.[32] The government must take public opinion seriously and court that opinion because the Japanese public takes voting seriously. In the highly regarded Japanese Election Study of both lower and upper house elections in 1983, 57 percent of the respondents disagreed that it is useless to vote if you don't think your party has a chance to win. Similarly, only 14 percent agreed that there are so many people who vote in an election that their individual vote doesn't really matter. In addition, 78 percent agreed that elections make it possible for one's voice to be heard in politics, and 66 percent agreed that the national legislature makes it possible for one's voice to be heard in politics.[33]

These figures demonstrate quite clearly the limits to both cynicism and apathy. The public does not give unquestioning and unconditional support to the state and government policies, but acquiesces in them. The government is committed to democratic institutions and recognizes that its existence depends on the continued acquiescence of the public. The voting public understands the relationship and uses it to send the government messages concerning its pleasure or displeasure. This is especially obvious in voting patterns. Although Japanese voters make their decisions for various and sometimes complex reasons, there is no doubt that they are very aware of the relative importance of political institutions in the system, the way those institutions work, and the effect of their vote on those institutions.

But, one can still ask, if the public distrusts politicians and feels relatively unempowered, why does it support the state? One of the main factors in creating support for the state in prewar years was coercion. Those who criticized the state or took other actions against it were jailed or harassed by the state. Coercion is of little significance today in maintaining compliance with the state. While the government will sometimes ask the press to voluntarily curb its reporting, such as in asking for a moratorium on reporting about the crown prince's hunt for a bride, the press has as much freedom as the press in the United States, and perhaps more than in Great Britain. Similarly, freedom of speech is highly respected in Japan, and a wide range of views in opposition to the government, from the far left to the far right, can be heard and read every day.

In other countries, tradition can also be a major reason why people support their state. To take Great Britain as an example, one can say that some political institutions such as Parliament have existed for so long that they have become a symbol of identification for the British people. In Japan, however, tradition plays a relatively minor role. With the exception of the emperor, Japanese political institutions are relatively young and have not been created through domestic social movements. Thus, there is no strong tradition of identification.

Neither is support for the state ideological, although there is support for the values of democratic capitalism. Both Marxism and, more successfully, democratic capitalism have taken root in Japan, but have not produced the same flowers as bloom in the West. Marxism has not been a truly popular ideology because of the lack of class consciousness and the success of democratic capitalism. Japanese believe their society to be egalitarian and do not perceive the existence of class conflict. What class polarization that does exist tends to be an elite phenomenon and not a mass phenomenon.

Democracy has succeeded, not because there is a spiritual and intellectual commitment to it, but because it works. This may sound cynical to an idealist, but it makes sense in the pragmatic, relativistic Japanese political culture. "To grasp the essence of a political culture that does not recognize the possibility of transcendental truths demands an unusual intellectual effort for Westerners, an effort that is rarely made even in serious assessments of Japan."[34] We cannot know the extent to which Japanese have committed themselves to democratic values because they have never been fully challenged in the postwar era. But it does appear that democratic political culture is taking root in Japan. Almost three-quarters of the respondents in the 1983 Japan Election Survey said they were proud of democracy in Japan.[35] Interest in politics has risen substantially over the past twenty years and is higher in Japan than in most other industrialized democracies. Similarly, voter turnout rates, discussing politics, joining grassroots political organizations, signing petitions, and other forms of conventional participation in Japan are roughly the same as in other developed democratic countries.

The most fundamental reason why Japanese support their political system is its success in putting out rewards for that support. It gives them what they want. As we have seen, Japanese believe that the role of the state is a paternalistic one—to take care of them—and they expect favorable outputs from government officials. The expectation of favorable outputs from the system has become especially strong in recent years as the rewards of economic growth became more apparent. Support for the system is also related to the perennial rule of the leading governmental institution, the Liberal Democratic Party. Although the LDP is the conservative party, they maintained an extensive social welfare system and have guided Japan's economy through what is arguably the biggest peacetime boom in modern world history, a boom that has brought both evenly distributed material gains and a level of international prestige superior to that of any other era of Japanese history. There are individuals and groups in Japan who believe their needs are not being served and who do not support the system, but on the whole most are content with the system, government policies, and government outputs. Even at the beginning of Japan's present boom:

Most political observers would grant that a very large share of the present government's hold on political power in Japan is attributable to the popular credit and support it has acquired as the self-proclaimed creator and sustainer of a boom economy. . . . The people now look to government as a normal means of producing or ensuring a vast variety of goods and services ranging from peace and order through transportation and communications to a broad range of welfare and social security measures, as well as serving as a planning and regulatory mechanism for the maintenance of general and increasing economic prosperity throughout the society. . . . The Japanese view of their political system has in this sense become output oriented.[36]

The PKO Bill

The twenty-month process of passing the PKO bill into law, and the ensuing deployment of forces to Cambodia, is a good example of many of the points made above concerning the problems of state-oriented nationalism and the dim prospects for future Japanese militarism. When the PKO debate first began, it was feared by many at home and abroad that the passage of the bill and an actual deployment of forces abroad would herald the end of Japan's international pacifism and increase the military's prestige and policy-making power at home. Now that SDF peacekeeping duties in Cambodia have finished, the results have belied the original negative expectations. Japanese SDF and police forces have done their job well, with little fuss or bother, and the power and status of the military at home has not changed from what it was before the deployment. Indeed, the exercise has simply demonstrated that Japan is capable of acting as a responsible member of the United Nations.

The history of the PKO bill began on August 29, 1990, twenty-seven days after the invasion of Kuwait by Iraq, when then Prime Minister Toshiki Kaifu announced the first-aid package for the multinational forces in the Gulf. At the same time he also proposed an idea for allowing Japan to work with United Nations peacekeeping forces without sending SDF forces abroad. The role of the SDF in any Japanese contingent sent to the Gulf was the prime area of discussion because it would have been the first time SDF personnel had been deployed outside Japan, setting a precedent for the future. In addition, the discussion of the use of SDF personnel abroad reopened the whole question of Article 9 of the constitution, a discussion that had been fairly dormant.

Kaifu was leery of including SDF personnel in a Japanese peacekeeping contingent, but one of his main advisers, Ichiro Ozawa, felt that the inclusion of SDF personnel was absolutely necessary. Ozawa was a young but rapidly rising member of the LDP inner circle who had already attained the position of secretary general of the party. Ozawa was also one of the leaders of the party's strongest factions, the Takeshita faction. Kaifu was not a member of the Takeshita faction, but needed its support in order to remain party president and therefore prime minister. Ozawa used his position to convince Kaifu to include the use of the SDF for support activities for the multinational force being assembled under the auspices of the United Nations Security Council.

There was an immediate national reaction against the proposed legislation as soon as it was introduced in the Diet on October 16, 1990. Popular demonstrations organized by opposition parties sprang up around the country, and the SDPJ immediately tried to put together a coalition of all opposition parties against the bill. A poll of registered voters taken at the time by the Kyodo News Service found that half the public opposed the bill and only 13 percent favored it. The poll also found that two-thirds of the electorate opposed any dispatch of SDF personnel abroad, while only 13 percent favored it.[37] Facing an unsure reaction, if not outright opposition, from the voters, unified opposition within the legislature, and a rapidly ending legislative session, the LDP was forced to rethink the bill and went into caucus in early November.

The fight then raged again within the LDP over the inclusion of the SDF in any Japanese force, with another heavyweight from the Takeshita faction, Shin Kanemaru, supporting a non-SDF force. It was obvious from the factional struggle over the inclusion of the SDF in the proposed Japanese contingent and the solid opposition from the other parties that the LDP had little chance of passing the bill. Consequently it beat a strategic withdrawal by abandoning the bill in the form first presented, simultaneously promising that a multiparty study group would be convened to write an alternative bill. Shortly thereafter the LDP and the two centrist parties, the Komeito (KMT) and the Democratic Socialist Party (DSP), agreed in principle on a plan that would send non-SDF personnel as a support group for the United Nations peacekeeping forces in the Gulf.

As the Japanese government and the opposition parties continued to discuss an appropriate response to the Gulf crisis, events in the Gulf proceeded apace. Although the LDP had signed a memorandum with the KMT and the DSP calling for a non-SDF contingent, Ozawa and other members of the LDP were still fighting for the inclusion of the SDF in any Japanese deployment. On the evening of January 16, 1991, the very eve of hostilities, Kaifu and his inner circle of advisers were meeting to determine what Japan's response should be when the war began. The Foreign Ministry had written a working paper calling for Japanese support to consist of (1) providing airplanes from Japanese commercial airlines to ferry refugees, (2) the dispatch of volunteer medical teams, (3) sending the Japan Disaster Relief Team to help with the cleanup after the war, and (4) financial support.[38] This formed the main body of Japanese policy when the war in the Gulf began, but with one major difference. In the final instance, Kaifu was prodded by Ozawa to announce that SDF planes might also be used in the evacuation of refugees if commercial aircraft could not be found.

The opposition parties remained adamant against the use of any SDF personnel, and again the LDP was forced to back down on its use of SDF aircraft. Kioshiro Ishida, chairman of the KMT, announced that he would support a $9 billion contribution for the Gulf forces, but that his support would be contingent upon not using SDF planes for evacuation. It was also agreed secretly between Ozawa, Kanemaru, and the secretary general and vice chairman of the KMT that the KMT's support would also be contingent upon a reduction of appropriations for the SDF.[39]

By the time the war ended Japan was no closer to resolving the debate over what its response should be than it was when the crisis first began. However, Prime Minister Kaifu did take a major step in sending SDF personnel abroad for the first time by sending SDF minesweepers into the Gulf to help clean up after the hostilities had ended. But the PKO bill was still nowhere near completion. LDP decision makers created a package that would include the SDF participation, but be as vague as possible, in an attempt to placate the factions within the LDP and the centrist parties whose support was essential. The LDP resubmitted a PKO bill in late September 1991 that maintained the provision that SDF personnel could be used abroad in a peacekeeping contingent, but the bill left many questions unanswered. The bill did have the support of the centrist parties because, although it allowed SDF participation, it did not allow the SDF to participate in combat. The debate over the bill centered upon its constitutionality, the conditions under which SDF personnel could fire their weapons,

whether the SDF contingent would be able to withdraw from the peacekeeping force once a cease-fire was broken, and whether the Diet would have to approve the dispatch and use of SDF personnel. After lengthy debate, the bill was eventually railroaded by the LDP and the KMT through the Ad Hoc Committee and the lower house.

The battle in the upper house loomed as a greater challenge because the LDP lacked a majority there. While it worked in cooperation with the LDP to pass the bill in the lower house, the KMT began to get cold feet when it came to passage in the upper house, because it had been somewhat tarred with the bully's brush when it acted in concert with the LDP to force passage in the lower house. This worried the LDP as it needed the support of the DSP and the KMT in the upper house in order to insure passage and to present a picture of consensus to the Japanese public. Consequently the two centrist parties were able to get the LDP to modify the bill. In agreeing to pass a PKO bill which, in theory, would allow for the dispatch of SDF troops overseas, and which included the United Nations command over SDF peacekeeping forces, they were able to get guarantees that (1) the use of SDF personnel in peacekeeping forces and in nonmilitary operations connected to military operations would be frozen for the time being, (2) the Diet would have to give prior approval every time the SDF was sent on a peacekeeping mission, and (3) the bill would be reviewed by a multiparty body after three years.

These modifications meant that the bill had to be reintroduced into the lower house for a third time. Ever since the original deliberation in the fall of 1990, the SDPJ and the Communist Party had been in total opposition, but as the LDP-KMT-DSP negotiations continued, they had been left on the sidelines. Now that things were coming to a head and the three parties had a final draft of the bill on which they could agree, the SDPJ was backed into a corner and was forced to resort to its traditional stalling tactics. In both the upper and lower house it boycotted sessions and did all it could to disrupt and delay voting, but at last, on June 15, 1992, the PKO bill became law.

Now that, under law, Japan has the ability to send its forces abroad as part of a United Nations peacekeeping contingent, it may seem to some that the lid is being lifted off Pandora's box, but that is not the case. First, the bill is very limited. The prime minister may order Japanese personnel to participate in the following peacekeeping operations without the approval of the Diet: transportation, communication and construction; international humanitarian relief activities; supervision of elections and referendums; and advising on administrative and policing activities. The prime minister may also order the use of SDF aircraft and ships to transport goods and refugees. That, however, is the extent to which the prime minister may act without the direct and express approval of the legislature. The prime minister must receive the approval of the Diet each time he sends SDF personnel to monitor cease-fire compliance, supervise the disarming,

redeployment, or withdrawal of troops, patrol buffer zones, supervise weapons movements, collect and dispose of weapons, demarcate cease-fire lines, and assist in exchanging prisoners of war. The SDF peacekeeping contingent is further restricted by a limit of two thousand members and in the use of its arms. Individual members of the SDF peacekeeping contingent can use only small arms and only in order to protect themselves and other members of the peacekeeping force. Any peacekeeping force operation can last for only two years before it again needs to be approved by the Diet. Finally, all of the above was academic at the point of its passing, as the heart of the compromise between the LDP and the centrist parties called for a freeze on all peacekeeping operations until separate legislation ended the freeze. This means that even though the bill was passed, SDF members could still not participate in peacekeeping operations until the legislature voted once again to end the freeze.

These severe restrictions on the use of SDF personnel in United Nations peacekeeping operations is more an indication of the military's lack of power in the Japanese political system than an indication of its strength. It demonstrates that conservatives in the LDP did not have the ability to push through the legislature a bill that would give the SDF significant powers to act abroad. It was unable to do so because the LDP itself was not unified on the policy, and because both the opposition parties and public opinion were able to keep the LDP pushing the legislation through. For one to argue that the PKO bill is a harbinger of a new militarism in Japan, one would also have to argue that the government will now have the power to push approval of the use of PKO forces through the legislature anytime it wants. That is not the case now, nor will it be the case in the future. Rather than free the SDF to participate in United Nations peacekeeping operations, the PKO bill has tied up its participation in a very tight knot which can only be untied after long and hard public debate and scrutiny in the Diet.

Even if SDF personnel are sent on peacekeeping operations, it seems impossible that the SDF will have the will or the ability to use their participation as a means of furthering Japanese interests abroad. Certainly many members of the SDF, both officers and enlisted personnel, have many doubts about their role in any peacekeeping mission. There was, at the time of this writing, no policy on compensation for those killed, wounded, or missing in action during peacekeeping operations, nor was there any policy on behavior when taken as a prisoner of war. Members of the SDF are uncomfortable with the controversial nature of their participation and are unclear as to what they are supposed to do if they find themselves in a combat situation. The bill says that they may use their weapons to defend themselves but that use must "be within a rational limit dictated by the circumstances." The meaning of this phrase is not entirely clear. If weapons are used, will each case be reviewed, and if so by whom? What are the liabilities a soldier faces if it is found that he violated this principle?

As was stated above, the use of Japanese SDF and police personnel in United Nations peacekeeping missions continues. On September 9, 1992, two years after the invasion of Iraq, the cabinet ordered SDF troops on their first peacekeeping missions. Eight officers were sent to Cambodia as cease-fire monitors, and six hundred troops were sent to repair Cambodian roads and bridges. That first contingent was replaced in April 1993, and the mission ended in September. A separate deployment of fifty SDF personnel was sent to Mozambique in May 1993, and that mission was extended to September 1994.

The Japanese public had settled down into acceptance of SDF forces as United Nations peacekeepers, but continued unrest in Cambodia has re-opened the national debate over sending Japanese personnel overseas on United Nations missions. Specifically, the Khmer Rouge faction has not agreed to the United Nations-sponsored vote scheduled for May 1993 and has been attacking United Nations peacekeeping forces. In April a Japanese United Nations volunteer (no connection to the SDF forces) was shot to death, and in early May one Japanese policeman was killed and three others wounded. The civilian volunteer was apparently not killed by the Khmer Rouge, but the police were attacked by the radical faction. The real question raised by the increased violence in Cambodia is whether Japan is willing to accept risks to its personnel that are stationed overseas. This question can only be answered by placing it in the larger context of what Japan perceives its role to be in the international relations system.

NOTES

1. See, for example, Kent Calder, *Crisis and Compensation*; William R. Nester, *The Foundation of Japanese Power*; Ishida and Krauss, eds., *Democracy in Japan*, all in the Bibliography below.

2. Chalmers Johnson, *MITI and the Japanese Miracle* (Stanford: Stanford University Press, 1982).

3. Michio Muramatsu and Ellis S. Krauss, "Bureaucrats and Politicians in Policymaking: The Case of Japan," *American Political Science Review* 78 (March 1984).

4. Gerald L. Curtis, *The Japanese Way of Politics* (New York: Columbia University Press, 1988), 39.

5. *Japan Times*, August 18, 1992, p. 3.

6. Masayuki Takagi, "The Japanese Right Wing," *Japan Quarterly* 36 (July–September 1989), 301.

7. David E. Kaplan and Alec Dubro, *Yakuza* (Reading, Mass.: Addison-Wesley, 1986).

8. Ronald Dore, "The Ethics of the New Japan," *Pacific Affairs* (June 1952), 148–49.

9. *Japan Times*, July 1, 1991, p. 2.

10. *Japan Times*, April 30, 1993, p. 3.

11. *Japan Times*, June 4, 1992, p. 3.

12. *U.S. News and World Report*, December 24, 1990, pp. 56–57.

13. Herman Kahn, *The Emerging Japanese Superstate* (Englewood Cliffs, N.J.: Prentice Hall, 1970), 165–68.

14. Prime Minister's Office, *Public Opinion Survey on the Self-Defense Forces and Defense Problems* (Tokyo, June 1988), 3.

15. Ibid., 6.

16. Ibid., 8.

17. *New York Times*, March 6, 1989, p. 6.

18. *Japan Times*, December 10, 1991, p. 20.

19. *Japan Times*, January 21, 1992, p. 4.

20. *Japan Times*, March 3, 1992, p. 2.

21. Lawrence W. Beer, "Law and Liberty," in Takeshi Ishida and Ellis S. Krauss, eds., *Democracy in Japan* (Pittsburgh: University of Pittsburgh Press, 1989), 85–86.

22. Prime Minister's Office, *Public Opinion Survey on Society and State* (Tokyo, June 1991), 1, 3.

23. Prime Minister's Office, *Public Opinion Survey on the Life of the Nation* (Tokyo, December 1989), 5, 12.

24. Prime Minister's Office, *Public Opinion Survey on the Self-Defense Forces and Defense Problems* (Tokyo, July 1991), 11.

25. Prime Minister's Office, June 1991, 5–6.

26. Ibid., 7, 9.

27. Prime Minister's Office, *Public Opinion Survey on the Self-Defense Forces and Defense Problems* (Tokyo, June 1988), 9.

28. *Japan Times*, June 13, 1991, p. 2.

29. Bradley Richardson and Scott C. Flanagan, *Politics in Japan* (Boston: Little Brown, 1984), 240–42.

30. Curtis Martin and Bruce Stronach, *Politics East and West: A Comparison of Japanese and British Political Culture* (New York: M. E. Sharpe,1992), 61–62.

31. See Richardson and Flanagan, *Politics in Japan*, chapter 6, and Martin and Stronach, *Politics East and West*, chapters 3–5.

32. Davis B. Bobrow, "Japan in the World," *Journal of Conflict Resolution* 33 (December 1989), 572.

33. Joji Watanuki et al., *Electoral Behavior in the 1983 Japanese Elections* (Tokyo: Sophia University Institute for International Relations, 1986), 127, 210.

34. Karel van Wolferen, *The Enigma of Japanese Power* (New York: Vintage Books,1990), 10.

35. Watanuki et al., *Electoral Behavior*, 210.

36. Robert Ward, "Japan: The Continuity of Modernization," in *Political Culture and Political Development*, ed. Lucian Pye and Sidney Verba (Princeton, N.J.: Princeton University Press, 1965), 64.

37. *Japan Times*, November 1, 1990, p. 1.

38. Akira Azabu, "Echoes from the Gulf in Japanese Politics," *Japan Echo* (Summer 1991), 35.

39. Ibid., 39.

5

Japan's Role in the World

The previous chapters have dealt primarily with the effects of nationalism within Japan, but Japanese nationalism is also an important factor in determining Japan's role in the world community. The problem faced by Japan today is not only that of understanding its own nationalism, but also understanding how that nationalism affects its role as an international economic and political power. This is no easy question. Japan's postwar economic success has made its linkages to the postwar international trade and finance system most obvious, but less obvious is that its success has also been dependent upon its place in the international political system. Even though Japan has a well-defined image of its place in the international trade and finance system, it has yet to come to grips with its role in the international political system.

Many of Japan's problems in determining its national identity are related to the way it perceives itself in a global context. During the Cold War it was easy enough to define Japan's role in the world as that of a secondary member of the Western bloc. But if Japan wants to be an international leader in the post–Cold War world, it must redefine its role and expand its perception of itself from that of secondary power in the Western bloc to a primary power in Asia and the world. This is easier said than done. The first problem it must confront is to determine what role it wants to play in the world's affairs and, as a corollary, its ability to make foreign policy decisions.

Traditionally, Japan's foreign policy has been isolationist, pragmatic, and opportunistic, and has had the tendency to follow the lead of a more powerful state. Particularly in the postwar period, its position as a secondary state on the political front allowed its foreign policy to be inward-directed in refraining from political involvement and allowed it to become involved only at those times when it was absolutely necessary, usually in such a way as to benefit its national interest above all other considerations. But it can no longer indulge in self-interested isolationism. Its economic success, and the demand for resources and markets upon which that success has been based, have made it interdependent with the rest of the world. The protector and benefactor that it has followed, the United States, is now calling on Japan to share political as well as economic burdens and responsibilities. The rest of the world expects Japan to step forward to accept both. The easy choices of the past are no longer available, and the time for a decision is fast approaching.

The conundrum Japan faces is this: it has attained great economic power by allowing the United States to lead politically and guarantee its security, thus freeing Japan to gain the advantages of trade without political conflict. Its foreign policy has been to separate trade from politics and maintain a low political profile (within the parameters set by loyalty to the United States and the most fundamental policies of the Western bloc) while concentrating on trade. The economic success of this policy has, however, brought pressures to bear on Japan to accept the very political leadership it has shunned because it can be disruptive to universal trade relations. It has been decades since Japan has staked out strong political positions in international politics, other than those necessary to maintain its alliance relationship with the United States, because it has feared such actions would have an impact on trade. It has even been willing to incur the wrath of the United States, if it believed that securing Japan's economic self-interest necessitated deviating from the American policy line. This was the case in 1973 when oil-producing Arab states slapped a partial oil embargo on Japan during the Yom Kippur War. The Japanese government successfully ended the embargo by officially endorsing the Palestinian cause and calling on Israel to withdraw to the pre-1967 border. This brought one of the sternest reprimands from the United States in postwar relations, but to no avail. Japan's need for Middle Eastern oil remains the dominant factor in Japanese-Israeli relations.

Maintaining a low political profile benefited Japan by aiding its accumulation of economic power, but there has also been a cost. Japan's policy of taking a back seat on political issues has also reinforced its image as less than a great power in the fullest sense of the term. Thus Japan has had a subordinate position in the international power hierarchy position vis-à-vis other, less economically powerful states. But as economic power becomes a more important element by which a state's comprehensive power status is defined, and as Japan's economic power increases, both its own population and other states expect increased Japanese political leadership—leadership commensurate with its economic and potential overall power. If one accepts the argument that Japan has been able to accumulate economic power by keeping a low profile, then the increased political activity of Japan may be detrimental to the further accumulation of economic power or perhaps even its maintenance. If Japan continues its low political profile, it may face the wrath of its citizens and other states, but taking greater political initiatives is counter to the very policies that were instrumental to its accumulating economic power.

The second problem that confronts Japan has to do with the way in which its nationalism is perceived by others. The extent to which Japan will be allowed to lead is related to the acceptance of Japanese nationalism by other states. This is especially true in Asia but may also have some importance in its relations with non-Asian states such as Great Britain and Russia. The Tokyo war crime trials may have given Japanese individuals specific sentences as punishment for their behavior but, other than the occupation itself, there was no sentence for Japan as a nation. Two questions remain: how long will Japan continue to be less than trusted, and what does it have to do to regain the trust of the world?

Japanese leadership is a manifestation of increased Japanese sociocultural nationalism in that it is an expression of increased pride and confidence, and if Japanese leadership is accepted, so must Japanese nationalism be accepted. Contemporary Japanese nationalism is substantially different from prewar nationalism: it is benign and sociocultural rather than state-oriented. However, the only way to convince others of the benign nature of contemporary Japanese nationalism is if Japanese themselves accept their immediate history and its ramifications. According to Barry Buzan, such a revision of history as it is known in Japan would have to meet three criteria. It would have to be true, acceptable abroad, and acceptable in Japan.[1] Only when Japan comes to terms with its past and accepts responsibility for it, will its leadership and nationalism be considered legitimate.

The third problem Japan must face is less a question of foreign policy but has more to do with the way in which the international relations system is organized and the way in which Japan perceives itself to fit into that organization. During the Cold War it was easy for Japan to accept the role of secondary power in the Western bloc because that role was thrust upon it by the United States. In addition, the organization of the international relations system gave it few options. American policy during the occupation was intended to insure that Japan remained a member of the Western bloc long after a peace treaty had been signed. Even if the United States had not molded it for that role, it is doubtful whether Japan would have chosen to join either the Eastern bloc or the non-aligned movement.

The breakdown of the Cold War international relations system has not only changed the Japanese-American relationship specifically but has also destroyed the order that was imposed by the Eastern and Western blocs. The world that Japan faces today has a much more complex set of possibilities and those outside powers that are attempting to force it in one direction or another are much weaker. The very concept of what comprises international power may be changing to include economic power as a much more important component, and as the concept of power changes, so does the hierarchy of states ranked by power. Equally important is the simultaneous drift toward both greater interdependence and nationalism. The breakdown of the old system has allowed previously integrated units such as North America, the European Community (EC), and the Association of South East Asian Nations (ASEAN) states to expend more of their resources and energies on greater integration, while other states, most notably those in the Eastern bloc, have reverted to old habits of irredentist nationalism.

Japan was brought into the Western international relations system after that system had matured. It was a system that relied on the concepts of national sovereignty, national security, and the de jure recognition of the equality of states. While much of the system remains intact, bloc formation during the Cold War and advances in transportation, communication, and weapons technologies have mortally wounded it. The decision as to what role Japan will play in the world will depend upon how the international system evolves and the extent to which Japan sees its own interest lying in a self-centered, or state-centric, vision of the world, or the extent to which it sees its interest being served by aiding the system as a whole.

JAPAN AS AN INTERNATIONAL LEADER

There is a frictional dichotomy in Japan's posture toward the international relations system. On the one hand, export-driven economic growth has created a high level of interdependence between Japan and the other trading states of the world which, in turn, has increased expectations at home and abroad that Japan will become a more active, high-profile player in the international arena. On the other hand, Japan's postwar success is in large part due to a foreign policy that has eschewed leadership, choosing instead to follow the lead of the United States while pursuing a low-profile but determined concern for economic self-interest.

The calls for the internationalization of Japan and its foreign policy have been ubiquitous. As a case in point, an EC report issued for their April 1993 foreign ministers' meeting took Japan to task for not demonstrating enough leadership, and called upon the EC and the United States to work together to "guarantee" that Japan play a role commensurate with the strength of its economy.[2] Japan's success in the international trading system has created pressures from abroad to become a true partner in the international economic, political, and social systems. Simultaneously, the government is pressured by its public to take what can be seen as its rightful position among the leading states of the world. But the increased expectation of Japanese leadership has been met with an increased concern as to whether Japan has the willingness and/or the capability to become a leading state.

Japan's lack of initiative and action during the Gulf crisis and the consequent war were a focus for these concerns, but it was only one of a series of events that have engendered concerns about Japanese leadership. The expectation of Japanese world leadership, for better or for worse, has existed ever since Japan began to flex her economic muscles in the late 1960s. But no matter how strong Japan's economy, as long as the international relations system was based on Cold War alignments, it could easily avoid taking any real action by pledging its support for the cause and following the U.S. lead like a good ally. Japanese leadership was always perceived as having future potential.

Part of Japan's problem is that the future is here, but in all of those years of speaking of future leadership, there does not seem to have been much coordinated policy making to prepare for the reality it now faces. The post–Cold War situation has cast the spotlight on Japan, a position in which it does not seem comfortable. Ideological conflict during the Cold War gave the appearance that the problems of the world were very focused. They were all in some way related to that conflict. Now that that focusing element has been removed, all the other problems previously there, such as the environment and migration, as well as others that have been exacerbated by the end of the Cold War, such as disintegration and nationalism, appear to be chaotic and unmanageable. In addition, the Cold War also sapped the U.S.'s economic strength and reduced its ability to spend its resources in order to help solve world problems. In these circumstances, the United States and many other countries in the world have turned to Japan for help. Japan's role in the post–Cold War world has been the subject of numerous books and papers and hundreds of conferences, but ultimately its response has been cautious.

Prime Minister Miyazawa's policy speech given at the opening of the 126th session of the Diet in January 1993 is indicative of the type of response given by the Japanese government concerning its role in the international community.

The Cold War between the East and West is over, and the tide of history has turned toward peace. Just as this situation has raised grave issues of how best to structure a new order for peace in the international community, it has also brought about major changes in the circumstances affecting Japanese foreign policy and Japan's own position within the international community. Japanese behavior today has come to have a major impact on the international community as a whole, and it is imperative that we assume a positive role and responsibilities for the establishment of this new order for peace, commensurate with our enhanced standing. . . .

These changes in the international environment and popular awareness demand changes in the entire socio-economic system created since the war, and it is politics that must take the lead in this effort.[3]

While the intention of such words is sincere, they have not always been followed by practical actions. The concern that Japan's words speak louder than its actions is exacerbated by people like Osamu Shimomura. He has stated that it may be necessary for Japan to write reports promising an internationalization that will never happen simply in order to present a "good face" to the rest of the world.[4]

Progress is beginning to be made in some areas. Japan is trying to exert some political leadership. It was the first state to present to the Soviet Union a comprehensive plan for economic restructuring. It has stepped in to guide Mongolia through its transition from dependence on the Soviet economy. It has increased its bilateral Overseas Direct Assistance (ODAs) and its payments to multilateral aid organizations. It is trying to play the honest broker between post–Tiananmen Square China and the West. It has played an important role in getting talks started between North Korea and South Korea. Its role in the Cambodian talks was praised by the French as being one of the factors in bringing about a peace treaty among the warring factions. But these efforts are limited to the Asia-Pacific region; Japan's actions as an international leader outside that region have been more limited.

Japan is under increasing pressure to demonstrate to the rest of the world and to its own citizens whether it is willing to lead and, if it is, what kind of leadership it will undertake in a post–Cold War, multipolar world. That does not mean that Japan must accept leadership. There is no law of morals, nature, politics, or even economics that commands Japan to accept a greater role in the international political system. Many would argue that Japan has done very well in the postwar years by following the lead of the United States, maintaining a low profile, and waiting to see which way the wind blows on major issues. This is a point upon which there is great ambivalence in Japan. If looked at rationally, it would certainly appear to be in Japan's best interest not to lead. It has prospered greatly under the protection of the United States, and, should the status quo be maintained, there is no compelling reason to leave the eagle's nest. But if Japan is pushed out of the nest, is it possible to adopt a foreign policy that reacts to international events in such a way as to look to its own interests without taking political initiatives?

This course of action would be feasible but difficult and might be counterproductive. Without an ability to guide events, Japan might find itself trapped by circumstances. Beyond the problems of policy "drift," there is also the antagonism that other states might feel toward Japan for pursuing its own national interests without regard for the interests of other states and the system in general. In addition, there is the irrational but very real desire to become a leader for pride's sake alone. Japan's national goal since the Meiji period has been to become a world power, and now that international leadership is available to it, it is too tempting a prize for either the public or the leadership elite to disregard.

Whether or not Japan decides to lead, the important point is that Japan must make its intentions clear to itself and the outside world. Japanese leaders keep giving speeches similar to that quoted above, and yet continued hesitancy to take concrete actions gives the impression that the decision to this point has been to avoid a decision. Although the Japanese public states in surveys that Japan should have a greater role in the world, there is anxiety that an increased political profile will disturb the peace, security, and affluence that Japan has attained. Whatever its economic power, Japan will be relegated to the backbench of the international political debate if it does not stake out a clear position in it. If other states continue to look toward Japan in the expectation that leadership will be forthcoming and none appears, then those states will be reluctant to accept Japanese leadership when, and if, Japan wants to lead. There is an increasing irritation in Japan over the way in which American and European policy makers consult each other, to the exclusion of Japanese policymakers, when taking policy initiatives that will have important international ramifications. This was especially obvious in the case of the Gulf War (1990–1991). There was a great deal of discussion in the Japanese press about how Japan was forced into a position of supporting the war with substantial payments while not being fully involved in decision making. There was, however, very little written about Japan's inability to take the initiative in putting its policy forward at the beginning of the crisis and its waffling stance throughout its course. If Japan continues to be as indecisive on the major issues and problems facing the international relations system as it has been to this point, it cannot expect to be treated otherwise.

The ambiguity of Japan's position on its leadership role is also demonstrated by the difference between word and deed. To quote again from Prime Minister Miyazawa's speech to the Diet:

> If the GATT Uruguay Round negotiations end in discord, it could spur the rise of protectionism and have a grave impact on the global economy. Japan is thus determined to join together with the other leading countries in continuing to work for an early and successful conclusion of the negotiations.
>
> While agriculture is an area in which all countries face difficult problems, I intend to make the utmost efforts for a solution based upon mutual cooperation under our basic policy.[5]

Miyazawa's speech came just days after GATT's Trade Negotiations Committee was unable to meet a deadline for agreement on trade liberalization rules, especially in agriculture. Japan's role throughout the Uruguay Round has been either passive, in staying in the background while the United States and the EC fought it out over agricultural liberalization, or defensive, stonewalling the tariffication of rice. Even the resolution of a long-standing dispute over agricultural subsidies between the United States and the EC failed to move Japan in any similar direction until the eleventh hour. The Japanese government has said the right words, but their actions have not spoken as loudly or clearly. As long as this is the case, the acceptance and the reality of Japanese leadership will continue to be problematical.

The hesitancy of Japanese leadership to take initiatives in world politics while stating its desire for leadership also creates a great deal of frustration among its citizens. Public pride in Japan's economic development leads to an assumption that leadership should be ascribed to it simply because its economy is strong. But leadership is not ascribed; it is achieved. States that want to lead must act in such a way that other states are willing to acquiesce in their leadership. That concept is not well understood in Japan. Many Japanese feel that other states should defer to Japan simply because it has become one of the top economic powers. When other states do not meet those public expectations of deference or acquiescence, it feeds old anxieties about other states' unwillingness to accept Japan as a power (for racial or other reasons) and increases the Japanese feeling of isolation and, as a result, nationalism. Although Japanese are more confident than ever when dealing with other states and nations, traditional feelings of inferiority and sensitivity to slights still lurk beneath the surface of the society.

What Style of Leadership?

Most of the debate over Japan's role as a leading state has focused on (1) the locus of its leadership, whether it would continue to work in harness with the United States or drift away from its dependence on the bilateral relationship; and (2) the type of power on which its leadership would be developed, especially the extent to which it would have to develop more military and political strength. While these are extremely important questions, the question of how Japan leads, its style of leadership, is of primary importance.

If one assumes that Japan wants to become a leader state, it must rely upon its strengths, reform its weaknesses, and resist acting on mistaken and inappropriate models of leadership. It is doubtful that Japan will ever become a leader state if it adopts the leadership style exhibited by the United States and the Soviet Union during the Cold War because the Japanese polity is unable to fulfill its most important elements. The United States and the Soviet Union acted as scouts for their allies during the Cold War. They went ahead, cut a path for their allies to follow, and then encouraged them to follow by using both persuasion and coercion. The success of this model of leadership depended upon the elements of unilateral decision making, initiative, material power, clearly stated goals and values, will, and an ability to respond rapidly to crises.

Although collaboration with allies is an important part of leadership, the United States and the Soviet Union have used collaboration with allies as a means to sell policy already created within the leader state. The leader state makes most foreign policy decisions unilaterally and then turns to its allies, or those states it wants to influence, and pulls them into alignment by means of bilateral or multilateral negotiations. Its diplomacy is, by definition, high profile. In order to implement its policy successfully, a leader state must maintain power sufficient to coerce and cajole the follower states' acquiescence in its leadership. A history of powerful initiatives from the leader state creates a habit of reaction in its allies and other states. Follower states can be driven into policy alignment either by the promise of reward or the threat of punishment, but a leader state must also be careful to understand its allies' concerns and be willing to cajole as well as coerce. A leader state's allies love to hate a strong leader and hate to love a weak leader. That is to say, there will always be a tension within allied states between the antipathy to dependence on a stronger state and the rewards and security that such dependence brings. When the leader state is acting unilaterally as a strong policy initiator, follower states will complain that they are being excluded from the decision-making process, but will also feel more secure in the belief that the leader state is strong in carrying out its commitment as a leader. When the leader state gives up the initiative, follower states may laud the sharing of responsibility, but they may also question the strength and will of the leader state and fear the dissolution of stability.

The above assumes that the leader state has material resources sufficient to reward and punish others, but its leadership does not rest on this material basis alone. It also rests on both the ideals it presents to the rest of the world as the foundation for its actions and the willingness of the polity to be involved in the international system as well as to pay the price for that involvement. It would be foolish to argue that any leader state in any period of world history acted from totally altruistic motives, but in fact leader states present global or regional ideals that act as a guide for others to follow. In the case of the United States and the Soviet Union, it was the safeguarding of an ideology; for lesser leaders, like France under General de Gaulle, it was an integrated, and European, Europe. If a state is perceived to be acting only in its own self-interest, then other states will follow its lead only if their national interests coincide or if they are coerced.

Similarly, no state can be a leader of other states if its polity is not willing to be involved in the international relations system nor willing to suffer the sacrifices inherent in such an involvement. Leader states pay a tremendous price for their position. It is their economies that must support the burden of aiding others and supporting the system. It is their citizens who must pay higher taxes. It is their young men who must die in the conflicts that are created. Leader states, being alone and out front, become the obvious target for opponents. They must brave castigation, terrorist acts, and even the threat of war from other states, and nonstate actors, who do not agree with their policies.

The final major element of this traditional style of leadership is an ability to respond rapidly to crises. In a world of instantaneous communications, the world has come to expect instantaneous reactions. Rapid and resolute reactions to crises are necessary to maintain the initiative. If the leader state does not react, that inaction will be taken as a sign of weakness and loss of power, and an open invitation to others to assert their authority. This is especially true of policies and actions perceived to have a seriously negative effect on the policies of the leader state and/or to be openly hostile toward the leader state.

THE PROBLEMS OF LEADERSHIP

If leadership is perceived as conforming to the above model, Japan cannot possibly become a leader state. A study of eighteen cases of Japanese international negotiations covering the period 1895–1941 demonstrated, in the words of the author, that Japanese diplomacy has a "cultural proclivity to oppose rather than propose, to be passive rather than active, defensive rather than offensive, and evasive rather than forthright."[6] The extent to which these traits are cultural proclivities may be open to question, but, whatever their cause, they are elements still plainly evident in Japanese diplomacy. They are *not* the traits of a leading state. The Japanese government's response to Iraq's invasion of Kuwait, its relations with Russia, its actions in the GATT negotiations, and its nonpolicy on Bosnia, to name but a few, have all clearly demonstrated that Tokyo has not yet formulated a policy for world leadership and will act only when prodded by others, that it is unsure of its people's willingness to support a stronger leadership role, and that the Japanese polity would be hard pressed to react rapidly to any global crisis.

The most fundamental problems that Japan must overcome in order to become a leading state are to be found in the "software" of leadership. Policy-making power is shared among the government, the agencies and ministries of the bureaucracy, and the legislature. Given the factionalized nature of past LDP governments, and the fragmented nature of the present coalition, this power sharing necessitates a time consuming (and often futile) process of building a consensus, and precludes any one central figure or institution from taking the lead and setting the direction for the whole polity. If one adds the impact of public opinion and interest groups to the equation, then the probability of reaching a rapid consensus is significantly lowered. Although all democratic states must deal with the encumbrances of power sharing among policy-making institutions, the situation in Japan is significantly worsened by the emasculation of the Japanese prime minister by the factional politics within past LDP governments. The recent election of the seven-party coalition has increased the government's inability to come to a decision on foreign policy matters, especially in a crisis.

The elements of delay and confusion in the Japanese government's formulation of its decisions during the Gulf crisis and war have been described in chapter four, but that is just one of many such cases. Japanese postwar policy toward the United States, policy toward China during the 1950s and 1960s, policy toward Vietnam during the 1960s and 1970s, trade policy, and almost every major foreign policy since reindependence in 1952 have been delayed and made more complex by interparty conflict, interbureaucratic rivalries, and, worst of all, intra-LDP factional contention. The first two elements are natural and healthy components of a pluralistic political system, but the third is disabling in the extreme. Factional reform as a means of streamlining decisionmaking and increasing Japan's ability to act as a world leader has been seriously discussed in the LDP and by the society at large since at least the mid-1970s, but the party has yet to reform itself.

Early in the winter of 1993, Japan faced a situation that called for unity and a comprehensive policy that could affect its major bilateral relationship and its role in the world for years to come. Bill Clinton was moving into the White House, presenting Japan with its biggest uncertainties and challenges in its relationship with the United States for more than a decade. The old comfortable figures of the Reagan/Bush years were gone; the new people of the Clinton administration were grumbling about a $46 billion deficit with Japan in 1992 and talking openly about managed trade. At roughly the same time the Secretary General of the United Nations, Boutros Boutros-Ghali, was in Tokyo urging Japan to get more involved in the United Nations, especially in peacekeeping efforts.

Coincidentally with these two events, Prime Minister Miyazawa was saying to the Diet that he intended "to move forward with political reform as if there were no tomorrow." Although the change in administrations in Washington, the increased pressure on Japan to be involved in the United Nations, and political reform in Japan may not seem directly related, they are. Political reforms are intended to give the Japanese political system more stability and unity, especially as they are, in part, intended to reduce the power of the factions within the LDP. Stability and unity are just what the LDP needs as Japan's relations with the United States and the world are approaching a crucial period.

But as President Clinton was beginning to put together his economic policies in the White House, and Boutros-Ghali was putting the pressure on in Tokyo, the leadership of the LDP was as disunited as is possible in a parliamentary political system that is supposed to have a unified cabinet.

Hiroshi Mitsuzuka, chairman of the LDP's Policy Affairs Research Council (one of the party's two top policy-making organs) and leader of one of the party's biggest factions, proposed the creation of an interparty panel to review the amendment of the constitution as a means of legitimizing the dispatch of Japanese troops abroad on peacekeeping missions. Miyazawa announced during a state visit to Brunei that he is opposed to such a constitutional revision. Mitsuzuka promptly announced he was calling for the review panel anyway and was joined by Michio Watanabe, foreign minister at the time and leader of another major faction. (He has since resigned from the post because of ill health.) Watanabe stated publicly that he supports the arming of Japanese peacekeeping forces, an idea that has been opposed by the prime minister. He was quoted as saying that the Miyazawa government was a "three-no" government: "No you can't. No, we won't. No, we don't want to."[7] However, Miyazawa and Watanabe do agree that the tariffication of rice under GATT is inevitable, while Mitsuzuka has promised that foreign rice will never be imported into Japan. As if this were not enough, it was actually overshadowed by the conflict between the LDP and opposition parties, and among LDP factions, over the testimony given by past prime minister Takeshita and past LDP secretary general Ozawa concerning their roles in the Sagawa scandal and their connections with ultranationalist organizations.

Nothing changed after the coalition took power. Hosokawa met President Clinton in Washington in February 1994 to discuss ongoing trade issues immediately after the conflict within the coalition and between it and the LDP over political reform and taxation. In such circumstances Hosokawa was perceived as a weak prime minister with little hope of being in power for long, representing a political system that had little to offer in a unified policy. As a result, there was no progress in the trade negotiations.

Such intraparty and intracoalition factional wrangling is entertaining to devotees of political intrigue, and can add a little interest and humor to otherwise staid proceedings, but it is a fatal weakness. It weakens the prime minister. He (there has never been a female prime minister) often is dependent upon a coalition of factions to remain in power, thus he is rarely able to speak for himself when treating with foreign leaders and is usually not around for a long time. The average tenure of Japanese prime ministers is about one-half of their British counterparts. When the policy conflicts that go on between the faction leaders surface, neither the Japanese public nor foreign observers know what is government policy. In the above LDP case, the chairman of the Policy Affairs Research Council made an announcement that was contradicted by the prime minister but supported by the foreign minister. At other times the prime minister has contradicted himself, according to the ebb and flow of factional pressures. Finally, creating a consensus within the government adds a tremendous amount of time to the already time-consuming process of building interparty and interbureaucratic consensus.

There is also the problem of individual leadership styles. Japanese leaders tend to come into power through developing a consensus among other leaders. In the past, the person chosen to lead the LDP may not have been the most powerful person within the party, but someone who belonged to a faction that was so politically weak it was not a challenge to other factions. That has been the case for Prime Ministers Takeo Miki (1974), Sosuke Uno, Kaifu (1989), and Miyazawa (1991). Not only were they dependent on others for their power and vulnerable to quick dismissal, but they were also more adept at chameleon-like political maneuvering than at initiating new policies. This is most clearly seen in the Kaifu and Miyazawa governments. Both prime ministers were beholden to the Takeshita faction for their selection as president of the LDP and as prime minister. Yet the faction itself was going through a long period of internecine struggle that began when Takeshita took control of the faction following the incapacitation of the past prime minister and faction head, Kakuei Tanaka. Neither politician was free to deal with either domestic or foreign policy initiatives because there was struggle and disunity within the party and even within the faction.

Interpersonal relationships between individual leaders is one important factor in a state's relations with other states, and there are few cases where Japan has had a leader who developed a warm personal relationship with another leader. Most of the other leaders they deal with, especially among the Group of Seven (G-7) countries, have risen to power as individual politicians that have attained their office either through some combination of personal charisma and policy initiatives. If they are not in better control of their parties than is the Japanese prime minister, at least their parties, and party factions, have less control over them and their actions. These differences in background make it more difficult for Japanese prime ministers to put forth Japan's point of view forcefully when meeting with the leaders of other states and also increase the probability of personality differences.

Even if policy making could be streamlined, it is unlikely that the people of Japan would be willing to undergo the sacrifices necessitated by a traditional model of leadership. Although one hears many private citizens and public figures in Japan demanding greater respect for Japan as a world leader and more chances to play a leadership role, few are willing to pay the accompanying price. Japan would have to develop an ability to project its military overseas, but the polity is still not willing to give up its pacifist status under the constitution. Young Japanese men are neither willing to volunteer for the military nor to be drafted into service. Defense costs would soar, but Japanese taxpayers are not willing to increase their tax burden significantly to pay for increased military spending. Neither are Japanese diplomatic and political leaders willing to make the sacrifices demanded of high-profile leadership. They lack confidence when aggressively pursuing policy initiatives in discussions with their Western counterparts. Neither the Japanese people nor members of the Japanese political and diplomatic elite would be willing to stand up against the pressures that opposing states would bring to bear against their policy initiatives. The Japanese are a very conservative people in that they resist change when the status quo is at least tenable. And now that, for the first time in its history, most Japanese people are affluent and materially comfortable, few want to take any action that might upset the status quo.

The situation in Cambodia in May 1993, just weeks before the elections Japanese personnel were supposed to monitor, presented just such a challenge to the Japanese people and their government. As was noted before, one Japanese policeman on duty with the United Nations peacekeeping forces was killed and four others wounded in a Khmer Rouge ambush, and one volunteer was also killed. The events brought home to Japanese the price a nation pays for taking an active role in world leadership. The initial reaction of the government was mixed. Immediately following the Khmer Rouge ambush, the government ordered the recall of all Japanese police to Phnom Penh in order to insure their safety. However, The United Nations Transitional Authority in Cambodia (UNTAC) rejected the request, saying that it could not allow Japan alone to withdraw its police monitors. At the same time the Japanese cabinet voted not to withdraw its peacekeepers from Cambodia, but it was also reported that the SDF had secretly started planning for a withdrawal of all Japanese forces.[8]

Japan's most apparent leadership potential exists in its material ability to influence others, but even that potential strength is more apparent than real. The preeminence of economic over political and military power has often been cited as one of the changes of the post–Cold War international relations system, and the increased expectations of Japanese leadership are directly related to its ability to transform economic power into political power. But, as Joseph S. Nye, Jr. has written, "power is becoming less transferable, less tangible, and less coercive."[9] This may be true for power in general, but it is especially true of economic power because the very process of accumulating economic power makes the state dependent upon other states. The problem not just for Japan but for any country in today's world is that economic strength can only be gained through interdependent relations. All economic superpowers are dependent upon the world economy. If any one state uses its economic power too coercively, it is vulnerable to retaliation by any number of other economic powers, either singly or in combination. It is, in essence, a kind of deterrence theory of economic relations. Boycotts, embargoes, and trade wars are the same type of mutually destructive tools as nuclear weapons. Their unlimited use would destroy the world's economy in the same way that the unlimited use of nuclear weapons would destroy the physical world. Japan, the United

States, and the EC all use brinksmanship in their economic negotiations, but none ever take actions so drastic that the international trade and finance system is totally destroyed. They all realize that their postwar economic growth has been dependent on that system. They all have a stake in the system. Thus, while Japan may have economic weapons that it can hold to the head of other countries, it can find itself hostage to the same weapons.

Overseas development assistance is often seen as one area where Japan can use its economic power to coerce others, and Japan's approach to ODA has been regional, commercial, and pragmatic. Japanese decisions on foreign aid are not based on moral or ideal principles, but are rational investment decisions based on the best future return to the Japanese economy and, secondarily, the receiver economy. Even if it is agreed, for the sake of argument, that Japan's foreign aid approach has been beneficial to both the Japanese economy and receiver economies, it has not brought Japan increased political power. Asian countries use Japan as a development bank, but they have not accepted its role as a regional or global political leader. They enjoy investments from Japan but are becoming less enthusiastic about a trade relationship that includes monthly increases in their deficit with Japan. As the economies of Asia become more similar, that is, as the number of manufactured goods as a percentage of total exports increases for all Asian countries, it becomes impossible for any one country to control the Asian economy.

On the other hand, the coercive use of Japan's economic power is limited in that Japan is dependent on foreign markets to a greater extent than foreign economies are dependent on the Japanese market. Any embargo or boycott initiated by Japan would stimulate a response that may well be more harmful to the Japanese economy. If Japan decreases its aid or investment to Southeast Asian states, they can embargo the export of natural resources, boycott Japanese manufactured goods, and nationalize Japanese assets. Another problem for Japan is that there are substitutes for its products. As an example, Shintaro Ishihara has argued that Japan can hold a great deal of power over the United States because of the importance of its computer chips to American weapons. "If Japan told Washington it would no longer sell computer chips to the United States, the Pentagon would be totally helpless."[10] It could threaten to withhold from the United States electronics technology vital to the operation of American military hardware, but that would simply encourage the United States to retaliate with devastating barriers against other Japanese goods. Also, as has been the case with embargoes throughout history, it would encourage the Americans to get serious about developing domestic production. In the long run it would severely hurt Japan's competitive position.

As is pointed out by Deborah Haber, Japan has no chance of becoming a hegemon,[11] and its chances of becoming a leader state are only slightly higher if it adopts the traditional model of leadership. But Japan does not have to accept that model. It has before it the opportunity not only to become a leader state but to redefine the concept of leadership. The international relations system appears to be in a state of metamorphosis, with new power configurations and relationships between states yet to be defined. This environment allows Japan to construct a new form for the old model of leadership and, in doing so, take an active role in the construction of a new international relations system.

Working in Harness

Japan must pursue a form of leadership based on its own abilities and within the limitations of the polity. Japan must develop a form of leadership based on low-key, quiet diplomacy, as opposed to high-profile, bold initiative, through which it can become a leader state by using its good offices to mediate the disputes of others, circulating its proposals among other states for feedback before going public with them, and by developing and initiating, whenever possible, its foreign policy in collaboration with supranational or international institutions. It must attempt to "push" other states from behind rather than "pull" from out front. But this nontraditional model of leadership still includes many of the same elements of traditional leadership that Japan lacks: initiative, material power, will, the ability to respond to crises, and clearly stated goals and values.

Given these continued deficiencies, it appears as if Japan will never be a primary power, but Japan can be an effective leader if it works in harness with a state that does have the elements of traditional leadership and is willing to be a partner in leadership with Japan. The most likely candidate for that position is the United States. This is by no means a new idea, nor does it have any one particular ideal formulation. Some of the best experts on Japanese-American relations and the international relations system, including Richard Holbrooke, Takashi Inoguchi, Kuniko Inoguchi, Joseph S. Nye, Jr., to name but a few, have put forth similar proposals all of which are variations on the joint United States-Japan leadership theme.

If the United States is the world's de facto policeman, then Japan and the United States in tandem would make the perfect "good cop/bad cop" combination. The Japanese-American relationship will not only be beneficial to both sides but can also act as a role model for the rest of the world. While the dominant trends in the world are toward integration and disintegration, the Japanese-American relationship is a good model of cooperation between states with significant differences. It has been generally believed that the strength and stability of alliance relationships has to a great extent depended upon a similarity of values, especially cultural values, and the ability to communicate. The United States and Japan have similar economic and political values, but their cultural values are quite dissimilar and they have a relative inability to communicate. Nevertheless, the relationship has weathered many hardships over the years because it has been in their own best interests to do so, and that will continue to be the case.

There is no doubt that the United States and Japan still have significant trade problems. When the Clinton administration began in 1993, Japan had just finished running up a $117.6 billion surplus in the current account of the balance of payments (the biggest in its history), $46 billion of which was with the United States. However, the American and Japanese economies will continue to remain both interdependent and integrated because each has become too important for maintaining the other's economic well-being. Although there has been much talk about Japan joining an Asian trading bloc, its main fear is being squeezed out of the North American Free Trade Agreement (NAFTA) and the EC. Neither can the United States do without the Japanese financial pipeline or its markets. American farmers may complain about the closed nature of Japanese agricultural markets, but it is the biggest single market for American agricultural exports.

The two countries' security is also still interdependent. Japan is not going to undertake a major rearmament program and will continue to rely on the United States to protect its shipping lanes and territorial integrity in a world that is becoming less and less stable with the breakdown of cold war sureties. Neither is the United States going to abandon its role as a world, or an Asian, military power. There is no doubt that a certain amount of downsizing has occurred and will continue to occur as a means of finding the "peace dividend" that supposedly came with the end of the Cold War. However, the rising strength of regional powers in Asia, such as China and India, and continued instability will keep a steady and successful pressure by Japan and other Asian states on the United States to maintain significant forces in the region.

Finally, as was outlined in the first chapter, the length of the relationship has moved both Japanese and Americans closer together culturally, and given them a greater understanding of one another. This has not necessarily meant that they have come to a mutual sense of understanding, far from it, but there is a friendship that has grown. On the Japanese side there is also an element of choosing to consort with "the devil you know." American culture has deeply infiltrated Japan at all levels, Japanese leaders have been dealing with Americans for a long time, and it has been Japan's most important bilateral relationship for a long time. Given the inertia of the relationship and the investment that the Japanese have in it, it will be long before they can build up another, alternative relationship.

Not only has the Japanese-American relationship been a model for the rest of the world to build a binding bilateral relationship between two countries that have dissimilar cultures, but it can also be a future model as to how the international relations system should be managed in the future. In order to work as partners in managing the international relations system in the future, both Japan and the United States will have to compromise in ways that will affect basic behavior patterns of the past. The United States will have to come to the realization that it is a multipolar world and begin to share decision-making power with Japan as well as with other states. Although the need for the United States to accept Japan as an equal partner in the international relations system has been recognized, it has not often been put into operation. On the other hand, Japan will have to rid itself of its tendency to see the world in terms of its own self-interest and truly internationalize. More specifically, the United States and Japan will have to be more explicit in defining their policies toward each other. The type and amount of burden of leadership will have to be precisely defined.

ASIAN REGIONALISM AND JAPANESE LEADERSHIP

The region of Asia[12] is Japan's laboratory for international leadership. If it does not or cannot play a leading role in its own backyard, then it will find it difficult to claim a leading role on the world stage. In determining its role in Asia, it must face all of the problems and questions it faces as a world power. It must choose its place between Asia and the West. It must deal openly and directly with its prewar actions in Asia. It must decide what level of involvement is appropriate. Its ability to take the initiative, to coerce, cajole, and influence other states, is greater in Asia than in any other region. Its ability to produce public goods is also highest there.

But it is in Asia that Japan faces its greatest challenges to leadership. While Asia looks to Japan with a high expectation of both leadership and reward, there is a simultaneous fear of Japanese leadership. The ambivalence that other countries feel toward increased Japanese political power and leadership is stronger in Asia than in any other region or country. A strong Japanese economy is needed to drive the continued development of Asia, and its political power is needed as an Asian voice in the councils of the chosen, but the lessons of the past are not soon forgotten. Asian states are unsure if their support for Japan is helping to bring the entire region into a position of economic and political strength in the twenty-first century, or whether it is simply helping to make a Frankenstein that, once revived, will run amok in the region.

If there have been few competing loyalties within Japan on the subnational level, there are no competing loyalties on the supranational level. There has never been a need to create a "supranationality" such as "British" or "Yugoslavian" to unite component nationalities, and neither has regional integration ever threatened national loyalties. Until the 1850s, its "regional" orientation was isolation. There was nothing in Japanese experience comparable to Europe's trading economies or rivalries. Since the Peace of Westphalia, Europe has had a system of relations based upon explicitly stated and implicitly understood principles that regulate a very high frequency of transactions. East Asian diplomatic tradition is rooted in the Chinese tributary system, in which a dominant, self-sufficient China was usually little concerned with seeking out relations with bordering "barbarian" nations. Japan's position as a tributary of China, in addition to its political isolation, limited Japan's impact on regional politics, although it occasionally encroached on the continent. This changed after Japan joined the Western international relations system upon its "opening" by the United States. It soon dominated East Asia by defeating both China and Russia. These military victories allowed Japan to build an empire that by 1940 stretched from Taiwan, through coastal China, to the Russian-Manchurian border. Japan's prewar role in Asia supplanted and superseded that of China. It became the dominant state, but whereas China cared little for relations with other nations, Japan was hegemonic. Armed with a Pan-Asian ideology, economic power, and military coercion, it attempted to put into effect the Greater East Asian Co-Prosperity Sphere.

Contemporary distrust and fear of Japan in the region stem from the fact that circumstances today somewhat resemble those that existed at the turn of the century. Japan's military defeat of China was only the resultant cause of its ability to replace China as the preeminent state in Asia. The primary cause was its ability to modernize and learn from the West. When Japan became the first non-Western great power, other Asians looked to Japan to provide leadership for Asia, to act as a representative for Asia in Western councils, and to help other Asian nations attain the same level of development. This perception of Japan was held most strongly by the Chinese, who were going through a significant identity crisis during the decay of the Imperial system and the birth of the Republic, although the Chinese were not alone in taking this view of Japan.

Beginning in 1896 and then increasing after the Boxer Rebellion of 1900, students flocked from China to Japan in order to gain the knowledge that would allow them to modernize as effectively as Japan. Between the years 1898 and 1911 there were sixty-six different periodicals published in Japan by Chinese, most of which were intended to "introduce new knowledge and stimulate patriotism."[13] Chinese admiration for Japan peaked in 1905 when its victory over Russia was hailed by many Chinese as the first step in a movement to reverse the European colonization of Asia. Within ten years, however, it had become apparent that Japan was not attempting to free Asia but to replace European colonization with Japanese domination. Anti-Japanese nationalist sentiments became, if anything, more violent than anti-Western sentiments because of this betrayal.

The past misdeeds of Japan have been forgotten to the extent that Asia again looks to Japan for leadership and as a model of development. Japan is again the place to learn; 92 percent of all foreign students in Japan come from other Asian countries. Most Asian countries are developing their Japanese language programs in order to increase their ability to communicate with Japan. The Japanese economy is a model for Asian development. Most famous in this regard is the "Look East" policy of Malaysia's prime minister, Dr. Mahathir bin Mohamad. In a speech in Tokyo commemorating Keio University's 125th anniversary, he said that Malaysia must learn from Japan by emulating its work ethic, its export strategies, its unity, its cooperation between the private and public sectors, and its education.[14] While culture and security play a role in Japanese leadership in Asia, most Asian countries are primarily concerned with the economic role that Japan can play in the region.

The future role of the Japanese military in Asia has been minutely examined over the past few years due to the end of the Cold War and the possible reduction of American forces. During the Cold War the very concept of Asia was different as it contained both communist and democratic powers, but past ideological distinctions have become meaningless in the post–Cold War era. More important, during the Cold War, Asian states, especially the smaller states of Southeast Asia, could depend on the presence of the United States to keep the major actors in the region—the Soviet Union, China, and Japan, in line. Today, however, the stability of the United States' commitment has been questioned in light of reduced ideological tensions, American economic problems, and a possible "peace dividend." There has been much concern expressed about a power vacuum in Asia with the decrease of American influence in the area and the possible withdrawal of American forces. There are both fears and hopes, depending upon one's point of view, that Japan will expand to fill this vacuum. In a sense, the desire of Southeast Asians is very similar to that of many in Japan. It is hoped that Japan will expand its concept of leadership to take on an increased military role in the area, but within the context of the United States-Japan security treaty and under the continued control of the Americans.

One of the most important areas of discussion has been the possibility of putting together a regional security pact to compliment a possible regional economic bloc. Japan has been rather hesitant on the point for a number of reasons. Any regional security pact would have to consider the inclusion of the Russians, and Russo-Japanese relations are going to continue to be very sensitive until Japan and Russia finally conclude a peace treaty formalizing the end of the Second World War, and that will not happen until the Northern Territories dispute is settled. Second, if there are problems in Russo-Japanese relations, the inclusion of the People's Republic of China into the equation vastly increases the difficulties. Not only does China have territorial disputes with both Russia and Japan, but it is highly unlikely that either the Chinese government or the Chinese people are as yet willing to enter into a security arrangement with the Japanese. Finally, there is the fear of cutting its ties with the United States. Japan does not want to go too far too soon in any direction in Asia without reassuring the

United States, and has taken pains in the past few years to include the United States in any plan concerning Asian security.

Within the last few years, however, Japan has taken the first tentative steps toward support for a regional security pact—as long as it retains an American component. Japan has proposed that the annual ASEAN talks also be a forum for political and security discussions. In addition, when Prime Minister Miyazawa visited Washington in the summer of 1992, he outlined a two-track approach to Asian-Pacific security that would promote subregional cooperation and a simultaneous regional political dialogue intended to enhance "a sense of mutual reassurance." He reiterated that the continued maintenance of the United States-Japan security treaty and the continued presence of American troops in the region are essential.

The relative vagueness and lack of content in Miyazawa's remarks, beyond the stress on maintaining an American presence in Asia, however, are indicative of the problems facing a regional security pact. In 1950 the United States tried to patch together a NATO-like collective security arrangement in the Pacific that would have included Australia, New Zealand, the Philippines, Indonesia, Japan, the United States, Great Britain, and Canada.[15] The natural divisions of the region, distrust of Japan, antipathy toward Great Britain, and the independence of Indonesia were but some of the reasons why the Pacific Pact was never realized. Although the world situation is quite different from what it was in 1950, the problems in creating an Asian security pact, or a Pacific security pact, are now even more formidable. There is no consensus on what is wanted. Asian states want a strong Japanese presence, but they do not want a strong Japan. They are tired of American domination, but they don't want America to leave the region. China would want a primary role in any pan-Asian pact, but most other states fear the Chinese military. Can there be an ASEAN security arrangement with the Northeast Asian subregion operating on an à la carte basis?

One positive note for the increased participation of a Japanese security force in the region is the commitment of Japanese SDF to peacekeeping operations in Cambodia and Japan's overall participation in the Cambodia crisis. Although the original announcement of Japanese participation in Cambodian peacekeeping forces was met by resistance in most other Asian countries, that resistance faded to reluctant acceptance, and is now becoming a more willing acceptance. The struggle of the government to get the PKO bill passed, the restrictions incorporated into the bill, and the actions of the SDF personnel in Cambodia have all gone a long way to reassure the other nations of Asia that Japan's military is under the control of its civilian government, that it will act responsibly, and that its presence does not mean Japan will run amok now that it has stationed its troops outside its borders.

Even if other Asian states are more willing to accept Japan's security role in Asia as legitimate, that role will evolve not as a single-nation hegemon but through Japan's role in some form of a regional grouping.

The problem is determining both what that Asian grouping will be and Japan's role in it. Japan's rise as a major economic force in the world two decades ago was soon followed by predictions of a rising Asia and the idea that the twenty-first century would be the century of Asia. This perception only increased following the rapid development of Asia NIEs (newly industrialized economies). Over that period of time the world has seen innumerable conferences and publications concerned with "The Pacific Rim," "The Pacific Basin," "The Northern Pacific Crescent," or simply "Asia," but these still tend to be geographical constructs in search of a broader, more meaningful reality.

Therefore, if Japan becomes an Asian leader, it seems more than likely that it will be as the leader of a subregional group comprised of the ASEAN states or some expanded version thereof. Its ability to lead in Northeast Asia seems highly constrained. Although the end of the Cold War has freed relations between states in Asia, it has also greatly confused the picture. On the one hand, Japan is now free to redevelop political and economic ties with Russia, but its capability and willingness to do so seem limited. The ideological barrier that has separated the two has been removed only to reveal other barriers that must be removed before a real rapprochement can take place. Although Russia and Japan are no more capable of geopolitical conflict over Manchuria or North Korea than the Koreans and Chinese are willing to allow them the struggle, both Russia and Japan still see the other as geopolitical antagonists. As the Chairman of the New England Japan Seminar in 1989, I was fortunate to have a senior member of the foreign ministry, an ambassador to a Southeast Asian country, address one of the meetings on the subject of Japan's relations in the era of perestroika and glasnost. The speaker's message was blunt: Russia was Japan's enemy before the Cold War, it was Japan's enemy during the Cold War, and it will continue to be Japan's enemy for geopolitical reasons.

Another factor is nationalism and domestic politics in both Russia and Japan. The Japanese government has consistently maintained a policy of demanding the return of the Northern Territories (the Kurile Islands consisting of Etorofu, Kunashiri, Shikotan, and the Habomai Islands). At the 1993 Northern Territories Day (February 7, the day in 1855 on which Japan and Russia signed an agreement that they were Japanese territory) rally in Tokyo, Prime Minister Miyazawa and Foreign Minister Watanabe told an audience of two thousand people that the Japanese government would never give up the fight for the islands. Although some of the more liberal members of the LDP have believed it necessary to compromise on the issue, the right wing has been able to hold the rest of the party hostage to the issue, in much the same way that farmers have been able to hold the party hostage on the rice issue. On the Russian side, the newfound freedom of Russia has unleashed a whole new wave of Russian nationalism that will not countenance the return of the territories that the Russians now see as legitimately theirs. Neither side seems to be willing to back down in the near future.

Russian President Boris Yeltsin was to travel to Tokyo in September 1992 but canceled the trip just four days before he was due to arrive. Although he initially said that domestic political problems forced him to cancel the trip, he later hinted that it was actually canceled because the Japanese were so uncompromising in their stance on the issue. He then set May 1993 as a tentative date for a new meeting in Tokyo, but that visit was also abruptly canceled in the first week of May after talks over the disputed territories made no progress. The end result has been to solidify feelings of mutual distrust on both sides. Although there was a drastic increase in positive feelings toward Russia in the aftermath of the Soviet Union's demise, negative feelings have once again emerged. In a poll conducted by the Prime Minister's Office in October 1992, 80 percent of Japanese responded that they felt little friendship toward Russia, up 10 percent over the previous year.[16]

Even though Russo-Japanese relations remain cool, it is one area in which Japan has changed its policy in order to demonstrate that it is a team player in G-7, and, by doing so, has also demonstrated its leadership by sacrificing for the good of the whole. Japan's original policy was to link economic aid to Russia to progress on return of the Northern Territories. This stance came under fire from the other members of the G-7 (as well as Yeltsin, of course) because it was believed that a united stand among G-7 members was necessary to convince those opposing Yeltsin and his reforms that Yeltsin had the support of the developed countries. The situation came to a head in the spring of 1993 when Yeltsin's referendum on economic reforms and presidential rule went to the Russian people. Both Yeltsin and the G-7 were concerned about Japan's support at that crucial time, especially because Tokyo was to host the G-7 meeting that summer. On May 14 the Japanese government announced that it would drop its policy of tying aid to progress on the Northern Territories issue, and the next day, at a G-7 ministerial meeting, it also announced that it was adding $1.82 billion to its aid to Russia. There is little doubt that Japan was hesitant in making the policy change, and that it made it only under pressure from the United States and other G-7 members, but in doing so Japan displayed the kind of leadership expected of it.

China and South Korea are equally problematical for Japan. On one level Japanese-Chinese relations seem to be warming. Although China consistently voiced misgivings about the dispatch of SDF troops as peacekeeping forces in Cambodia, it has been relatively quiet on the issue after the troops were actually sent. Japan certainly won points in China by being the first developed state to upgrade its political and economic relations with China after the Tiananmen Square incident. The visit of the Japanese emperor and empress to China in the fall of 1992 had been opposed by ultranationalists in Japan and China, but the fact that it was conducted without incident demonstrates a major step forward in Sino-Japanese relations. Beneath the surface, however, there are many problems that will not be so easily dispelled.

The general secretary of the Chinese Communist Party, Jiang Zemin, traveled to Japan in April 1992, but no major results came from the meetings with Prime Minister Miyazawa. On the contrary, Jiang chose to highlight the problems of the dispatch of the SDF, concerns over the emperor's visit, the ownership of the Senkaku (Daioyu) Islands, and compensation from Japan for war atrocities. While Miyazawa was telling the press that Sino-Japanese relations were as important as Japanese-American relations, few took the remarks at face value. Indeed, at the very same time an unnamed Japanese official was reported in the press as saying that Japan was unfortunate in not being able to choose its neighbors, and that any opening to China would increase the number of unwanted Chinese boat people invading Japan.[17] Similarly, following the emperor's trip to China, a Chinese military journal published a report purporting to demonstrate that Emperor Showa not only condoned the war against China in the 1930s but actively pushed for it and commended Japanese troops after the Rape of Nanjing.[18] In addition, China has announced a plan to increase its ability to operate outside its coastal waters by building three large naval bases, one in the north, one near Shanghai, and one in the south, and by possessing an aircraft carrier by the end of the decade. These would give China a greatly expanded ability to press its claims both over the Spratly Islands (disputed with Taiwan, Malaysia, Vietnam, the Philippines, and Brunei) and the Senkaku Islands (disputed with Japan).

Korean-Japanese relations are better than Sino-Japanese relations, but fundamental problems remain. Korean culture had a very important impact on the roots of Japanese culture, and today Korea has followed Japan in everything from the development of its economy to the naming of its ruling Democratic Liberal Party. But for all of the history that they share, and for all of the superficial similarities in Seoul and Tokyo, Japan's history as the colonizer of Korea, and contemporary economic competition, have created a deep distrust and a cultural antipathy that keep them at arm's length. Feelings have run so high that it was not possible for a Japanese prime minister to visit South Korea until the mid-1980s. Anti-Japanese sentiment in South Korea is still so strong that Kim Dae Jung stated in December 1990 that United States troops should remain in South Korea after the cold war in order to protect South Korea from a Japanese remilitarization. South Korea's essential concerns were expressed in the 1991–92 National Defense Ministry white paper which stated explicitly that it fears a remilitarization of Japan, including the adoption of nuclear weapons, which would directly threaten South Korea.[19] Once, while attending a security studies conference at Keio University in the early 1980s, a Japanese participant was discussing the possibility of Japanese support for South Korea if it were ever attacked by North Korea. Immediately following the end of the presentation, a South Korean participant responded by saying that if Japanese were ever to get involved, both sides would stop their fighting, turn their guns on the Japanese, and then resume after the Japanese had left—he was not joking.

There are three basic problems between Japan and Korea. The first is that the Japanese colonization of Korea and their actions during the colonial period (1910–45) have created a visceral dislike among the Koreans toward Japanese. Koreans have a long and proud cultural heritage and have always had to fight to keep it distinct and independent from the Chinese, Manchurians, Mongols, Japanese, and Russians that have encroached upon their peninsula. They still deeply resent the attempted "Japanization" of Korean culture during the period of colonization. They still remember the humiliation and privations they were forced to undergo as conscripted soldiers, laborers, and prostitutes for the Japanese.

Second, their unforgiving attitude toward Japanese is hardened by the perceived superiority of Japanese toward Koreans and continued Japanese discrimination against them. Although most people will not talk about it, many Japanese do have feelings of superiority toward Koreans. Japanese attitudes toward Koreans were formed long before the colonization of Korea and were reinforced by it. These attitudes are especially evident in the discrimination against Koreans living in Japan. Many Koreans were forced to move to Japan to act as laborers during the period of colonization, and their descendants remain there today. However, these ethnic Koreans, the largest ethnic minority group in Japan, are not allowed to become citizens of Japan, even though they may be the second or third generation to have been born in Japan. Neither are the rights of those victimized by the colonization readily recognized by the Japanese government. The Japanese government refuses to give veteran's benefits to Korean and Taiwanese soldiers who were conscripted into the Japanese Imperial Army. It refuses to compensate Korean laborers who were forced to work for Japanese companies.

The classic case, and the one that has created the most interest of late, is the Japanese government's handling of the "comfort women" (women who were forced to be prostitutes for Japanese soldiers) scandal. Immediately after the war, some of the estimated 70,000–200,000 comfort women who were forced to have sex with Japanese soldiers made accusations, but for decades the Japanese government totally denied any such program ever existed. Then in January 1992 evidence was uncovered which conclusively proved that the program did exist. Faced with this evidence the Japanese government admitted that it did exist, but denied any involvement in it and immediately stated there would be no compensation. As late as August 1992 the chief cabinet secretary was quoted as saying that a government investigation "has so far found no evidence that the government was involved in the *forceful* [author's emphasis] recruitment" of comfort women.[20] The purpose of this statement was to claim that, while it had been conclusively demonstrated that Japanese police, military, and government officials were involved in the rounding up of women to be used as prostitutes, force was not used. Finally the prime minister offered an official apology to Korea. The Japanese government promised that a compensation program would be announced by the end of 1992, but it failed to meet that self-imposed deadline. South Korea's attitude toward Japanese foot-dragging on the issue is summed up by a speech given to the United Nations Commission on Human Rights by the South Korean representative: "My delegation is convinced that a friendly relationship between Japan and other countries in our region cannot be realized until Japan willingly cleans itself of its guilty past whose infamous legacy is still lingering in the minds of the Asian people."[21] Finally, in the summer of 1993, the Japanese government acknowledged that Asian women had been forced to serve Japanese soldiers as prostitutes.

The Japanese response to a unified Korea must also be taken into consideration. Although the Japanese government is on record as supporting the reunification of Korea, most observers put as much stock in that as they do Japan's contention that force was not used to recruit comfort women. A Korea unified on the model of South Korea (as most assume it will be) is the proverbial dagger aimed at the belly of Japan. It would give Korea a drastically increased economic capacity which could soon make it an even greater economic rival. Add to that the combined military power and fighting spirit of both Koreas, in combination with their will to be involved in regional politics, and you have a first-class threat to everyone in the region. A reunified Korea could even challenge Japan as the primary power in Asia.

The situation in Northeast Asia is extremely complicated and fluid. In it Japan is faced with two other major powers and two minor powers, each with a strong military. The three major powers of the region—Japan, the People's Republic of China, and Russia—all belonged to separate ideological blocs during the Cold War, and have had a long history of mutual suspicion and conflict. Just in the modern era, the Japanese have warred with both Russia and China and attempted to colonize the latter, in competition with the former, for most of the first half of the twentieth century. The domestic political system in Russia is still in turmoil, no one is sure how the People's Republic of China will evolve, and the unification of Korea is also uncertain. Under these conditions, there has never been, and will probably never be, an equivalent of "Western Europe"—a region including several proximate, equal, and interdependent powers in Northeast Asia.

One thing is certain: all states want a continued American presence in Asia that will insure that any increase in Japanese power and leadership will be in harness with (and harnessed by) the United States. In very general terms the instabilities created by the end of the Cold War make all the Asian states look to an outside arbiter that can insure the security of all against all. The vacuum that an American withdrawal would create would be a temptation for China, India, and Japan, and no one wants that. While the Southeast Asian nations have, to greater or lesser degrees, accepted Japan's presence in Cambodia, within the confines of a United Nations peacekeeping force, there is still a great fear of the Japanese. Even as Malaysia's prime minister continues to "Look East," and simultaneously moves to exclude the United States from Asia, other officials of the Malaysian government have expressed different opinions. General Yaacob Zain, head of the Defense Forces, has been quoted as saying that if you combine Japan's past history of aggression, its reliance on external sources of raw materials, and its technological capabilities, "there is a greater chance of Japan being a threat to the region than China."[22] In a regional security conference held in Kuala Lumpur shortly after the PKO bill was passed by the Diet, speakers from China and Southeast Asia constantly expressed anxieties about an increased Japanese role in Asia outside an American partnership.

But it does not appear as if the Japanese government is any more desirous of an end to the Japanese-American relationship than are other Asian states. Japan realizes the problems that are inherent in taking on a greater security role in Asia, and would rather work with the United States than shoulder them alone. It is also mindful that its increased presence in the region—economic, political, and military—will be facilitated by working with the United States as a guarantee of security to other Asian states. Finally, Japan continues to need American help in its own defense. Growing Russian nationalism, the possible unification of Korea, and the growing economic and military strength of China are only some of the more obvious future contingencies for which Japan must prepare.

There are calls for Japan to create a more independent security policy, but they have been more calls in the wilderness than mainstream thought. The Japanese government has been consistent in its statements that Japan's future security policy will continue to be linked with the United States through the security treaty. Japan's desire to continue the status quo in its relationship with the United States is evident in its hesitant attitude toward the East Asian Economic Community (EAEC) or any other regional economic or security group which does not include the United States. The two-track approach to Asian-Pacific regional security that Miyazawa announced in the summer of 1992 depends upon a strong American presence in the region, the continuation of the security treaty, and a continued positive overall relationship between the United States and Japan. Miyazawa continually reiterated this policy in his swing through Southeast Asia in January 1993.

PAX NIPPONICA?

In the words of Deborah L. Haber, "People who [fear Japan will become a hegemon] should take solace in the knowledge that a 'Pax Nipponica' is an impossibility now and in the near future."[23] Japan will continue to build its role as a leader in the Asian-Pacific region, but it will not do so unilaterally or without restraint. The United States, China, Russia, Korea, and India will all act to buffer and constrain Japan, while the smaller states of Southeast Asia will work both individually and in concert to avoid being dominated by Japanese economic power. Japan will certainly be *a* leader in Asia, but it will not be *the* leader of Asia.

Indeed, the very transference of that economic power to other forms of leadership is a problem for Japan. Although Asian students flock to Japan and Japanese studies programs are developed in those countries that want to do business with Japan, it does not mean that Japanese culture will become a legitimizing factor for leadership as has British and American culture in the past. American popular culture is still the standard, and Asians thrive on American fast food, movies, music, and television shows. As one Malaysian put it: "We may use Japanese products in our daily lives, but that's about it. For intellectual leadership, we still look to countries like the United States."[24] The rise of Asian nationalism in the postwar world has made most governments wary of outside cultural influences, but memories of attempted Japanization of Asian countries in the prewar world have made them especially resistant to Japanese culture, contemporary pan-Asianism not withstanding.

Increased Japanese investment in Asia during the mid-1980s sparked fears that Japan would "buy up Asia" and control Asian economies in a modern co-prosperity sphere, but that perception is a vast misunderstanding of the situation. Japanese investment in Asia has been decreasing since 1989, but more important, intra-Asian trade has been increasing since 1986. Intra-Asian trade is becoming increasingly more complex as the economies of Asian states develop into broader markets and varietal producers. In the past the relationship has been the classic colonial relationship: a flow of manufactured goods and investment from Japan to other states, while depending on those states for cheap labor and raw materials. Now those states are also demanding a greater share of the Japanese market for their manufactured goods, and a greater acceptance of their surplus labor to feed the Japanese labor shortage. The countries of Asia that host Japanese transnational corporations (TNCs) are no longer naïve and are more than able to get their quid pro quo from both TNCs and their home countries. Although the Japanese economy is two-thirds of the Asian economy, savings rates throughout the major Asian economies are now about 30 percent (as compared to 8 percent in the G-7 countries), which means that they are creating enough capital to fuel development on their own.[25]

Japan has also had difficulty creating a perception of itself as a state willing to give priority to regional interests over self-interest. It has been noted by many that Japan continued to do business as usual with both Thailand and Mynmar after coups in those countries retarded the progress of democratic governments. It was also the first government to reestablish normal relations with China after Tiananmen Square. While Japan has said in all these cases that it was using its relations to urge the furtherance of democracy, the image that other states received was that pragmatic economic concerns were of primary importance. Similarly, Japanese ODA has been perceived in the past to be structured in such a way as to help the domestic Japanese economy as much as it benefited recipient countries. Japan has made an effort to eliminate tied aid and has instituted a new ODA policy that stresses basic human needs, environmental protection, and population control, but many remain skeptical of its ability to implement these policies.[26]

For all the talk about Japan adopting a new role as the leader of Asia, Japan itself has appeared to be ambivalent about adopting the role. During Miyazawa's trip to Southeast Asia in early 1993, Indonesia's President Suharto, the chairman of the Non-Aligned Movement, reflected the desires of many other Southeast Asian leaders by asking the Japanese prime minister to represent the interests of the developing nations at the 1993 G-7 meeting to be held in Tokyo. Specifically, Suharto asked to be invited to the summit in order to address the delegates as the representative of the non-aligned nations. Miyazawa's response was polite but dissembling. Japan is obviously uncomfortable in any role that portrays it as the leader of a group of developing countries. Japan is still not far enough removed from the time when it was also perceived as a developing country to be secure in its status as a legitimate member of the G-7. But, on the other hand, it has also grown so far from the developing world that its ability to represent developing nations as an equal is questionable. Although Japanese ODAs and technology transfer have increased drastically in the 1980s, there is concern that not enough of it is appropriate technology. There is also little understanding of the needs of third world countries within Japan, as reflected by the lack of educational programs designed to teach development studies in Japanese universities and graduate schools.

Both Japan's attitudes toward other Asian nations and its inability to come to grips with past events are also important factors that constrain Japan's ability to be accepted as a legitimate leader in Asia. Continued distrust of Japanese can be boiled down to two basic points: Japanese do not see other Asians as equals, and they have not yet apologized for their prewar behavior. For all the talk about Japan working as an equal with other

Asian nations, there are also hints that Japan, at the very least, believes itself to be both economically and culturally *supra inter pares*. Japanese tourists come to Southeast Asia on golf or sex tours and never leave their hotels or hermetically sealed buses and tour groups. There is much investment by Japanese companies in other Asian countries, but their employees tend not to assimilate into the local culture, and local employees are not blended into the upper management of those companies. A study of ten local subsidiaries of Japanese companies in Southeast Asia showed that local employees thought that Japanese employees had no interaction with them, did not include them in management decision making, and that Japanese employees were not straightforward with local employees.[27]

There is a strong attempt by the Japanese government and private foundations to export Japanese culture to the south, but not much effort to introduce other Asian cultures into Japan. Japanese attitudes toward greater economic cooperation have also stimulated stricter immigration laws. As mentioned in Chapter 2, immigrant laborers in Japan, legal or illegal, are tolerated at a minimum level when they are deemed useful or necessary, such as with "entertainer" bar-girls from the Philippines, but they are not welcomed or assimilated into Japanese society—especially laborers from other Asian countries. Even Korean and other Asian ethnic groups who have lived in Japan for decades are not given equal treatment there.

Of greater importance, however, is the perception of Japan's unwillingness to deal with the past or to apologize for past behavior. Korea, China, and all of the Southeast Asian states, with the exception of Thailand, felt the brunt of Japanese military aggression and domination during the 1930s and 1940s. They are willing to give Japan the benefit of the doubt because they recognize that the contemporary world is quite different and that Japan has changed. But each time that Japan has stepped forward to make an official announcement concerning the colonization of Korea, or the invasion of China, its words have been hedged. The inability of Japan to issue a clear "mea culpa" beyond such phrases as Emperor Akihito's pronouncement that he regretted China's great suffering at the hands of the Japanese, force other Asian states to take a wait-and-see attitude.

The earliest statements of then Prime Minister Hosokawa and other members of the governing coalition have raised the hopes of many in Japan and Asia that Japan is now more willing to reexamine its past. Hosokawa was the first prime minister to state explicitly that Japan waged a "war of aggression" and that the war was wrong.[28] While on a trip to South Korea, Sadao Yamahana, head of the SDPJ and a minister in the coalition cabinet, apologized to the South Korean government and people for Japan's atrocities during their occupation of the Korean peninsula.[29] It is too early to know how deeply and how broadly the reexamination of Japan's past will progress, but the extent to which it does progress is a measure of the extent to which Japan is willing to make the hard decisions necessary for respect and leadership in Asia.

Beyond the government's position, other Asians also see a whole nation unwilling to deal with the past. Likhit Dhiravegin, head of the department of political theory and philosophy at Thammasat University, noted the attitude of many Japanese participating in the first Japanese-ASEAN round table held in Tokyo. The air was filled with words of cooperation and harmony until the topic of Japan's role in the Second World War arose. At that point the Japanese participants began reciting a well-known litany: Japan invaded Asia not to colonize but to liberate Asia from the West; many so-called atrocities did not occur because history was written by the victors; those that did occur were not as bad as those perpetrated by the Western powers.[30] This desire to dissemble and prevaricate on topics concerning its role in prewar Asia can only serve to maintain distrust. There is no rational, logical reason to issue a clear "mea culpa." As seen in the case of Germany, admitting war guilt does not guarantee an automatic end to feelings of nationalism and national superiority. But it is an emotional need felt by other Asians that as yet goes unfulfilled.

MAKING NATIONALISM SUBSERVIENT TO LEADERSHIP

Unilateral decision making and the perception of international relations as a zero-sum game have always been fundamental principles of the nation-state system and are essential components of traditional leadership. The utility of these principles may now be held in question, however. The end of bipolarity has thrown the international relations system into a period of transition, most likely with one of two outcomes: (1) the world may regress to an earlier, prewar form of the nation-state system in which national interest and nationalism grow unchecked by supranational constraints such as ideology and multilateral agreements on international trade; or (2) nation-states may meld into blocs in a continuation of the interdependencies developed during the Cold War. If one agrees with the normative assumption that the latter is preferable to the former, Japan could help push the world in that direction by adopting a lower-key, more consensus-oriented leadership in cooperation with a more traditional American leadership.

This style of leadership would be based on the principle of a nonzero-sum game in that it tries to create the conditions under which competitive situations are not perceived as conflict and in which gains do not have to equal losses. It is also based upon the principle of making consultations and negotiations with outside actors an integral part of the foreign policy-making process within each state. Such principles of diplomacy are essential for the relations among states within blocs, the relations between blocs, and the relations among states, blocs, and international institutions. If Japan can conduct its diplomacy based on such principles, and encourage others to do so, it will be perceived as a leader of the international relations system without resorting to the aggressive use of power. It is, however, essential that Japan resist by all means the tendency of most people within Japan and in the international community to define leadership only in terms of the traditional model. It must adhere to its own model of leadership and in doing so present an ideal goal for others to follow.

Even leadership based upon these principles and supported by the United States will be difficult for Japan and will necessitate fundamental changes.

1. There must be more consolidation of political power within the government. As long as the prime minister is subservient to party factions and party policy-making organizations, and as long as the government is dependent upon the civil administrative service for the development of policy, the Japanese government will be unable to lead its own polity, to say nothing of the rest of the world. Japan must create a more powerful executive while balancing his or her power with institutionalized controls in the legislature. This is necessary because diplomacy is the art of interpersonal relations, and successful diplomacy is most often conducted by strong personalities. Most especially, it is a strong executive leader that creates policy momentum within policy-making institutions, sells that policy at home and abroad, and takes responsibility for policy.

2. Modern Japanese foreign policy has essentially been reactive and pragmatic. Ever since Japan's relatively recent entry into the European-derived international relations system, it has been forced to react to the initiatives of more powerful members, steering a course with the fewest risks and the greatest rewards to the national interest. Its position has made it both self-absorbed and dependent upon greater powers with whom it has aligned itself. Taking the initiative and carrying it out through the early period of innovation will take more perseverance and will than the Japanese polity and its elite have so far displayed. Japan must also do a much better job of convincing other states that whatever actions are taken, they are taken in the interest of all parties concerned, and not just in Japan's own self-interest.

3. In order to lead, Japan must be able to transcend its self-centeredness and homogeneity. Homogeneity has made the Japanese people and their polity inward-looking and unaccustomed to dealing with others outside the group. Although the discussion to this point has been about the ability of the Japanese political and diplomatic elite to treat with the political and diplomatic elites of other states, there is also the broader question of Japan's interdependent ties with other countries. Japan has benefited a great deal from its interdependence with the United States and other countries in the postwar era, but interdependence has two lanes and one leads into Japan. The Japanese people must be ready to accept the fact that a more active role in world leadership means that their borders will have to become more open to foreign peoples, their markets more open to foreign goods, and their minds more accepting of foreign behaviors and cultures.

4. While the emphasis in Japanese society is on consensus building, consensus building works best, perhaps only, on the micro level in person-to-person communications where there is a preexisting ability to communicate through the acceptance of mutually shared values. These shared values and the resultant ability to communicate have made Japan a society of consensus and harmony. But in those instances where values are not mutually shared, such as in the struggle against the state by those who oppose the Narita Airport, the Japanese demonstrate an absolute lack of negotiation or consensus building. This poses great problems for Japanese diplomacy since one cannot expect the hothouse conditions under which consensus building flourishes in Japan to exist in the international environment. On the contrary, negotiations take place among elites with different means of communication, with widely varying values, and with widely varying goals. The Japanese diplomatic and political elite are going to have to learn to communicate, not just speak a foreign language, with people of varying values and outlooks in order to become a leader state.

Although making these fundamental changes in the Japanese polity and its policy-making processes will be difficult, this style of leadership holds much more promise for Japan than the certain failure of traditional leadership. Japan has a history of making rapid and radical changes at times when such changes are absolutely necessary. They are necessary now if Japan wants finally to fulfill the goal of world leadership first proposed by the Meiji restoration. But Japan must act, and act soon. The international conditions that exist now may not last long, and Japan's chance to influence the future direction of the international relations system may pass. Of equal importance, Japan is also losing internal direction. It has fulfilled its goals in achieving domestic affluence and international economic power, but those successes have left it with a lack of future purpose. Now is the time for Japan to reassess itself and its role in the world community and to decide its future direction.

NOTES

1. Barry Buzan, "Japan's Future: Old History versus New Rules," *International Affairs* 64 (Autumn 1988), 563.

2. *Japan Times*, April 27, 1993, p. 6.

3. *Japan Times*, January 23, 1993, p. 12.

4. Masaya Ito and Osamu Shimomura, "The Folly of Structural Adjustment," *Japan Echo* 13 (August 1986), 36.

5. *Japan Times*, January 23, 1993, p. 12.

6. Michael Blaker, *Japanese International Negotiating Style* (New York: Columbia University Press, 1977), as quoted in Lloyd Jensen, *Explaining Foreign Policy* (Englewood Cliffs, N.J.: Prentice-Hall, 1982), 52.

7. *Tokyo Journal*, February 1993, p. 11.

8. *Japan Times*, May 8, 1993, p. 2.

9. Joseph S. Nye, "The Changing Nature of World Power," *Political Science Quarterly* 105 (Summer 1990), 183.

10. Shintaro Ishihara, *The Japan That Can Say No* (New York: Simon and Schuster, 1991), 21.

11. Deborah Haber, "The Death of Hegemony," *Asian Survey* 30 (September 1990), *passim*.

12. Asia is a vast continent reaching from Turkey to New Zealand, but for the purposes of the discussion here I will use the word "Asia" as a shorthand to denote the area from India in the west to Indonesia in the east and north from Indonesia to China. Specifically not included in the "region of Asia" that would look to Japan as a leader are Australia, New Zealand, Russia, India, and states west of India.

13. Fu-ch'ing Huang, *Chinese Students in Japan in the Late Ch'ing Period* (Tokyo: Centre for East Asian Cultural Studies, 1982), 271–75.

14. Andrew J. Armour, ed., *Asia and Japan* (London: Athlone Press, 1985), 150–59.

15. U.S. Department of State, *Foreign Relations of the United States*, vol. 6 (Washington, D.C., 1950), 121–23, 149–52.

16. *Japan Times*, January 19, 1993, p. 2.

17. *Japan Times*, April 14, 1992, p. 3.

18. *Japan Times*, January 14, 1993, p. 3.

19. *Japan Times*, October 29, 1991, p. 1.

20. *Japan Times*, August 1, 1992, p. 1.

21. *Japan Times*, February 21, 1993, p. 2.

22. *Japan Times*, September 23, 1992, 2.

23. Haber, "The Death of Hegemony," 906. Those interested in understanding Japan's broader role in the world and the difficulties of hegemony generally are encouraged to read this excellent article.

24. *Japan Times*, November 30, 1992, p. 21.

25. Testimony by Kenneth Courtis given before the U.S. Congressional Committee on Foreign Affairs, February 17, 1993.

26. *Japan Times*, July 18, 1992, p. 3.

27. *Japan Times*, December 10, 1991, p. 3.

28. *New York Times*, August 21, 1993, p. 2.

29. *Japan Times*, September 7, 1993, p. 1.

30. *Japan Times*, September 27, 1990, p. 24.

6

Conclusion

George Santayana's axiom—those who do not know the past are bound to repeat it—haunts Japan like a nightmare. States that refuse to forget Japan's past actions hold it captive to a history it desperately wants to escape. They will not allow Japan to escape its past because they are captives of a corollary to Santayana's axiom: those who see only the past cannot see the future. All of Japan's actions are judged by the standard of history. The world cannot think of a rich Japan, a strong Japan, a proud Japan, an active Japan in terms other than the authoritarianism, militarism, and colonialism of the prewar era.

But Japan's inability to escape the past is deceiving. Japanese may believe that dwelling on the unpleasant past is embarrassing and shameful, but the wrongs of the prewar era have had their effect on contemporary society. The democratic nature of Japanese political institutions and political culture is a clear indication that it has learned from the past and has applied those lessons to bring about substantive, positive changes. Japan may exhibit a form of national stubbornness and denial behavior by not considering the claims of those who suffered, by refusing to examine its actions, and by refusing to issue a clear "mea culpa." But while its denials are insulting to the victims of its behavior, and deprive Japanese youth of their historical education, it does not mean that contemporary Japan is set on a course for the past. Quite the opposite. The actions of the Hosokawa government have demonstrated that Japan may be more willing to openly debate and examine its recent past.

Events in Japan since the election of 1993 have only strengthened the main contentions of this book that Japan is headed on a course away from its prewar past, and that the changes in the forms and manifestations of Japanese nationalism are a clear indication of the changes in Japanese society. The world should continue to guard against Japanese nationalism, but to no greater or lesser extent than it needs to guard against nationalism in the United States, France, the Netherlands, or any other developed democracy. Japan has adopted democratic political institutions and developed a supporting political culture that are both stable and deeply rooted. Japan should continue to be held accountable for its prewar actions, but they should not be used as a standard of judgment for contemporary actions, especially as regards Japanese nationalism. Nationalism in prewar Japan was used by the political elite as the ideological cement that bound together the people and the state. Theories of *tennosei* and *kokutai* linked one's identity as a Japanese directly to loyalty to the state. The resultant state-oriented nationalism was then harnessed to support authoritarianism, militarism, and colonialism.

Japanese nationalism today is not a state-oriented, political form of nationalism but a sociocultural one. It is manifested not as a means of linking the citizen to the state but as a means of identifying with the nation. As such, Japanese are among the most nationalistic people in the world. Their country is an almost pure nation-state. Japanese share intensely held in-group feelings and widely believe that all Japanese are part of an inseparable whole. They tend to believe that what is in the best interest of the group is in their own best interest, and also that it is necessary to give up individual social and behavioral freedoms to conform to social values and behavioral norms of collectivity, conformity, homogeneity, and uniformity set by the group. There is pressure to conform, to submit one's will to the group, but it is a social pressure and not political coercion.

Although exceptions may abound, values and norms are very widely shared in Japan. A variety of racial, ethnic, and social out-groups exist in Japanese society, but the vast majority of Japanese are ethnically and racially homogeneous. While Japanese nationalism can be isolating, it has also been a powerful tool that has aided the Japanese in their postwar development. Japanese were driven to sacrifice in order to develop economically by many motives—pride and materialism not the least—and were aided by many structural benefits, such as technology transfer and the support of the United States, but there is no doubt that a major factor in the postwar development of Japan has been sociocultural nationalism. It has allowed Japan to avoid the draining and costly internecine struggles that have limited the development of other states. It has provided a motive for sacrifice.

The type of Japanese nationalism described above is distinct from prewar nationalism in that it is essentially nonpolitical: it exists separate from the state, it does not define itself by political values, it does not express itself in political manifestations, nor does it attach itself to the symbols of the state. In addition, it is a grassroots nationalism whereas prewar nationalism was enforced from the top down. "Identification of the people with their nation, after 1945, was far deeper and broader than in the earlier period. . . . Still another difference was that after 1945 the nationalist tune was no longer being called by the rulers in response merely to *state* needs, but was being called principally by the ruled, who were concerned more directly with the needs of the people."[1]

That is not to say, however, that state-oriented nationalism does not exist in Japan, but its existence is primarily an elite phenomenon. Many within the LDP and the bureaucracy, as well as in corporate interest groups and ultranationalist organizations that have the ear of the LDP and the ministries, hold strong attitudes supporting the de-democratization of Japan, greater respect for the symbols of the state, the reinstitution of moral values in education, and the elimination of article 9 of the constitution, to name just the most obvious. But the question remains as to how the nationalistic attitudes of those elites who hold such attitudes can be transferred to the mass in order to create a grassroots state-oriented nationalism.

At present, it would be difficult to link state-oriented nationalism to sociocultural nationalism. The mass would either have to accept willingly the weakening of democratic values and political institutions, or the political elite would have to enforce such changes. There would have to be a bridging of the gap between the political elite and the mass. In order for state-oriented nationalism to be transferred to the mass, two things would have to occur: Japanese people would have to stop being "spectators" of the political system and become motivated to move out of their social environment and participate in the political world, and that participation would have to be in support of anti-democratic forces.

Before the election of 1993, Japanese citizens generally demonstrated very low levels of pride in the institutions of the state, low levels of trust in politicians, low levels of patriotism, low levels of efficacy, and a desire to maintain the status quo, all of which indicated a sense of removal from the political system and a low level of involvement. That may be changing, but it is too soon after the fact to analyze the effect of the election on Japan's political institutions and political culture. Although the public did not initiate the downfall of the LDP or the reform movement by any direct action, the disintegration of the LDP was undoubtedly caused in part by sensitivity to public opinion. When the system has changed to allow greater expression of public opinion, for example, open-line audience response broadcasts during the election, the public has shown a willingness to express its opinions. One can make a case that the Japanese public may now be more willing to become more active in politics, but they have demonstrated such a proclivity only in support of more liberal democratic institutions and policies. They have not been generally supportive of more conservative political institutions and policies.

While the mass have little motivation to become involved in a state-oriented nationalism sponsored by the political elite, they in turn have few authoritarian powers to force a nationalistic ideology on the masses, as was the case in prewar nationalism. In the prewar years there was a coherent ideology based upon state Shinto, *kokutai*, and *tennosei*, but no such coherent ideology exists today, outside democracy. However, even if a prewar, *kokutai* ideology were created by the elite, through what means could they coerce the mass into accepting it? Democratic political institutions have taken root in Japan, and they are strongly supported by the mass. There is little support for more authoritarianism. The United States-Japan Security Treaty riots of 1960 are evidence of what can occur when the public believes that the government behaves in an authoritarian manner. The Sagawa scandal and the PKO bill both demonstrate that government policy is obviously constrained by public opinion.

In a more general sense, if we assume that conservative politicians have harbored a desire to implement policies that would create a state-oriented nationalism in Japan, they have been extremely unsuccessful. The LDP simply was not able to create a public opinion in support of its policies which would lead to a greater state-oriented nationalism in Japan, and it is highly unlikely that future governments will be able to do so through coercive action. Laws like the Peace Preservation Law and the Peace Police Law, which were the cornerstones for state coercion in prewar Japan, would be unacceptable to today's Japanese public. What authoritarianism that exists in Japan today is not the authoritarianism of the state but of its social mores. The strong pressure to conform in Japanese society, and to obey authority, is a result of peer pressure and social pressure, not government coercion. The words of John Stuart Mill in *On Liberty* are never truer than when applied to Japan: "When the society is itself the tyrant—society collectively, over the individuals who compose it—its means of tyrannizing are not restricted to the acts which it may do by the hands of all its political functionaries."

There is the expectation by many inside Japan and abroad that state-oriented nationalism is a horror waiting to happen. This concern is supported by indelible memories of prewar Japan, the economic power and arrogance of contemporary Japan, the hierarchical nature of its society, and the solidarity of its citizens. A resurgence of this type of nationalism has been awaited for decades, but the prophecy will not be realized: conditions necessary to support a linking of mass sociocultural nationalism to elite state-oriented nationalism no longer exist. Indeed, state-oriented nationalism is the weakest form of nationalism in Japan.

The image of Japan that portrays it as a country of unified groups has given rise to a popular image of vast, sprawling cabals consisting of politicians, businessmen, ultraconservatives, and *yakuza* who use their hidden power to control the masses and drive Japan back to the authoritarianism and aggressive nationalism of the past. While relations among these elites exist, they are not nearly as unified as portrayed by this image. There are points of agreement and contact, but factionalism within the governing party, power struggles between it and the bureaucracy, and the non-mainstream nature of the ultraconservatives all add up to a great deal of conflict among these various elites.

Neither do they have the ability to change the democratic capitalist system as it now exists without the support of the public. There have been many attempts to change the peace constitution, remilitarize Japan, bring back more traditional Confucian values, and restore the emperor's prewar powers, but none of them have been successfully implemented because they lack support. Public support for such policies will not be forthcoming. The Japanese public is not at all oriented toward the state. They do not have a sense of patriotism toward the state and its symbols. They do not want to be involved in the state and politics. They do, however, want to be recipients of its outputs, and they believe that they can be served best by maintaining the status quo. A return to the nationalism of old presents a dangerous challenge to the peace and affluence that has been accumulated in the postwar era.

Although Japanese citizens feel removed from the world of politics, they have internalized democratic political values to the extent that they are willing to be involved in the political process as a way of securing the status quo. Democratic political institutions and values have become a fundamental part of Japanese society, and overriding them will be no easy matter. Thus Japanese politicians are very sensitive to public opinion.

Above all, Japan is not about to return to militarism. That threat, the fear held most deeply by those who are wary of a resurgent Japanese nationalism, will be the most difficult to realize. In the forty years since its inception, the Japanese public has come to accept the need for the SDF and even support its existence as a necessary component of development and great power status, but it is still somewhat of a pariah. The vast majority of Japanese will not join its ranks, will not fight to defend their country, will not allocate the financial resources necessary to make it a larger force, and are not willing to give up the nation's status as an international pacifist. Even if all that were to change, neither the other states of Asia nor the great powers of the world would stand by and watch Japan once again become a military threat to the region or the world.

The weakness of state-oriented nationalism will most likely last for the indefinite future, but it also includes inherent dangers. Since the end of the war, the gap between the state-oriented nationalism of the elite and the sociocultural nationalism of the masses has not been bridged, but one can think of situations in which a spark might bridge that gap to fuse the two.

Perhaps the most obvious is a change in economic conditions. Because the public's support for the political system is in part instrumental, economic instability, a reduction of living standards, or a reduction in government outputs would lead to decreased support for democratic political values. In such circumstances it would be easier for nationalistic elements in the elite to convince the public that a change in the status quo is necessary. The ubiquitous and deeply rooted nature of sociocultural nationalism would then become a potent force for the support of state-oriented nationalism.

Self-determined nationalism exists in Japan's differentiation of itself from other nations of the world and in its perceived role in the international relations system. The Western powers have been the unit of measurement by which Japan has gauged itself since Japan began the process of modernization in the mid-nineteenth century. Although Japan prides itself on its cultural uniqueness, there is no doubt that it has internalized Western values, political institutions, and economic institutions. When nationalism first came to Japan it was in emulation of the West. The development of centralized political and economic institutions and the creation of an ideology that tied the citizens directly to the nation-state was undertaken as a means of competing with the Western powers on their own terms. Japan wanted to join the club and become a voting member. But while nationalism was originally adopted as a means of becoming like the West, the very nature of nationalism gave rise to both nativist concerns about a loss of traditional values and an increasing competition that eventually led Japan into a war with the Western liberal democracies.

Japan was again forced to turn to the West after it was defeated in that war, but its reaction—the adoption of Western institutions and culture—has been very different from the retreat into the ultranationalism of the 1930s and 1940s. Japan has not drawn away from the West. It has, instead, continued to use its strong economic power and growing political power to claim its heritage as one of the developed nations and, in doing so, its place as an equal among the Western powers. Although it lays a strong claim to cultural uniqueness, its fundamental political and economic institutions remain those of a liberal democracy and capitalist economy. Even culturally, its food, architecture, clothing, entertainment and leisure activities, and general world view maintain strong Western, and especially American, influences. This is not to say that Japanese culture, political institutions, and economic institutions have not also been adapted to fit native culture and behavior—they have. But if one were to compare Japan in 1850, or even 1940, with Japan in 1992, then the fundamental impact of the West becomes obvious.

Japan is still faced with the original conundrum that existed in Meiji Japan of maintaining uniqueness and separation while at the same time having a highly interdependent relationship with the West. Although attuned to the West, Japan also uses its current conflicts with the West as a means of defining itself. When foreign states put pressure on Japan to change trade regulations or open their domestic markets, or when the internal pressures of internationalization become too strong, Japanese have sometimes taken the attitude that the world is against them. There have been, and continue to be, native reactions to *gaiatsu* and internationalization, and Japanese still sometimes feel they are being unfairly criticized by the other developed countries, but this native reaction has existed now for decades and does not appear to have any significant impact on Japan's orientation.

As Japan realizes its goals of economic development, political rehabilitation, and leadership in the international relations system, old questions once again come to the fore. The strong sense of pride in Japanese culture, the belief that Japanese culture has allowed them to progress economically beyond their rivals in the developed world, and the rapid growth of the national economy have led to an increase in national pride among Japanese. This pride is based on the transference of a belief in the superiority of Japanese products to a belief in the superiority of the Japanese people. In other words, if Japanese people make better products than other peoples in the world, then the Japanese people must be superior.

The belief in the superiority of Japanese products in comparison with the products of other countries raises, especially in combination with the desire to maintain the status quo, important questions about the future of Japan's trade relations with other countries. If Japanese people continue to buy native products and do not support the opening of markets, it will put even more strain on the balance of trade. Neither does it bode well for Japan's future role as a leading power in the international political system. There has been in recent years an inherent contradiction in the belief of many Japanese that Japan's increased economic power in the international relations system should be transmuted into political power and leadership. However, Japan has been unwilling to take any aggressive action to attain leadership, such as political and bureaucratic reform or opening its agricultural markets. It appears as though Japan will continue this trend of assuming the right of world leadership without being willing to actuate it. In addition, it might also mean that Japanese will not actively support changes in Japan's economic policies toward the outside world, if they see the policies of today as maintaining their present affluence. These frictions will increase if Japanese perceive that Western countries, especially the United States, have purposely thwarted their ambition to take a leadership role in the international relations system. The perception among Japanese that the rest of the world is in collusion against it would be a major factor in allowing mass support for state-oriented nationalism.

Japan must avoid a realist perception of the international relations system and not base its foreign policy on zero-sum game competition for economic power in a multipolar world. Japan has benefited tremendously from the postwar international trading system and its increased economic interdependence, but it must also accept the responsibility of reciprocity that accompanies interdependence. As Japan becomes more interdependent, the pressures one sociocultural nationalism increase because economic interdependence has brought about pressure for greater cultural interdependence, especially through the movement of foreigners into Japan. Japanese are, to a greater extent than ever before in their history, experiencing the outer world firsthand. The expansion of Japanese direct investment has sent a flood of Japanese businessmen, workers, and managers to foreign markets. The rapid appreciation of the yen in both the mid-1970s and the mid-1980s has led to a fivefold increase in the number of Japanese tourists abroad. Conversely, the lure of the Japanese economy has attracted many foreigners to Japan. Foreign professionals and businessmen, either working for their firms in Japan or hired by Japanese companies, demand that the old barriers separating foreigners and Japanese be torn down. The diversity of racial and ethnic groups in other countries to which Japanese are tied economically has created a need for greater sensitivity toward these groups by Japanese. But, most important, it must be understood that the isolating effect of the perception of uniqueness and the reality of homogeneity, both of which are inherent in sociocultural nationalism, must give way to a more open perspective on Japan's role in the world.

One final point must be made concerning the question of reciprocity in the world's definition of nationalism and the world's perception of nationalism in Japan. Americans, to use the most prominent example, and others such as the French, British, Koreans, and Australians, hold Japan to a double standard of nationalism. Those actions and behaviors that raise the specter of nationalism in the eyes of foreign observers, both in Asia and the West, are accepted as standard practices in those same countries that wring their hands over nationalism in Japan. This double standard of nationalism for Japan begs the question of trust that other countries have in Japan. In the words of one prominent and knowledgeable American observer of Japan, the use of patriotic symbols in the United States is a glue necessary to hold its component parts together, while patriotic symbols in Japan simply intensify an already strong feeling of national solidarity and superiority.

Obviously the double standard originates in Japan's past actions, and contemporary fears of Japanese nationalism are directly related to an uncertainty as to whether Japan can again take pride in itself and project a sense of assuredness in its dealings with the rest of the world, both politically and economically, while maintaining a responsible role in the international relations system. The ultimate conclusion of this study is that these fears and concerns are misplaced. Japanese nationalism is not so much a threat to other countries as it is a threat to Japan. A growth of Japanese nationalism in any of the forms outlined here can only frustrate and hurt Japan. Arrogant and coercive use of its economic power and, potentially, its military strength, or a chauvinistic isolationism, will only serve to incur a retaliation that will severely damage its economy, which is so dependent on trade. Thus, in the end, Japan will curb its nationalism because, if for no other reason, it is in the best interest of the nation to do so.

NOTE

1. Delmer M. Brown, *Nationalism in Japan* (New York: Russell and Russell, 1955), 252.

Bibliography

Ahern, Jerry, and Sharon Ahern. *The Kamikaze Legacy*. New York: Pocket Books, 1990.

Armour, Andrew J. L., ed. *Asia and Japan*. London: Athlone Press, 1985.

Azabu, Akira. "Echoes from the Gulf in Japanese Politics." *Japan Echo* 18 (Summer 1991): 35–40 (translated from and first published in *Shokun*, pp. 172–79. Tokyo: April 1991).

Bailey, Thomas A. *A Diplomatic History of the American People*. 10th ed. Englewood Cliffs, N.J.: Prentice-Hall, 1980.

Beer, Lawrence W. "Law and Liberty." In Takeshi Ishida and Ellis S. Krauss, eds., *Democracy in Japan*. Pittsburgh: University of Pittsburgh Press, 1989, pp. 67–88.

Beer, Samuel, and Adam Ulam, eds. *Patterns of Government: The Major Political Systems of Europe*. 3rd ed. New York: Rodman, 1973.

Befu, Harumi. "Internationalization of Japan and Nihon Bunkaron." In *The Challenge of Japan's Internationalization*, ed. Hiroshi Mannari and Harumi Befu, pp. 232–65. Tokyo: Kodansha International, 1983.

————. "Cultural Construction and National Identity: The Japanese Case." Culture and Communication Working Papers No. 5. Honolulu: Institute of Culture and Communication, the East West Center, 1992.

Block, Jonathan M. "A Transformation of the Japanese Popular Music Market: The Position of Western Popular Music." Honors thesis, Harvard University, 1990.

Bobrow, Davis B. "Japan in the World: Opinion from Defeat to Success." *Journal of Conflict Resolution* 33 (December 1989): 571–604.

Booth, Ken. "Security in Anarchy: Utopian Realism in Theory and Practice." *International Affairs* 67 (July 1991): 527–45.

Borg, Dorothy, and Shumpei Okamoto, eds. *Pearl Harbor as History*. New York: Columbia University Press, 1973.

Breuilly, John. *Nationalism and the State*. Manchester: Manchester University Press, 1982.

Brown, Delmer M. *Nationalism in Japan*. New York: Russell and Russell, 1955.

Brzezinski, Zbigniew. *The Fragile Blossom: Crisis and Change in Japan*. New York: Harper and Row, 1972.

Budner, Stanley. "United States and Japanese Newspaper Coverage of Frictions between the Two Countries." Draft paper prepared for the Mansfield Center for Pacific Affairs, University of Montana, Missoula, 1992.

Burstein, Daniel.*Yen!: Japan's New Financial Empire and Its Threat to America*. New York: Simon and Schuster, 1988.

Buruma, Ian. "A New Japanese Nationalism." *New York Times Magazine*, 12 April 1987.

Buszynski, Leszek. "Southeast Asia in the Post-Cold War Era." *Asian Survey* 32 (September 1992): 830–47.

Buzan, Barry. "Japan's Future: Old History versus New Roles." *International Affairs* 64 (Autumn 1988): 557–73.

Calder, Kent. *Crisis and Compensation: Public Policy and Political Stability in Japan, 1949–1986*. Princeton, N.J.: Princeton University Press, 1988.

Campbell, Karen L. "Ultranationalism in the English-language Classroom." *Japan Quarterly* 34 (January–March 1987): 46–50.

Chamberlin, William Henry. *Japan over Asia*. Boston: Little, Brown, 1937.

Chapman, William. *Inventing Japan*. New York: Prentice Hall, 1991.

Cole, Wayne S. "The Role of the United States Congress and Political Parties." In Dorothy Borg and Shumpei Okamoto, eds., *Pearl Harbor as History*. New York: Columbia University Press, 1973.

Crichton, Michael. *Rising Sun*. New York: Alfred A. Knopf, 1992.

Curtis, Gerald L. *The Japanese Way of Politics*. New York: Columbia University Press, 1988.

Cussler, Clive. *Dragon*. New York: Pocket Books, 1990.

Dale, Peter N. *The Myth of Japanese Uniqueness*. New York: St. Martin's Press, 1986.

Deutsch, Karl W. *The Analysis of International Relations*. 3d ed. Englewood Cliffs, N.J.: Prentice Hall, 1988.

———. *Politics and Government*. 3rd ed. Boston: Houghton Mifflin, 1980.

———. *Tides among Nations*. New York: Free Press, 1979.

Dietrich, William S. *In the Shadow of the Rising Sun*. University Park, Pa.: Pennsylvania State University Press, 1991.

Dogen, Mattei, ed. *Comparing Pluralist Democracies: Strains on Legitimacy*. Boulder, Colo.: Westview Press, 1988.

Dore, Ronald. "The Ethics of the New Japan." *Pacific Affairs* 25 (June 1952): 147–59.

Dower, John W. *War without Mercy*. New York: Pantheon Books, 1986.

Emmerson, John K. *Arms, Yen and Power*. Dunellen, 1971.

Emmerson, John K., and Leonard A. Humphreys. *Will Japan Rearm?* Washington, D.C.: American Enterprise Institute for Public Policy Research, 1973.

Fairbank, John K., Edwin O. Reischauer, and Albert Craig. *East Asia: The Modern Transformation*. Boston: Houghton Mifflin, 1965.

Flanagan, Scott C. "Changing Values in Advanced Industrial Societies: Inglehart's 'Silent Revolution' from the Perspective of Japanese Findings." *Comparative Political Studies* 14 (January 1982): 403–44.

———. "The Genesis of Variant Political Cultures: Contemporary Citizen Orientations in Japan, America, Britain and Italy." In *The Citizen and Politics*, ed. Sidney Verba and Lucian W. Pye, pp. 129–63. Stamford, Conn.: Greylock, 1978.

Friedman, George, and Meredith LeBard. *The Coming War with Japan*. New York: St. Martin's Press, 1991.

Funabashi, Yoichi. "Japan and the New World Order." *Foreign Affairs* 70 (Winter 1991–92): 58–74.

Girvin, Brian. "Conservatism and Political Change in Britain and the United States." *Parliamentary Affairs* 40 (1987): 154–71.

Gluck, Carol. *Japan's Modern Myths*. Princeton: Princeton University Press, 1985.

Haber, Deborah L. "The Death of Hegemony." *Asian Survey* 30 (September 1990): 892–907.

Haitani, Kanji. "The Paradox of Japan's Groupism." *Asian Survey* 30 (March 1990): 237–50.

Haley, John O. *Authority without Power*. New York: Oxford University Press, 1991.

Harada, Tadashi. "Seijiteki Taido no Kozo to Sejiteki Kanshin, Seijiteki Chishiki to no Kanei ni Tsuite" (The Structure of Political Attitudes and Their Relations to Political Interests and Political Knowledge in Undergraduates). *Japanese Journal of Educational Psychology* 33 (1985): 327–35.

Hasegawa, Michiko. "The Tyranny of Internationalization." *Japan Echo* 13 (Autumn 1986): 49–55 (translated from and first published in *Shokun*, pp. 154–74. Tokyo: December 1985).

Hayashi, Chikio. "The National Character in Transition." *Japan Echo* 15 (special issue 1988): 7–11 (translated from and first published in *Next*, pp. 98–102. Tokyo: August 1985).

Heald, Gordon. "A Comparison between American, European and Japanese Values." Paper presented at the Annual Meeting of the World Association for Public Opinion Research, May 21, 1982.

Holbrooke, Richard. "Japan and the United States: Ending the Unequal Partnership." *Foreign Affairs* 70 (Winter 1991–92): 41–57.

Holstein, William J. *The Japanese Power Game: What It Means for America*. New York: Scribners, 1990.

Hoyt, Edwin P. *The Militarists*. New York: Donald I. Fine, 1985.

Huang, Fu-Ch'ing. *Chinese Students in Japan in the Late Ch'ing Period*. Tokyo: Centre for East Asian Cultural Studies, 1982.

Inglehart, Ronald. "Changing Values in Japan and the West." *Comparative Political Studies* 14 (January 1982): 445.

Inoguchi, Takashi. *Japan's International Relations*. Boulder, Colo.: Westview Press, 1991.

Inoguchi, Takashi, and Ikuo Kabashima. "Status Quo Student Elite." In *Electoral Behavior in the 1983 Japanese Elections*, ed. Joji Watanabe et al. Tokyo: Institute of International Relations, Sophia University, 1986.

Iritani, Toshio. *Group Psychology of the Japanese in Wartime*. London: Kegan Paul International, 1991.

Ishida, Takeshi. *Japanese Political Culture*. Oxford: Transaction Publishers, 1989.

Ishida, Takeshi, and Ellis S. Krauss, eds. *Democracy in Japan*. Pittsburgh: University of Pittsburgh Press, 1989.

Ishihara, Shintaro. *The Japan That Can Say No*. New York: Simon and Schuster, 1991.

Ito, Masaya, and Osamu Shimomura. "The Folly of Structural Adjustment." *Japan Echo* 13 (Autumn 1986): 33–36 (translated from and first published in *Chuo Koron*, pp. 188–94. Tokyo: June 1986).

Iwao, Sumiko. "The Japanese: Portrait of Change." *Japan Echo* 15 (special issue 1988): 2–6.

———. "Recent Changes in Japanese Attitudes." In *Same Bed Different Dreams: America and Japan-Societies in Transition*, ed. Alan D. Romberg and Tadashi Yamamoto. New York: Council on Foreign Relations Press, 1990.

———. "Shinjuwan Go-ju Shunen Terebi Hodo Bangumi no Nichi-Bei-Hikaku" (A Comparison of Japanese and American News Broadcasts on the 50th Anniversary of Pearl Harbor). Paper produced for CULCON, February 10, 1993.

Japan Statistical Yearbook, 1991. Tokyo: Management and Coordination Agency, 1992.

Jensen, Lloyd. *Explaining Foreign Policy*. Englewood Cliffs, N.J.: Prentice-Hall, 1982.

Johnson, Chalmers. *MITI and the Japanese Miracle*. Stanford: Stanford University Press, 1982.

Johnson, Sheila K. *American Attitudes toward Japan, 1941–1975*. Washington, D.C.: American Enterprise Institute for Public Policy Research, 1975.

———. *The Japanese through American Eyes*. Stanford: Stanford University Press, 1988.

Kahn, Herman. *The Emerging Japanese Superstate*. Englewood Cliffs, NJ: Prentice Hall, 1970.

Kahn, Herman, and Thomas Pepper. *The Japanese Challenge*. London: Harper & Row, 1988.

Kamenka, Eugene, ed. *Nationalism: The Nature and Evolution of an Idea*. London: Edward Arnold, 1973.

Kaplan, David E., and Alec Dubro. *Yakuza*. Reading, Mass.: Addison-Wesley, 1986.

Kataoka, Tetsuya, ed. *Creating Single-Party Democracy: Japan's Postwar Political System*. Stanford: Hoover Institution Press, 1992.

Kedourie, Elie. *Nationalism*. 3rd ed. London: Hutchinson, 1966.

Keizai Koho Center. *Japan 1990: An International Comparison*. Tokyo: 1990.

Kennedy, Paul. *The Rise and Fall of the Great Powers*. New York: Random House, 1987.

Kober, Stanley. "Idealpolitik." *Foreign Policy* 79 (Summer 1990): 3–24.

Kohn, Hans. *Nationalism: Its Meaning and History*. Malabar, Fla.: Robert K. Kreiger, 1982.

Komori, Yoshihisa. "A Critique of Japan's Nationalists." *Japan Echo* 17 (Winter 1990): 39–47 (translated from and first published in *Chuo Koron*, pp. 90–109. Tokyo: March 1990).

Koppel, Bruce, and Michael Plummer. "Japan's Ascendency as a Foreign Aid Power." *Asian Survey* 29 (November 1989): 1043–56.

Koshida, Ryo. "Wakamono no Heiwa Ishiki" (The Peace Consciousness of Youth). *Heiwa Kenkyu* 10 (1985): 62–72.

Kyogoku, Junichi. *The Political Dynamics of Japan*. Tokyo: University of Tokyo Press, 1987.

Lebra, Takie Sugiyama. *Japanese Patterns of Behavior*. Honolulu: University of Hawaii Press, 1976.

Livingston, Jon, Joe Moore, and Felicia Oldfather, eds. *Imperial Japan: 1800–1945*. New York: Pantheon Books, 1973.

Lodge, George, and Ezra Vogel. *Ideology and National Competitiveness*. Boston: Harvard Business School Press, 1987.

Mannari, Hiroshi, and Harumi Befu, eds. *The Challenge of Japan's Internationalization*. Tokyo: Kodansha International, 1983.

Martin, Curtis, and Bruce Stronach. *Politics East and West: A Comparison of Japanese and British Political Culture*. New York: M. E. Sharpe, 1992.

Maruya, Saiichi. "The Folly of Language Reform." *Japan Echo* 16 (special issue 1989): 31–34 (translated from and first published in *Nihongo no Tame ni*. Tokyo: Shinchosha, 1974).

Maruyama, Masao. *Thought and Behavior in Modern Japanese Politics*, ed. Ivan Morris. Oxford: Oxford University Press, 1969.

Merkl, Peter H. "Comparing Legitimacy and Values among Advanced Democratic Countries." In *Comparing Pluralist Democracies: Strains on Legitimacy*, ed. Mattei Dogan, pp. 19–57. Boulder, Colo.: Westview Press, 1988.

Miyachi, Soshichi. "The Dangerous Tide of 'Soap Nationalism.' " *Japan Echo* 14 (Spring 1987): 51–54 (translated from and first published in *Chuo Koron*, pp. 89–97. Tokyo: December 1986).

Morimura, Stephanie F. "Japan's Marriage Industry Is Booming." *Japan Scope* 2 (Spring 1993): 39–43.

Morley, James William, ed. *Forecast for Japan: Security in the 1970s*. Princeton, N.J.: Princeton University Press, 1972.

Murakami Yasusuke, and Yutaka Kosai, eds. *Japan in the Global Community: Its Role and Contribution on the Eve of the 21st Century*. Tokyo: University of Tokyo Press, 1986.

Muramatsu, Michio, and Ellis S. Krauss. "Bureaucrats and Politicians in Policymaking: The Case of Japan." *American Political Science Review* 78 (March 1984): 126–46.

Murotani, Katsumi. "The Japanese Disease at the Seoul Olympics." *Japan Echo* 16 (Spring 1989): 61–64 (translated from and first published in *Voice*, pp. 172–77. Tokyo: December 1988).

Nakano, Osamu. "A Sociological Analysis of the 'New Breed.' " *Japan Echo* 15 (special issue 1988): 12–16 (translated from and first published in *Seiron*, pp. 30–39. Tokyo: November 1986).

Nester, William R. *The Foundation of Japanese Power*. New York: M. E. Sharpe, 1990.

Nippon Hoso Kyokai (NHK). *Nihonjin to Amerikajin* (Japanese and Americans). Tokyo: Nippon Hoso Shuppan Kyokai, 1982.

Nishimura, Hidetoshi. "Flag and Anthem, Symbols of Distress." *Japan Quarterly* 35 (April–June 1988): 152–56.

Nye, Joseph S. "The Changing Nature of World Power." *Political Science Quarterly* 105 (Summer 1990): 177–91.

Okimoto, Daniel I., and Thomas P. Rohlen, eds. *Inside the Japanese System*. Stanford: Stanford University Press, 1988.

Olsen, Edward A. *U.S.-Japan Strategic Reciprocity*. Stanford: Hoover Institution Press, 1985.

Ooka, Makoto. "Sitting, in a Circle: Thoughts on the Japanese Group Mentality." *Japan Echo* 17 (Winter 1990): 152–58. (translated from and first published in *Kokusai Koryu*, pp. 22–31. Tokyo: vol. 53, 1990).

Otsuka, Eiji. "Teen-age Fans of the 'Sweet Emperor.' " *Japan Echo* 16 (Spring 1989): 65–68 (translated from and first published in *Chuo Koron*, pp. 243–49. Tokyo: December 1988).

Packard, George R. III. *Protest in Tokyo: The Security Treaty Crisis of 1960*. Princeton, N.J.: Princeton University Press, 1966.

Perry, John C. *Beneath the Eagle's Wings*. New York: Dodd & Mead, 1980.

Prestowitz, Clyde V., Jr. *Trading Places*. New York: Basic Books, 1988.

Prime Minister's Office. *Public Opinion Survey on Society and State*. Tokyo: August 1986.

——— . *Public Opinion Survey on the Self-Defense Forces and Defense Problems*. Tokyo: June 1988.

——— . *Public Opinion Survey on Society and State*. Tokyo: September 1989.

——— . *Public Opinion Survey on the Life of the Nation*. Tokyo: December 1989.

——— . *Seishonen no Shakai Sanka ni Kansuru Seiron Chosa* (Public Opinion Survey on the Social Involvement of Youth). Tokyo: 1990.

——— . *Public Opinion Survey on Society and State*. Tokyo: June 1991.

——— . *Public Opinion Survey on the Self-Defense Forces and Defense Problems*. Tokyo: July 1991.

Pye, Lucian W., and Sidney Verba, eds. *Political Culture and Political Development*. Princeton: Princeton University Press, 1965.

Pyle, Kenneth B. "The Future of Japanese Nationality: An Essay in Contemporary History." *Journal of Japanese Studies* 8 (Summer 1982): 223–63.

——— . "The Burden of Japanese History and the Politics of Burden Sharing." In *Sharing World Leadership: A New Era for America and Japan*, ed. John H. Makin and Donald C. Hellmann. Washington, D.C.: American Enterprise Institute, 1989.

Richardson, Bradley, and Scott C. Flanagan. *Politics in Japan*. Boston: Little Brown, 1984.

Roberts, Adam. "A New Age in International Relations?" *International Affairs* 67 (July 1991): 509–25.

Robson, J. M., ed. *The Collected Works of John Stuart Mill*, vol. 18. Toronto: University of Toronto Press, 1977.

Rose, Richard. "National Pride in Cross-National Perspective." *International Social Science Journal* 36 (1985): 85–96.

Rosencrance, Richard, and Jennifer Taw. "Japan and the Theory of International Leadership." *World Politics* 60 (January 1990): 184–209.

Sansom, Sir George B. *The Western World and Japan*. New York: Alfred A. Knopf, 1965.

Sato, Ikuya. *Kamikaze Biker: Parody and Anatomy in Affluent Japan*. Chicago: University of Chicago Press, 1991.

Sato, Seizaburo. "The Foundations of Modern Japanese Foreign Policy." In Robert
    A. Scalapino, ed., *The Foreign Policy of Modern Japan*. Berkeley: University
    of California Press, 1977.
Satow, Sir Ernest. *A Diplomat in Japan*. Tokyo: Charles E. Tuttle, 1983.
Scalapino, Robert A., ed. *The Foreign Policy of Modern Japan*. Berkeley: University of
    California Press, 1977.
Scherer, Dr. James A. B. *Japan—Whither?* Tokyo: Hokuseido Press, 1935.
Seton-Watson, Hugh. *Nations and States*. London: Methuen & Co., 1977.
Skidmore, Max J. *Ideologies: Politics in Action*. New York: Harcourt, Brace and
    Jovanovich, 1989.
Smith, Anthony D. "The Myth of the 'Modern Nation' and the Myths of Nations."
    Ethnic and Racial Studies 11 (January 1988): 1–19.
Spence, Jonathan D. *The Gate of Heavenly Peace*. New York: Penguin Books, 1982.
Statistic Bureau, Management and Coordination Agency. *Japan Statistics Yearbook*.
    Tokyo: 1988.
Stronach, Bruce. "Deference, Pride and Political Culture: The Social Context of
    Japanese Political Participation in Comparison with Great Britain." Paper
    presented at the annual meeting of the Canadian Asian Studies Associa-
    tion, Windsor, Ontario, June 1988.
Tagore, Sir Rabindranath. *Nationalism*. New York: Macmillan, 1917. Reprinted
    Westport, Conn.: Greenwood Press, 1973.
Takagi, Masayuki. "The Japanese Right Wing." *Japan Quarterly* 36 (July–September
    1989): 300–305.
Thomson, James C., Peter W. Stanley, and John C. Perry. *Sentimental Imperialists*.
    New York: Harper & Row, 1981.
Treat, Payson J. *Japan and the United States: 1853–1921*. Reprinted New York:
    Johnson Reprint Corp., 1970.
Trezise, Philip H. "Japan, the Enemy?" *Brookings Review* (Winter 1989–90): 3–13.
United States Department of State. *Foreign Relations of the United States*, vol. 6.
    Washington, D.C.: 1945.
_____ . *Foreign Relations of the United States*, vol. 6. Washington, D.C.: 1950.
_____ . *Foreign Relations of the United States*, vol. 6. Washington, D.C.: 1951.
van Wolferen, Karel. *The Enigma of Japanese Power*. New York: Vintage Books, 1990.
Verba, Sidney, and Pye, Lucian W., eds. *The Citizen and Politics*. Stamford, Conn.:
    Greylock, 1978.
Vogel, Ezra F. *Japan as Number One*. Cambridge, Mass.: Harvard University Press,
    1979.
Wagatsuma, H. 1984. "Some Cultural Assumptions among the Japanese." *Japan
    Quarterly* 31 (October–December 1984): 371–79.
Ward, Robert E. "Japan: The Continuity of Modernization." In *Political Culture and
    Political Development*, ed. Lucian Pye and Sidney Verba, pp. 27–82. Prince-
    ton, N.J.: Princeton University Press, 1965.
_____ . *Japan's Political System*. 2d ed. New York: Prentice-Hall, 1978.
Watanabe, Shoichi. "The Emperor and the Militarists: Reexamining the Prewar
    Record." *Japan Echo* 18 (Summer 1991): 72–79 (translated from and first
    published in *Chuo Koron*, pp. 268–82. Tokyo: April 1991).
Watanuki, Joji et al. *Electoral Behavior in the 1983 Japanese Elections*. Tokyo: Sophia
    University Institute of International Relations, 1986.

White, James W. "Civic Attitudes, Political Participation and System Stability in Japan." *Comparative Political Studies* 14 (October 1981): 371–400.

——— . *Migration in Metropolitan Japan*. Japan Research Monograph, Institute for East Asian Studies. Berkeley: University of California Press, 1982.

White, Theodore H. "The Danger from Japan." *New York Times Magazine*, 28 July 1985.

Wolf, Martin J. *The Japanese Conspiracy*. New York: Empire Books, 1983.

Yanaga, Chitoshi. *Japan since Perry*. 1949. Reprinted Hamden, Conn.: Archon Books, 1966.

Zubaida, Sami. "Nations: Old and New." *Ethnic and Racial Studies* 12 (July 1989): 329–39.

Index

About the Author

BRUCE STRONACH is Dean, Graduate School of International Relations, International University of Japan in Niigata. His primary areas of interest include Japanese political culture and popular culture with an eye to the Japanese-American relationship. His recent books include *Politics East and West: A Comparison of Japanese and British Culture* (1992) with Curtis Martin, and *Japan and America: Opposites That Attract* (1989).